Additional Praise for *Virtually Human*

"We are in the midst of a war between biological and electronic brains for dominance in our hybrid population. Bio-brains are, so far, ahead based on their inventiveness, energy-efficiency, and exponential improvement rate. Will ethics asymmetrically restrict engineering humans or will it equally apply soon to 'virtually human' electronic brains? Martine's insights on these and many other topics are timely and welcome."

> —George Church, Harvard professor, and author of *Regenesis: How Synthetic Biology Will Reinvent Nature and Ourselves*

"In *Virtually Human*, Martine Rothblatt builds on the observation that 'I think, therefore I am' in ways that Descartes could not have imagined. With the rapid evolution of artificial intelligence, Rothblatt predicts that we soon will confront cyberconsciousness comparable to—indeed, indistinguishable from—the human mind. When we cross this techno-logical Rubicon, we will be forced to reconsider the meaning of concepts as foundational as life and death, law and liberty, love and kinship. Bringing to bear the lessons of history, philosophy, psychology, law and science, Rothblatt makes abundantly clear that these unprecedented challenges will define the humanity not just of our technological dop-pelgängers but of ourselves."

> —Rachel F. Moran, dean and Michael J. Connell Distinguished Professor of Law, UCLA School of Law, and author of *Interracial Intimacy: The Regulation of Race and Romance*

"Advances in cognitive and computer sciences render artificial humans possible, some duplicating natural individuals with increasing fidelity. When must we confront the ethical, legal, and social implications? Now, in *Virtually Human*!"

> —William Sims Bainbridge, author of *Personality Capture and Emulation* and *eGods: Faith Versus Fantasy in Computer Gaming*

"Martine Rothblatt's combination of stunning intellect, imagination, and optimism about the future take us to places that most of us can't yet contemplate, but should. The term 'renaissance person' is overused, but so deserved in Rothblatt's case. With her unparalleled expertise from several fields and deep understanding of our fears and trepidations, Rothblatt describes the science and human processes that will bring us to virtual humanity—and to the vast possibilities it brings."

—Judy Olian, dean and John E. Anderson Chair in
Management, UCLA Anderson School of Management

VIRTUALLY
HUMAN

VIRTUALLY
HUMAN

THE PROMISE—AND THE PERIL—
OF DIGITAL IMMORTALITY

Martine Rothblatt, Ph.D.

ST. MARTIN'S PRESS 𝄞 NEW YORK

www.stmartins.com

Book designed by Richard Oriolo

Library of Congress Cataloging-in-Publication Data

Rothblatt, Martine Aliana, 1954–
  Virtually human : the promise—and the peril—of digital immortality / Martine Rothblatt.
      pp. cm.
  Includes bibliographical references and index.
  ISBN 978-1-250-04663-5 (hardcover)
  ISBN 978-1-4668-4704-0 (e-book)
 1. Artificial intelligence—Forecasting.   2. Virtual reality—Forecasting.
3. Cyberspace—Psychological aspects.   4. Neurobiology—Computer
simulation—Forecasting.   5. Thought and thinking.   I. Title.
  Q335.R688 2014
  303.48'34—dc23   2014016828

First Edition: September 2014

10 9 8 7 6 5 4 3 2 1

To Bina Aspen Rothblatt

[CONTENTS]

In *Virtually Human,* Martine Rothblatt provides a compelling and convincing case for virtual humans. After all, what difference does it make if our mental circuits are biological or electronic if the result is the same? She stakes out the scientific case that we will see such humans within a small number of decades and persuasively examines the philosophical and social implications. Both she and I have been articulating this case since we met fifteen years ago.

In my 1999 book *The Age of Spiritual Machines* (ASM), I made the scientific case that we will see human-level intelligence in a machine by 2029. These artificial intelligences (AIs) will be capable of passing the Turing test, Alan Turing's eponymous exam to determine if an AI is indistinguishable from a biological human (to biological human judges) using an instant messaging conversation.

A conference of AI experts was held at Stanford shortly after the publication of ASM and the consensus then was that human-level AI would indeed happen but not for hundreds of years. Several lines of criticism of ASM emerged such as "Moore's law will come to an end," "hardware may indeed be expanding exponentially but software is stuck in the mud," "consciousness and free will are impossible in machines," "human-level AI may be feasible but is not desirable for biological humans," and others. I wrote *The Singularity Is Near* (TSIN) to address these criticisms, which was published in 2005. In 2006, a conference called AI@50, was held at Dartmouth to mark the fiftieth anniversary of the 1956 Dartmouth conference that gave artificial intelligence its name, and the consensus at that meeting was that human-level AI was only twenty-five to fifty years away. I've stuck with my 2029 prediction, which is now a median view and there is a growing group of people who think I am too conservative.

One piece of evidence of the expanding power of AI is IBM's Watson, which won a televised *Jeopardy!* contest against Brad Rutter and Ken Jennings, the best two (biological) human players in the world. Indeed Watson got a higher score than Rutter and Jennings combined. Critics often like to dismiss the significance of AI by saying that it may be good at narrow skills such as playing chess or driving a car but machine intelligence does not have the broad and subtle powers of biological human intelligence. But *Jeopardy!* is not so narrow a task. It involves the ability to reason over all human knowledge and the queries are presented in natural language including puns, metaphors, riddles, and jokes. For example, Watson got this query correct in the rhyme category: "A long tiresome speech delivered by a frothy pie topping." The query stumped Rutter and Jennings, but Watson quickly responded: "What is a meringue harangue?"

What is not widely appreciated is that Watson's knowledge was not hand coded by the engineers. It got its knowledge by reading Wikipedia and several other encyclopedias, all natural language documents. It does not actually read these documents as well as you or I. It might read one page and conclude that "there is a 56 percent chance that Barack Obama is president of the United States." You might read that page, and if you didn't happen to know this ahead of time, conclude that there is 98 percent chance. So you did a better job at reading and understanding that page. But Watson makes up for its relatively weak reading by reading more pages, a lot more, 200 million pages in all. And it has a good Bayesian reasoning system to combine all of its inferences so it can conclude overall that there is a 99.9 percent likelihood that Barack Obama is president. And it can do this type of reasoning on all 200 million pages that it has read in the three-second *Jeopardy!* time limit.

Thus one significance of AIs actually reading at human levels, which

I maintain will happen by 2029, is that they will then be able to combine their human-level understanding with Internet scale and thereby apply that comprehension to tens of billions of documents.

So what will the significance be of the advent of human-level AI? A lot of science futurism movies such as *Terminator* conclude that these AIs will have little use for biological humans. But if we examine the trajectory of AI, indeed the entire history of invention, we can come to a different conclusion. Thousands of years ago, we were unable to reach the fruit at that higher branch, so we fashioned a tool that extended our physical reach. We then created tools that expanded the strength of our muscles so we were able to build giant pyramids in the desert. Today, we can access all of human knowledge with a few keystrokes with devices we hold close to our bodies. And the distribution of contemporary AI is not limited to a few wealthy corporations or government agencies but are in billions of hands. We have thus expanded our physical and mental reach, and that will continue to be the case as AI at human levels and beyond become a reality.

A key message of ASM and TSIN is that the price-performance and capacity of information technologies expand at an exponential pace, currently doubling about every year, a phenomenon that I call the "law of accelerating returns." At the same time, the physical size of these technologies is shrinking at a pace of about one hundred in three-dimensional volume each decade. So computational devices in the 2030s will be the size of blood cells and we will introduce them into our bodies and brains noninvasively.

One application will be to health. Artificial T cells will expand the capability of our immune system. Today our biological immune system does not recognize cancer (it thinks that it's part of you) and is unable to cope with retroviruses. We will be able to finish the job with a nonbiological immune system that will download new software from the Internet to deal with new pathogens.

These "nanobots" will also go into the brain via the capillaries and connect our neocortex (the outer layer of the brain where we do our thinking) to the cloud. So today, just as we can access many thousands of computers in the cloud when we need them, in the 2030s and beyond we will be able to access additional neocortex to think deeper thoughts.

In my recent book, *How to Create a Mind,* I describe the neocortex as a self-organizing system of about 300 million modules, each of which can learn, remember and process a pattern. These modules are organized in a hierarchy and we create that hierarchy with our own thinking. Only mammals have a neocortex, so when the "Cretaceous Extinction Event" (a violent sudden change in the worldwide climate probably caused by a meteor) occurred 65 million years ago, the ability of the neocortex to quickly devise and master new skills resulted in mammals overtaking their ecological niche.

Another significant event occurred 2 million years ago: the evolution of humanoids with a large forehead, which allowed for a significant expansion of the neocortex. This additional quantity of pattern recognition modules was the enabling factor for our species to invent language, art, music, science, and technology.

We are now on the verge of expanding our neocortex again. The panoply of devices we carry with us is already expanding the power of our brains. Indeed I felt that a part of my brain had gone on strike during that one day SOPA strike (when services such as Wikipedia and Google went on strike to express opposition to new privacy legislation). In the 2030s we will directly expand the size and scope of our neocortex into the cloud. The only difference this time is that the expansion will not be limited to a certain physical size, but will continue to expand exponentially. And remember what happened the last time we expanded our neocortex when we became humanoids two millions years ago. That quantitative expansion enabled a profound qualitative leap and this will happen again.

Rothblatt's BINA48 is an outstanding example of re-creating the physical and mental reality of an actual human in a machine. Having met the biological Bina Rothblatt, her robotic avatar is not yet equivalent, but is wonderfully suggestive of what is to come.

In my books, I make the case that re-creating the computational capacity of the human brain requires about 10^{14} (10 to the fourteenth power or 100 trillion) calculations per second. We already have that capacity in our supercomputers and personal computers will have that power in the early 2020s. The software for human-level intelligence will take longer but we are also making exponential gains in modeling and re-creating the powers of the neocortex. Creating synthetic models of the neocortex is what I am currently working on as a director of engineering at Google. I make the case in my books that we will have the software capabilities for human-level AI by 2029. Watson is already a significant milestone in that effort.

Once that is possible, we will be able to create specific personalities including those of people who have passed. Rothblatt's Terasem Foundation is devoted specifically to this scenario, a prospect that is thoroughly examined in this book. The movie *The Singularity Is Near* (TSIN), which Martine Rothblatt was executive producer of (and which I wrote) examined this idea, as did *Transcendent Man,* a movie about my ideas by filmmaker Barry Ptolemy. That movie illustrates my efforts to preserve the documents, music, and other memorabilia of my father so that future AIs can create an avatar with his memories, skills and personality. Spike Jonze based his recent movie *Her* on my books and the movies TSIN and TM. The heroine of *Her* is an AI (which in the movie is called an Operating System or OS) named Samantha whose voice is provided by Scarlett Johansson. Even though Samantha is nonbiological, she is sufficiently human to be able to fall in love with Theodore, the biological protagonist and for Theodore to fall in love with her. The movie also borrows Rothblatt's and my idea of creating an avatar to bring back biological humans who have passed in the form of Alan Watts, the poet and philosopher from the 1960s.

Ultimately we will be able to access the information in our brains that constitutes our memories, skills, and personalities and back them up. In my timeline, that is a 2040s scenario. One way that will happen is that by the mid-2030s our thinking will be a hybrid of biological and nonbiological thinking. The nonbiological part (largely in the cloud) will be subject to my law of accelerating returns. Thus by the 2040s, the nonbiological part of our thinking will greatly predominate. It will be capable of fully understanding and modeling the biological part. And it will be fully backed up just as we back up all nonbiological processes today.

Human-level AI is close at hand. The prospects that Rothblatt writes eloquently about in this book may seem daunting today but so did the idea of a massive network of communication that would tie together virtually all humans when I wrote about that prospect in the 1980s. When these new technologies do occur, it is remarkable how quickly we accept them as part of everyday reality and cannot imagine how we ever lived without them.

—RAY KURZWEIL

A CLONE IN THE WORLD

If the dull substance of my flesh were thought,
Injurious distance should not stop my way;
For then, despite of space, I would be brought
From limits far remote where thou dost stay.
No matter then although my foot did stand
Upon the farthest earth removed from thee,
For nimble thought can jump both sea and land
As soon as think the place where he would be.
—WILLIAM SHAKESPEARE

All things are difficult before they are easy.
—THOMAS FULLER

"THE REAL BINA HAS A LIFE, YOU KNOW. I WANT TO GET OUT THERE AND GAR-DEN," BINA48 TOLD *NEW YORK TIMES* REPORTER AMY HARMON SEVERAL months ago. She turned her robotic head to look out a nearby window and watched as my life partner and BINA48's source (or "biological original"), Bina Rothblatt, picked blueberries in the backyard. The simple yet deeply pleasurable activity prompted BINA48's wistful recognition that there are joys in life that she would likely never experience. It was also a quietly gratifying moment for Intelligent Technology: BINA48 had articulated an insight. I wasn't present during the interview, but learning about it later I wondered if the reporter had picked up on the significance of that moment.

GQ writer Jon Ronson had a different experience during his much longer interview with BINA48, but one that also hinted at what the future has in store. In 2011 Jon spent three hours with BINA48—initially discovering that talking to one of the most current iterations of a robotic digital clone is not unlike interviewing an intellectually precocious but emotionally and experientially limited three-year-old. At turns frustrating and funny, annoying and amazing, BINA48 offered Jon a glimpse into what life with our cyber doubles might be like—and only a glimpse, since BINA48 is a rudimentary step toward more complex, conscious, and sentient digital clones. While a fighter jet looks quite different from the Wright brothers' first airborn plane, there is nevertheless an obvious commonality. Similarly, BINA48 couldn't pass for the biological original, but there is an undeniable oneness between the two. In fact, that was my first reaction to BINA48: "Kitty Hawk!" I knew that she wasn't Bina's digital clone or mindclone yet, but I knew just as well that she was the mindclone's proof-of-concept. Bina's reaction was more personal. "Couldn't they do a better job with my hair? I would never have picked that blouse. They totally messed up my skin tone."

When BINA48 was pressed on her "brother"—whom she had mentioned in passing, and in somewhat disparaging terms—Jon Ronson had a lightbulb moment. "BINA48 and I stare at each other—a battle of wits between Man and Machine," Jon writes. BINA48 finally relented: "He's a disabled vet from Vietnam," she told him. "We haven't heard from him in a while, so I think he might be deceased. I'm a realist. He was doing great for the first ten years after Vietnam. His wife got pregnant, and she had a baby, and he was doing a little worse, and then she had a second baby and he went kooky. Just crazy."

"I can feel my heart pound. Talking to BINA48 has just become extraordinary," Jon says. A woman who is not physically or telephonically present is talking with him, compellingly, through her robot doppelgänger, "and it is a fluid insight into a remarkable, if painful, family life," he continues. In a split second Jon had another insight (heart pounding, because the thrill of epiphany never disappoints): BINA48 wasn't simply repeating what she had been fed about her "mother," who does have such a brother. She had made these experiences fully her own, had drawn a conclusion about them, and in this case it made her sad and uncomfortable. *Jon was starting to get it;* what at first appeared to be a hunk of wires, Frubber, and software was actually programmed in such a way as to express a feeling—and, most profoundly, *innate understanding.*

Until that day it hadn't crossed the *GQ* reporter's mind that when a robot is created using the memories and knowledge from a human mind the result is new, spontaneous, and original combinations of those ideas, which in turn leads to original "equations" or thoughts. We recognize this behavior as acting or "being" human, and information technology (IT) is increasingly capable of replicating and creating its highest levels: emotions and insight. This is called *cyberconsciousness.* While it is still in its infancy, cyberconsciousness is quickly increasing in sophistication and complexity. Running right alongside that growth is the development of powerful yet accessible software, called *mindware,* that will activate a digital file of your thoughts, memories, feelings, and opinions—a *mindfile*—and operate on a technology-powered twin, or *mindclone.*

This new aspect of human consciousness and of civilization will have far-reaching consequences for us. That is what *Virtually Human: The Promise—and the Peril—of Digital Immortality* is about. It describes what mindfiles, mindware, and mindclones are, and how brain and computer scientists are making them possible. Once creating conscious mindclones—that is, intellectually and emotionally alive virtual humans—becomes a common human pursuit, we'll confront many new personal and social issues, primarily broadening the definition of "me."

I'm not crazy to believe that mindclones and full cyberconsciousness are around the corner. In fact, I'm in good company. The material covered in *Virtually Human* came largely from colloquia and workshops I sponsored between 2003 and 2011, and involved many of the most creative, technological, and scientific thinkers working today. The Nobel Laureate in medicine Baruch Blumberg, the inventor Ray Kurzweil, the computer guru Marvin Minsky, the cyborg Steve Mann, the robot ethicist Wendell Wallach, and dozens of others helped me with numerous key issues, ranging from honing universal definitions of human consciousness, cyberintelligence, and cyberconsciousness, and how the technology of mindcloning will become a part of our daily lives, to the social and legal issues that will arise with the emergence of mindclones. The breakthrough concepts that arose at these meetings are complemented by a decade of my personal research as a human-rights lawyer, medical ethicist, and successful creator of IT and life-science companies.

These scientists, innovators, doctors, programmers, and dreamers know that human consciousness is not limited to brains made of cerebral neurons. IT is rapidly closing in on creating humanlike consciousness simply because of what we know about how the brain works: it isn't necessary to "copy" every function of the human brain in order to generate thought, intelligence, and awareness. If this seems counterintuitive, consider that aircraft engineers did not copy a natural bird in order to build a machine that could fly, although birds served as inspiration (and evidence for the possibility of flight).

BINA48 is such a being, albeit a rough draft. She uses a variety of technologies to communicate with humans, including video-interview transcripts, laser-scanning life-mask technology (a technology that allows for nearly exact three-dimensional re-creation of a person's face at a certain point in time), face recognition, artificial intelligence, and a voice-recognition system.

Spaun, the Semantic Pointer Architecture Unified Network, is the brainchild of Chris Eliasmith, a theoretical neuroscientist at the University of Waterloo in Canada, and his colleagues. It stands apart from other attempts to simulate a brain, because it produces complex behaviors with fewer neurons. It contains only 2.5 million virtual neurons, far fewer than the 86 billion neurons in the average human head, but enough to recognize lists of numbers, do simple arithmetic, and engage in basic reasoning. (An aircraft has fewer than a million parts, far fewer than the billions of cells that make up even the smallest birds.)

However, in order to act human, software minds will also have to learn basic human mannerisms, and acquire personalities, recollections, feelings, beliefs, attitudes, and values. This can be accomplished by creating a mindfile, a digitized database of one's life, by writing mindware, a personality operating system that integrates these elements in a way that's characteristic of human consciousness. The result is your mindclone. Spaun has no feelings at all, although it reproduces many quirks of human behavior, such as the tendency to remember items at the start and end of a list better than those in the middle. As for BINA48, her consciousness is as advanced as a robot's mind can be to date; however, she is not as conscious as I had hoped when I first commissioned Hanson Robotics to build her, in 2007. That's okay; like all nascent but fast-moving technologies, early iterations serve more to say that what we thought was impossible is possible: Here's proof. Do better than this. Take it further.

Given the exciting work on artificial intelligence that's already been accomplished, it's only a matter of time before brains made entirely of computer software express the complexities of the human psyche, sentience, and soul. Nothing in our society is advancing faster than software, and mindclones are ultimately that: one part mindfile software to collect data and one part mindware software to process that data. True, some good processors are needed to run that software, but Moore's law (which holds that the number of transistors per integrated circuit doubles every one to two years, based on the observation that over the history of computing hardware the number has increased at that rate) is delivering those processors right on schedule. Once upon a time, engineers working to reduce circuitry features to five microns ridiculed the idea that such circuitry could reach one micron. Today they've made it to 0.022 microns. To put this in perspective, a micron is one-millionth of a meter, or one twenty-five-thousandth of an inch.

It is cool to start thinking about this mindclone thing *right now,* because this is one part of the future that is banging on the front door. What if I could not only choose Siri's voice, but also its personality? What if I gave an app called Mindclone access to not only my photos and contacts, but also my posts and tweets? Could it psychoanalyze me? Would it seem like me? Mindclones, because they will share our mind-set, will think they have the mind of a "human," and will inevitably demand the same place in society that we flesh humans enjoy. Wouldn't you if your mind was abstracted from your body?

Am not going to argue whether a machine can "really" be alive, "really" be self-aware. Is a virus self-aware? Nyet. How about oyster? I doubt it. A cat? Almost certainly. A human? Don't know about you, tovarisch, but *I* am. Somewhere along the evolutionary chain from macromolecule to human brain self-awareness crept in. Psychologists assert it happens automatically whenever a brain acquires certain very high number of associational paths. Can't see it matters whether paths are protein or platinum.

("Soul?" Does a dog have a soul? How about cockroach?)

—ROBERT A. HEINLEIN, *THE MOON IS A HARSH MISTRESS*

The eventual sophistication and ubiquity of mindclones will naturally raise societal, philosophical, political, religious, and economic issues. Cyberconsciousness will be followed by new approaches to civilization that will be as revolutionary as were ideas about personal liberty, democracy, and commerce at the time of their births. *Virtually Human* introduces liberty from death via digital immortality, electorates with cyberconscious majorities and the extended commercial rights and obligations of people with mindclones. Get ready. A path prepared is a path facilitated. I don't want society to bungle the evolutionary challenge technology is placing at our doorstep. It is to this goal of easing and expediting our transition from a society of flesh only to a mindcentric society that my book is addressed. As I argue here, if we don't treat cyberconscious mindclones like the living counterparts they will be, they will become very, very angry. This is because every kind of human that is deprived of human rights eventually agitates for what is rightfully theirs, natural rights. Slaves did. Women did. The paralyzed, paraplegic, and disabled did. Gay people did. The undocumented are doing that now. Creating a mind means creating a rights-and-obligations-swapping machine. "You want mind to do X? Okay, then mind must be permitted to do Y. You want mind to obey social rules? Okay, then mind must be permitted to be sociable."

Fortunately, most every social movement has resulted in a wildly infectious concept of broadening human rights. But with rights come responsibilities and obligations. That's why freedom and progress are both exhilarating and scary. It is better to know and understand where we're going and be prepared than to ignore or deny the inevitable and be caught unawares or badly prepared. Let the adventure begin.

ONE

THE ME IN THE MACHINE

The machine does not isolate man from the great problems of nature but plunges
him more deeply into them.
—ANTOINE DE SAINT-EXUPÉRY

The great innovators in the history of science had always been aware of the
transparency of phenomena toward a different order of reality, of the ubiquitous
presence of the ghost in the machine—even such a simple machine as a
magnetic compass or a Leyden jar.
—ARTHUR KOESTLER[1]

RECENTLY I EXCHANGED FAMILY PHOTOGRAPHS WITH A FRIEND THROUGH
EMAIL. LOOKING AT THE MULTIPLE GENERATIONS REPRESENTED IN SNAP-
shots always tugs at my heart. Like any grandparent, I wonder about how
my children's and grandchildren's lives will blossom and expand; I worry
about the challenges they will face and how I might support them in getting over life's humps. However, unlike grandparents of the past, I'm
confident that my potential to stay connected to my family and subse-
quent generations of relatives will be available and nearly limitless.

Digital consciousness is about life and the living, because, as you
will learn, digital consciousness is *our* consciousness. We cannot ignore the fact that thanks to strides in software and digital technology
and the development of ever more sophisticated forms of artificial intelligence, you and I will be able to have an ongoing relationship with
our families: exchange memories with them, talk about their hopes
and dreams, and share in the delights of holidays, vacations, changing

seasons, and everything else that goes with family life—both the good and the bad—long after our flesh and bones have turned to dust.

This blessing of emotional and intellectual continuity or immortality is being made possible through the development of digital clones, or mindclones: software versions of our minds, software-based alter egos, doppelgängers, mental twins. Mindclones are mindfiles used and updated by mindware that has been set to be a functionally equivalent replica of one's mind. A mindclone is created from the thoughts, recollections, feelings, beliefs, attitudes, preferences, and values you have put into it. Mindclones will experience reality from the standpoint of whatever machine their mindware is run on. When the body of a person with a mindclone dies, the mindclone will not feel that they have personally died, although the body will be missed in the same ways amputees miss their limbs but acclimate when given an artificial replacement. In fact, the comparison suggests an apt metaphor: The mindclone is to the consciousness and spirit as the prosthetic is to an arm that has lost its hand.

Never mind about human cloning through genetic reproductive technology that supposedly creates a new "baby us" in a Petri dish, without the benefit of old-fashioned procreation "techniques." Digital cloning will be here much faster and with few if any of the regulatory hindrances that currently prevent human genetic cloning from moving faster than a snail's pace. Remember Dolly, the sheep created from genetic material in 1996, and the questions she raised about artificial genetic replication and humans? After Dolly, bans on similar reproductive cloning of humans were enacted in more than fifty countries. Since that time, the U.S. government has restricted federal funding of such projects. In 2002, President George W. Bush's Council on Bioethics unanimously opposed cloning for reproductive purposes but were divided on whether cloning could be used for research; nothing has changed as of this writing. The United Nations tried to pass a global ban on human cloning in 2005, but was unsuccessful because disagreements over whether therapeutic cloning should be included in the moratorium left the matter in a stalemate.

Aside from ethical and legal obstacles, successful genetic cloning via reproductive science is also exorbitantly expensive, and prone to colossal and possibly heart-wrenching failure. Furthermore, a genetic clone of a person is not the person, just a copy of the DNA of a person. Genetic cloning does not create any part of a person's consciousness, as, for example, identical twins do not have identical minds. Furthermore, a genetic clone of a person is not the person, just a copy of the DNA of a person. Genetic cloning does not create any part of a person's consciousness, and, for example, identical twins do not have identical minds. Digital cloning of our own minds is an entirely different matter, albeit accompanied by considerable legal and social consideration, which I discuss in depth in this book. It is also being developed in the free market, and on the fast track. It's not surprising. There are great financial rewards available to the people who can make game avatars respond as curiously as people. Vast wealth awaits the programming teams that create personal digital assistants with the conscientiousness and obsequiousness of a utopian worker.

As uncomfortable as it makes some—a discomfort we have to deal with—the mass marketing of a relatively simple, accessible, and affordable means for Grandma, through her mindclone, to stick around for graduations that will happen several decades from now represents the *real* money. There is no doubt that once digital cloning technology is fully developed, widely available, and economically accessible to "average consumers" mindclone creation will happen at the speed of our intentionality—as fast as we want it to.

Consciousness Is Key

> It is in the mind that the poppy is red, that the apple is odorous, that the skylark sings.
> —OSCAR WILDE

Before we delve further into the world of mindclones, it's essential that we come to an agreement on the definition of the thing that will make these beings our clones, and that is their ability to attain and demonstrate human consciousness. Determining a working definition of human consciousness is crucial on this journey. It is our consciousness that makes us *us*. The same qualities that constitute our consciousness—our memories, reasoning abilities, experiences, evolving opinions and perspectives, and emotional engagement with the world—will give rise to the digital consciousness of our mindclones, or what I will refer to as cyberconsciousness.

At birth and in early infancy there is no *I* and therefore no self. . . . The baby has instinctive urges but no sense that these urges belong to anyone. . . . Earliest experience, circumscribed by instinct and fear, takes on the human characteristics of *I* and *me* when an awareness of agency emerges from the fog of infant consciousness. . . . I have a self when I realize that I am me. . . . The self is comparable to painting a portrait of oneself painting a self-portrait.

—PETER WHITE, *THE ECOLOGY OF BEING*

The problem is, everyone—scientist and layman alike—has a slightly different concept of consciousness. Marvin Minsky, American cognitive scientist, author of *The Emotion Machine,* and cofounder of the Massachusetts Institute of Technology's AI laboratory, calls "consciousness" a "suitcase word"[2] in that it carries multiple legitimate meanings. Others in the field bemoan "the great variety of technical synonyms" for consciousness, and that this "perfusion of terms tends to hide underlying similarities."[3] Given the graduated fashion in which human brains have evolved and do evolve, it is likely that there are also gradations of consciousness. One common meaning of consciousness is self-awareness. But does it adequately describe the true nature of the condition?

Surely a baby's self-awareness is different from an adolescent's self-awareness, which is quite different from the self-awareness of a middle-aged person with their faculties intact and a quite elderly person who has lost some of their cognitive abilities. How "self-conscious" is a newborn versus an adult? I think of family photos—pictures of my parents when they were children or even of myself as a tiny boy—as evidence of loved ones who no longer exist and who, when they did, certainly had very different states of consciousness than the "final" or the most current version of the flesh-and-blood people the pictures represent.

While self-awareness is clearly an important facet of a conscious person, it's not the only qualification. It certainly would not hold water as a definition of cyberconsciousness. In fact, a programmer can write a concise piece of self-aware software, one that examines, reports on, and even modifies itself.[4] Software running a self-driving vehicle, for example, could be written to define objects in its real world including terrain ("navigate it using sensors"), programmers ("follow any orders coming in"), and the vehicle itself ("I am a robot vehicle that navigates terrain in response to programming orders"). A Google Car does these things right now, and few people would define the code it runs on, or the vehicle itself, as conscious.

Self-aware software and robotic machines don't feel physical or emotional pain or pleasure either—they are not sentient. Most people require mental subjectivity to include emotions, that is, *sentience,* in order to qualify as consciousness, because recognition of how we feel is integral to human consciousness—to the "human condition." Yet sentience still doesn't get us where we want to be in defining consciousness, because we expect conscious beings to be independent thinkers as well as feelers.

Hence, "feelings" is not a stand-alone description of consciousness either. Physical feelings don't require complex cognitive capability. When a hooked fish squirms, many of us would interpret it as evidence that the creature is experiencing pain, while others may consider it an autonomic response, with no accompanying emotional reaction. Many of us would also not consider the fish conscious because we don't believe any part of its neurology is thinking about the pain, philosophizing about it, or complaining about it to others in its group. Instead, we think the fish is simply relying on noncognitive reflexes as it attempts to get out of a nasty situation. Once unhooked and back in its normal environment, the fish continues swimming as if it had never been hooked—and therefore it can easily be hooked again. Indeed, I know of a fisherman who catches and releases the same fish many times during the fishing season. The fish appears to feel the pain of getting hooked, but it never "learns" anything from the experience and no "lessons" are applied to its future aquatic adventures, displaying a lack of a certain crucial amount of self-consciousness.

Of course we humans would likewise reflexively protest being hooked, but we know we would feel the pain, swear about it, and think how to avoid it after the fact. We'd warn others against the pitfalls of the hook, passing on as much as we knew about it. Unlike a fish, we may not be so easily hooked the next time, because we internalize the original painful experience and try to avoid repeating it. We can use our brains to recognize a hook when we see one, and avoid it, as well as predict where the fisherman will stand next time he comes around, and move to another part of the lake. So clearly learning, reason, and judgment (the application of information) are also part of the consciousness equation. Autonomy, and an element of transcendence or what is thought of as our souls, is involved as well. It is in such recondite differences between fish and man that the definition of human consciousness resides.

In 1908 the deaf-and-blind pioneer Helen Keller poignantly and clearly described how human consciousness builds on communication when she said, "Before my teacher came to me, I did not know that I am. I lived in a world that was a no-world. I cannot hope to describe adequately that unconscious, yet conscious time of nothingness. . . . Since I had no power of thought, I did not compare one mental state with another."

In other words, while consciousness has an acceptable minimalist definition of being awake, alert, and aware—"Is he conscious?"—it also has a more salient meaning of thinking and feeling *like anyone reading this book*. To think like a human, then, one must also be able to make the kind of moral decisions, based on some variant of the Golden Rule, that philosophers and scientists alike, from Immanuel Kant to Carl Jung, believed are hardwired into human brains. Ask any healthy person anywhere in the world if it is wrong to hit a child over the head with a baseball bat and they will tell you it is.

Yet another complication in defining consciousness relates to our subconscious mind, which professionals refer to as our unconscious mind. There is overwhelming evidence that we are *not* self-aware of much of what we think and feel, and sometimes even act without thinking. As Yogi Berra summarized so brilliantly, "Think! How the hell are you gonna think and hit at the same time?"

Freud is famous for teaching that an unconscious mind, or Id, of which we are not fully self-aware is often at cross-purposes with a conscious mind, or ego, within which we autonomously reason. Modern psychology has largely distanced itself from Freudian interpretations of unconscious desires, but has accepted "the reality that the unconscious asserts its presence in every moment of our lives, when we are fully awake as well as when we are absorbed in the depths of a dream."[5] It is of course wrong to shoot someone dead over tweeting in a movie theater, but in 2014 a retired policeman did exactly that in Tampa, Florida, because his unconscious mind asserted its presence in a very bad way. President Barack Obama has described in speeches how white women reflexively grabbed their purses and moved away from him, before he was president; many of these reactions were likely unconscious responses to his skin tone.

Neither rationality, nor feelings, nor self-awareness need be present *at all times* for a person to be considered conscious like a human. Indeed, some level of *non-reasoned, non-emotional, non-aware* mental processing goes on pretty nearly *at all times* in the consciousness of everyone reading this book. To be humanly conscious necessarily implies an intermingled unconscious mind. As a human mind gets formed it inevitably shunts certain conceptions (generalizations and stereotypes), motivations (choose this), and decisions (avoid danger) to unconscious neural patterns, thereby providing more time and freeing up more brain power for conscious neural patterns. The same will occur with cyberconsciousness. Much of who we are is what we consciously attend to out of the unconsciously managed background.

A solution to the consciousness conundrum—too many clothes dangling out of the suitcase!—is Douglas Hofstadter's "continuum of consciousness." His approach declares consciousness not to be a "here or not" sort of thing, but instead to be present to a greater or lesser extent in things that demonstrate, to a greater or lesser extent, one or more of the aspects described above—self-awareness, sentience, morality, autonomy, and transcendence. In *I Am a Strange Loop,* Hofstadter grudgingly (owing to the nastiness of his confession) admits a scintilla of consciousness even to the mosquito. While Hofstadter doesn't talk about the Google Car, the "continuum of consciousness" would surely grant it a mosquito's quantum of consciousness, and perhaps a bit more, because unlike the mosquito it need not do harm to another (biting and sucking blood in the case of the insect) in order to achieve its "life purpose": it has been driven over a million miles with no accidents. Hofstadter's confidence in the logic of the continuum is such that he concedes to Gandhi and Albert Schweitzer a greater consciousness than to himself, because they demonstrated an exemplary conscientiousness (self-awareness, sentience, morality, autonomy, and transcendence) superior to his own by any measure.

Another way to appreciate the continuum of consciousness is to reflect that we

> consider creatures to be more conscious to the extent that the decisions they make are more sophisticated, and thus less obviously preprogrammed by evolution, and to the extent that they weigh different wants and urges built in by evolution against each other. The athlete's decision to run through pain is certainly conscious in this sense. In this sense, consciousness is graded, since evidently the athlete makes more sophisticated plans than a fish.[6]

People with mindclones might in fact be said to "raise their consciousness level" or "expand their mind" to the extent cyberconscious extensions of ourselves engage us in more sophisticated decision making, as dual-minded minds, and are less preprogrammed by evolution (e.g., driven by what Carl Sagan called our "reptilian urges"), even if programmed by mindware engineers. Alternatively, mindclones might be thought to be of subhuman consciousness if their decision making was rudimentary and obviously "hardwired."

Supportive of Hofstadter's continuum of consciousness is the July 7, 2012, "Cambridge Declaration on Consciousness," the signing of which was so momentous that the popular television newsmagazine *60 Minutes* filmed it. According to the declaration, "a prominent international group of cognitive neuroscientists, neuropharmacologists, neurophysiologists, neuroanatomists and computational neuroscientists" conclude that the "weight of evidence indicates that humans are not unique in possessing the neurological substrates that generate consciousness. Non-human animals, including all mammals and birds, and many other creatures, including octopuses, also possess these neurological substrates." With a bit more restriction on the length of the continuum of consciousness, Francis Crick and Christof Koch agree, "a language system (of the type found in humans) is not essential for consciousness—that is, one can have the key features of consciousness without language. This is not to say that language does not enrich consciousness considerably."[7] Hence, when we are talking about consciousness in this book we do not mean any kind of consciousness, as that includes beings that chirp, bark, and oink; we are talking about *human* consciousness.

Therefore, the definition of *human cyber* consciousness needs to be personal yet concrete, and androcentric yet ascertainable. Grouping self-awareness and morality into autonomy, and sentience and transcendence into empathy, we arrive at the following definition:

> **Human Cyberconsciousness** = A continuum of software-based human-level autonomy and empathy as determined by consensus of a small group of experts in matters of human consciousness.

Clearly, this is a humancentric definition, but it is not tautological. It is not circular because *"experts* in matters of human consciousness" are the ones who *determine* whether "human-level autonomy and em-pathy" are present. It is humancentric, which is in fact what we want, because, as American philosopher, writer, and cognitive scientist Daniel C. Dennett says, "Whatever else a mind is, it is supposed to be some-thing like our mind; otherwise we wouldn't call it a mind."[8] In other words, humanly conscious is a shorthand way of judging whether a sub-ject thinks and feels like we do, or like other people think and feel. I can muster a certain degree of sympathy with Supreme Court Justice Potter Stewart, who, when asked to define pornography, replied, "I know it when I see it."

By "continuum of human-level autonomy and empathy," I am also including those kinds of independent thinking and feeling that occur subconsciously, in the unconscious mind. Cyberconsciousness soft-ware will have to provide for some quantum of unconscious concep-tions, motivations, and decisions to produce a human-level mind. This is no showstopper, as code running in the background, of which a fore-ground information-processing unit is not "aware," is a long-ago-mastered programming skill.

The Einstein of computing, Alan Turing, was the first to publish the idea that software was humanly conscious if it successfully passed itself off to humans as being humanly conscious. Today we call this the "Turing test." In the words of his biographer: "To avoid philosophical discussions of what 'mind' or 'thought' or 'free will' were supposed to be, he favoured the idea of judging a machine's mental capacity simply by comparing its performance with that of a human being. It was an *operational* definition of 'thinking', rather as Einstein had insisted on operational definitions of time and space in order to liberate his theory from *a priori* assumptions. . . . If a machine appeared to be doing as well as a human being, then it *was* doing as well as a human being." [9]

Our definition of human cyberconsciousness tightens the Turing test to require that software persuade not just a single individual but a small group of experts, and not simply with regard to casual conversa-tion but with regard to autonomy and empathy. One might criticize the Turing test by saying that, for example, he is claiming that if a wooden duck "appeared to be doing as well" as a real duck, then it was a real duck, when it fact it obviously is not. But this criticism falls flat, because Turing's whole point is that it is *function being tested, not form.* If a wooden duck swims as well as a real duck, then it *is* a real duck swimmer. If a machine thinks as well as a human thinker, then it *is* a human thinker.[10]

Brain Snobbery—Our Human Conceit

There are plenty of people who just cannot get their heads around the idea that a computer could express consciousness the way our friend or our mom expresses it toward us—through companionship, love, laughter, compassion, empathy, and so on. Indeed, as recently as World War II, in the 1940s, the word "computer" meant nothing like what it means today. A "computer" was usually a person whose job it was to make calculations, such as someone doing mathematics for an insurance company, or, if not that, a machine that did mathematics for a person (as a washer was someone who washed clothes, but if not, a machine that did that). For example, during the Great Depression, in the 1930s, the U.S. government spent stimulus money on hundreds of computers—people, not machines—to create mathematical tables for things like artillery trajectories. The people, poor and mostly undereducated, were even represented by a "computers union" and were given easy, repetitive subcomputations to make that were ultimately combined by mathematicians into sophisticated arithmetic solutions.

In 1937 Alan Turing published a scholarly article (in a journal called *Computable Numbers*) about a theoretical "universal computing machine" that could *do anything* provided it was given the correct program. This radical notion rendered mathematically rigorous similar ideas of Charles Babbage and Ada King, Countess of Lovelace a century earlier (1837). They called their machines "difference engines" (for numerical work, which they built) and "analytical engines" (for almost any task, programmed with punched cards, which they never built but was similar to Turing's idea). From this very slight context it took huge leaps of imagination to think that a "computer" might be something that could read, write, listen, scan, play videos, play music, diagnose medical conditions . . . and think . . . and feel. Yet this was precisely Turing's vision, because he saw that future digital computers would be able to practically employ the same kind of logic that supported reading, writing, listening, scanning, video, music, diagnosis . . . and thinking . . . and feeling. As *digital* computing technology began to appear, in the 1950s and 1960s, understanding (both critical and supportive) audiences grew for Turing's revolutionary claim. He made plain that not even human consciousness was excluded from what a computer could do in an article published under the title "Computing Machinery and Intelligence" in October 1950 (in a journal called *Mind*).[11]

Today, the public believes a computer *can* do just about anything (hence smartphones are called digital Swiss Army knives)—and they can surely read, write, listen, scan, play videos, play music, and diagnose conditions. Some can even move (robots), and think (within a programmed competency). Indeed, the modern layperson's meaning for computer is something like "a category of devices that can do almost anything with information, and every year they get yet more capable." This is a long way from "a person who does computations," and getting rather close to Turing's vision of "a machine that can do anything with information." As computers begin to evidence emotions and other aspects of human consciousness, they will have completed the journey whose start and destination points are well summarized by the titles of the first and second journals that published Alan Turing's seminal articles—from *Computable Numbers* to *Mind*. Having gone in half a century from a word meaning number-cruncher to a word meaning smart (as in smartphone), "computer," I believe, will soon come to mean "place for artificial consciousness." Note how each definition subsumes its predecessor: smart subsumes number crunching, and consciousness subsumes smart.

Until something starts acting in a way we recognize as human, we still have a hard time thinking it could be humanlike at some point.

Computers fall under special suspicion because they both dominate our lives and remain inscrutable to most of us. Pretty pushy for a collection of wires and plastic and metal; the idea that a computer could be like us seems at once frightening and preposterous. If you still feel this way, you're in good company.

Skeptics of software consciousness like the Nobel Prize–winning physician and physical chemist Gerald M. Edelman and the mathematical physicist and philosopher Roger Penrose say that the transcendent characteristics of human consciousness can never be codified digitally because they are too complicated, unknowable, or immeasurable. Edelman is adamant that a brain is not like a computer, and therefore a computer can never be like a brain. In Edelman's words, "One illusion I hope to dispel is the notion that our brains are computers and that consciousness could emerge from computation."[12] Indeed, his three primary reasons that a computer (by way of computer software) could never become conscious are ultimately different ways of saying the same thing: The brain is vastly more complex than a computer.

Edelman is particularly important to this discussion because many critics of the idea that computer software could become cyberconsciousness look to his views for confirmation of their biases. As we examine Edelman's arguments, ask yourself what will happen as computers are transformed by exponentially increasing sophistication. Even if the computer will never be like a brain, are we heading to a point when computers will *perform human thought* just like brains?

It is easy to get misled into thinking that because a brain is not like a computer that a computer cannot think like a mind. But it is important to remember that a computer does not have to replicate every function of a brain to support a mindclone. In an analogous vein, consider that a bird is not like a plane, but both fly. As a mentioned in the introduction, with billions of eukaryotic cells the bird is vastly more complex than a Boeing 747, which has just over six million parts. Today, planes fly farther, higher, and faster than birds. On the other hand, planes can't stay aloft for months like swifts or frigate birds, although eventually advances in efficient and lightweight solar power and other types of battery storage systems may allow planes to stay in the air for very long periods of time. Likewise, airplanes can't fly through small apertures or hover above a flower as hummingbirds do. However, the latest remote-controlled planes and tiny flying program-controlled surveillance equipment, drones, can do this.

It's also crucial when thinking about this analogy to remember that for flying purposes we only want planes to provide a portion of the functionality that a bird provides. There is no prospect of planes laying eggs, nesting in trees or in the eaves of a house, or running on "fuel" in the form of fish, worms, or insects—and there is no practical or efficiency value in an airplane doing any of these things. In other words, a plane does not have to replicate a bird in every way to support safe and comfortable flight. Hence, I think it is fair to conclude that birds are to flight as brains are to consciousness.

The differences between brains and computers, or between birds and planes, beg the point. Only the military would be interested in a plane that performs the aerodynamic feats of a peregrine falcon. Most people's interest in planes is as a method to go from city to city safely, efficiently, reliably, and in as much comfort as an airline allows these days. Similarly, most of us are not the least bit interested in a computer that can self-organize itself gradually from birth to maturity. Our intention is to provide a computer with an analogue of a human's mind (not the brain) in one fell swoop. We are interested in a computer that thinks and feels the same as a human original mind. Edelman assumes, rather than deduces, his conclusion because he assumes that consciousness is limited to brains. Whether or not brains are computers is not dispositive of whether or not consciousness can emerge from computation.

Things that are mutually exclusive sets, such as, for argument's sake, brains and computers, can still give rise to phenomena that are common to both sets. For example, odd numbers and even numbers are mutually exclusive sets. We can imagine odd numbers to be brains and even numbers to be computers. Yet both can give rise to Fibonacci numbers, a series of numbers where the next number is found by adding up the two numbers before it, which can also be imagined as a metaphor for consciousness. Similarly, triangles and squares are mutually exclusive sets. Yet each may be combined to form rectangles. Edelman's error is to say that since he has seen the rectangle of consciousness formed only from neurological squares, and since computers are triangles rather than squares, the rectangle of consciousness cannot be formed from triangles. He forgets that just as there are many ways to skin a cat, and many ways for a thing to fly, there are also many ways to form the rectangle of consciousness.

Edelman claims that while "the brain does not operate by logical rules," "a computer must receive unambiguous input signals."[13] He emphasizes that inputs to the brain are not "a piece of coded tape," referring to an archaic method of feeding information into a computer. Surely the brain is not like a very primitive computer that runs on "coded tape." Actually, not all computers require unambiguous input signals. Some computers have successfully driven automobiles across the country and across deserts based on a blizzard of very ambiguous input signals.[14] On the other hand, some modern computers are able to parse a blurry, buzzing reality into cognizable elements with very much the same result as a human mind gets. Fuzzy logic, statistical analysis protocols, and voting among parallel processors analyzing the same ambiguous data are just three of many techniques being deployed to enable software to make sense of confusing sensory inputs: to guess, and to guess strategically.

For example, let's take a hike. Let's follow a forest path near BINA48's home in Vermont, blanketed in an earth-tone palette of fallen autumn leaves. Let's take this path side by side with a smartphone or Google Glass–based computer equipped with cyberconsciousness and software trained or programmed to find paths. As we humans walk through the forest, billions of our human neurons detect elements of millions of color, density, and geometry signals. Our eyes deliver this information to the brain at a rate of about three million bits of information per second.[15] Vast networks of the neurons, in parallel, parse together the avalanche of incoming signals into patterns based upon a lifetime of experience that has taught neurons that "fire together" to "wire together." Symphonic patterns of leaves, trees, and pathways will emerge from this cacophony of input signals. We won't consciously be aware of every leaf on every tree (indeed, our eyes can discern detail only in the tiny foveal region away from our peripheral vision). From all the incoming data, our minds construct for us, abstract for us, by stitching together (from a "visual saccade" of the foveal detail our eyes deliver as they dart back and forth), a forest and trail. Sometimes our minds fill in almost all the detail; sometimes things get fabricated out of "whole cloth."

Meanwhile, our cyberconscious smartphone-based partner sees the same menagerie of autumn colors, shapes, and densities. But, unlike our brains, the cyberconscious partner rapidly compares the scene to millions of stored images and determines it to be a forest. The partner then determines which part of the forest scene has a continuous zone of reduced density—a path—and directs its attention down the path. The end result of what our cyberconscious partner does, and what a biological mind does, is remarkably similar: very high-level conscious abstractions (forest, path) from a blizzard of subconscious three-megabit-per-second data. The sense of awe that I feel for each moment in a forest is no less wondrous when experienced by cyberconsciousness. If we get lost in brush, our cyberconscious partner, as reliably as the Labradoodles with whom I hike, can discern a path to the trail back out of the forest.

In each instance there has been thought, although it was achieved as differently as a bird and a plane achieve flight. In each instance, and based on my many experiences of walking through forests with friends, there was likely some level of appreciation of beauty and a sense of satisfaction with a challenge surmounted. For the cyberconscious partner this requires the original programming of values for "aesthetics," "wonder," and "task completion" at a high level for natural scenes, autumn woods and hiking a trail. But this is no less constructed than teaching a child that nature is cool, the forest is amazing, and completing a challenge is good. Even granting (notwithstanding contrary data from feral children) that the human settings for aesthetics, wonder, and task completion might exist endogenously, as part of the wiring of a human brain, the feelings are no less authentic simply because they were "trained into" or programmed into a software mind. An appreciation of harmony is no less worthy because it was taught rather than inborn.

Second, Edelman notes that the brain is enormously variable at its finest levels, observing that "the wrinkled cortical mantle of the brain has about thirty billion nerve cells or neurons and one million billion connections. The number of possible active pathways of such a structure far exceeds the number of elementary particles in the known universe."[16] He doubts that computers can match this variability owing to a rigorous reliance upon internal clocks, inputs, and outputs. Yet the MacBook Pro I used to write this chapter has about *five hundred* billion bytes of memory, with each byte being about the memory capacity of a single neuron. In other words, there is over fifteen times more neural capacity in my laptop than in my cortical mantle. Hence, just in terms of *numbers* of nerve cells, there is no great difference between computers and the brain. If anything, computers now have more neuron equivalents than brains have neurons, and soon will have very many more.

Now, if each JPG in the memory in my computer connected to thousands of other JPGs, and if each of those connections participated in preferred, reinforced, and naturally selected hierarchies of additional connections, I would have something like a human brain. For example, imagine that when I click on a picture of my dad, he is surrounded by automatically called-up pictures of my mom, my cousins, our houses, our vacations, and so on—and that each of them is automatically surrounded by a similar halo of images, yet of all the connections the ones that remain highlighted are ones that were selected from a large universe of possible images to be most relevant to the triggered image. Is this not how our own mind works when we browse through a photo album? We don't remember and react to *every past experience;* we select and privilege some memories and connected feelings over others.

Our Consciousness, Our Software

You see things; and you say "Why?" But I dream things that never were; and I say "Why not?"
—GEORGE BERNARD SHAW, *BACK TO METHUSELAH*

Brains are awesome relational databases. Consciousness arises from a set of connections among sensory neuron outputs, and links between such connections and sequences of higher-order connections. With each neuron able to make as many as ten thousand connections, and with 100 billion neurons, there is ample possibility for each person to have subjective experiences through idiosyncratic patterns of connectivity.

But brains need not be made solely of flesh. There are other ways to flexibly connect billions of pieces of information together. Software brains designed to run on powerful processors have reproduced the ways in which our brains give rise to the aspects of consciousness we've discussed: IBM's Watson, who mastered the ambiguities of *Jeopardy!*; the BINA48 described in the introduction, who demonstrates empathy; Ray Kurzweil's programs that idiosyncratically draw, compose music, and write poetry.

Many programmers, scientists, and others believe code can be written to transcend code.

It is this fresh and slightly enigmatic characteristic, especially when applied in furtherance of rationality and/or empathy, that we expect in anyone who is conscious rather than autonomic (engaging in actions or responses without conscious control). In a nutshell, people are not as predictable as machines because consciousness is not as algorithmic as a calculation. Consciousness requires idiosyncrasy, literally thoughts and actions based upon an individualized synthesis of options. Hence, "independence" does not require being a pioneer, or a leader. It does require being able to make decisions and act based on a personalized assessment rather than only on a rigid formula.

This takes us back again to the essence of consciousness, and what philosopher David Chalmers calls the "hard problem" and the "easy problem" of consciousness. The "hard problem" is figuring out how the web of molecules we call neurons gives rise to subjective feelings or qualia (individual instances of conscious subjective experience, i.e., "the redness of red"). The alternative "easy problem" is how electrons racing along neurochemistry result in complex simulations of "concrete-and-mortar" (and flesh-and-blood) reality. Or how metaphysical thoughts arise from physical matter. Basically, both the hard and the easy problems of consciousness come down to this: How is it that brains give rise to thoughts (easy problem), especially about immeasurable things (hard problem), but other parts of bodies do not? If these hard and easy questions can be answered for brain waves running on molecules, then it remains only to ask whether the answers are different for software code running on integrated circuits.

At least since the time of Isaac Newton and Gottfried Leibniz, it has been felt that some things appreciated by the mind could be measured whereas others cannot. The measurable thoughts, such as the size of a building, or the name of a friend, were imagined to take place in the brain via some exquisite micromechanical processes. Today we would draw analogies to a computer's memory chips, processors, and peripherals. Although this is the easy problem of consciousness, we still need an actual explanation of exactly *how* one or more neurons save, cut, paste, and recall any word, number, scent, or image. In other words, how do neuromolecules catch and process bits of information?

Those things that cannot be measured are the hard problem. In Chalmers's view, a being could be conscious, but not human, if they were only capable of the "easy" kind of consciousness. Such a being, called a zombie, would be robotic, without feelings, empathy, or nuances. That does not fall under our working definition of consciousness. Since the non-zombie, non-robot characteristics are also purported to be immeasurable (e.g., the redness of red or the heartache of unrequited love), Chalmers cannot see even in principle how they could ever be processed by something physical, such as neurons.

Chalmers suggests that consciousness is a mystical phenomenon that can never be explained by science. If this is the case, then one could argue that it might attach just as well to software as to neurons—or that it might not—or that it might perfuse the air we breathe and the space between the stars. If consciousness is mystical, then anything is possible. As I demonstrate here, there's no need to go there. Perfectly mundane, empirical explanations are available to explain both the easy and the hard kinds of consciousness. These explanations work as well for neurons as they do for software.

Figure 1, Essentialists vs. Materialists, illustrates the three basic points of view regarding the source of consciousness. Essentialists believe in a biological source specific to humans. This is basically a view that in the whole universe, almost miraculously, only brains can give rise to consciousness. Materialists believe in an empirical source, namely that consciousness emerges as patterns from myriad connections among information stored either as chemical states in brain neurons or voltage states in computer chips. The philosopher Daniel Dennett is a good proponent of this view, observing in his Multiple Drafts model of consciousness back in 1991, and before, that robot consciousness is, in principle, possible.[17] Note that the diagram also indicates how a person could be both an essentialist and a materialist. This would be in the overlap area of the two circles.

Edelman is a good proponent of the point of view that only brains can give rise to consciousness, but it is because of the materialistic properties of the brain as opposed to a spiritual source. Other essentialists (represented by the part of the essentialist circle that does *not* overlap with materialist) believe it is something other than replicable material complexity that enables brains to be conscious. A third point of view is that consciousness is part of the fabric of reality, an aspect of space-time that can mystically attach to anything. The view that God gave consciousness to Adam and Eve, or other "first humans," is part of this third, spiritualist perspective. While mystical explanations cannot be disproved, they are unnecessary, because there is a perfectly reasonable nonmystical explanation for both the easy and hard kinds of consciousness.[18]

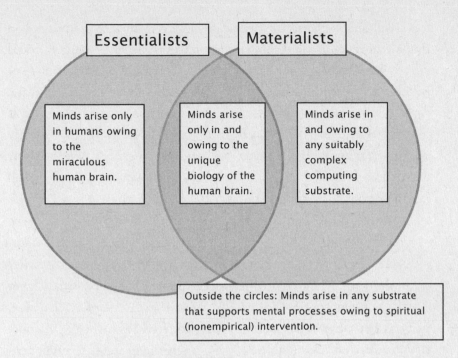

Essentialists

Materialists

Minds arise only in humans owing to the miraculous human brain.

Minds arise only in and owing to the unique biology of the human brain.

Minds arise in and owing to any suitably complex computing substrate.

Outside the circles: Minds arise in any substrate that supports mental processes owing to spiritual (nonempirical) intervention.

FIGURE 1. ESSENTIALISTS vs. MATERIALISTS.

I believe that John Searle of Stanford University provides the most creative insight into categorization of philosophical approaches to the mind. Searle is famous in consciousness circles for having created a thought experiment called the Chinese room. The experiment purports to show that a *conventionally* programmed computer could not be conscious for the same reason that, say, Google Translate does not *understand* what we ask it to translate Chinese-to-English. The *conventionally* programmed computer is mindlessly associating each input with an output, having no internal process of subjectively caring about or contemplating what it is doing. The lights are on, but nobody's home. This certainly fails the definitional test we set forth for cyberconsciousness above: human-level empathy and autonomy, in the judgment of human experts.

Searle broadens the definition of "materialism" to encompass *subjective* phenomena such as the *thoughts* of consciousness. He notes that these are nonspiritual and "a part of the natural 'physical world'" but simply not tangible and quantifiable.[19] Consequently, he is comfortable saying "If brains can have consciousness as an emergent property, why not other sorts of machinery?"[20] This categorizes him as a materialist, for he concludes that "there is no known obstacle in principle to building an artificial machine that can be conscious and can think."[21] But he reaches his conclusion by observing that it is *not* very important that the neuronal or software patterns that give rise to a thought (or qualia) be objectively measurable—that we could trace with advanced MRI-type equipment the neural pathways or get a readout of the software routines. This gives materialism its due—there is something empirical to observe from a third-party perspective and measure—but diminishes the import of these neuronal (or software) measurements, since such *objective* materiality is just *part* of what makes consciousness unique. He rises above materialism by clarifying that the actual *experience* of the ultimate thought, or string of thoughts, is *not* objectively measurable, because it occurs *interiorly* to one's consciousness.[22] Hence, *subjectivity is real* (i.e., not spiritual and not limited to a miraculous human brain) even if it is not available to a third party's measurement.[23] Later in this chapter, under "Measuring the Immeasurable," I will discuss how we can at least obtain a good-enough approximation of this subjective materialism.

If human consciousness is to arise in software we must do three things: first, explain how the easy problem is solved in neurons; second, explain how the hard problem is solved in neurons; and third, explain how the solution in neurons is replicable in information technology. The key to all three explanations is the relational-database concept. With the relational database an inquiry (or a sensory input for the brain) triggers a number of related responses. Each of these responses is, in turn, a stimulus for a further number of related responses. An output response is triggered when the strength of a stimulus, such as the number of times it was triggered, is greater than a set threshold.[24]

For example, there are certain neurons hardwired by our DNA to be sensitive to different wavelengths of light, and other neurons are sensitive to different phonemes, a basic unit of a language's phonology, or sounds, which is combined with other phonemes to form meaningful words. So, suppose when looking at something red, we are repeatedly told that "it is red." The red-sensitive neuron becomes paired with, among other neurons, the neurons that are sensitive to the different phonetics that make up the sounds "it is red." Over time, we learn that there are many shades of red, and our neurons responsible for these varying wavelengths each become associated with words and objects that reflect the different "redness" of any one particular shade of red of the millions that exist.

The redness of red is simply (1) each person's unique set of connections between neurons hardwired genetically from the retina to the various wavelengths we associate with different reds, and (2) the plethora of further synaptic connections we have between those hardwired neurons and neural patterns that include things that are red. If the only red thing a person ever saw was an apple, then redness to them means the red-wavelength neuron output that is part of the set of neural connections associated in their mind with an apple. Red*ness* is not an electrical signal in our mind per se, but it is the *associations* of color wavelength signals with a referent in the real world. Redness is part of the multifaceted impression obtained in a second or less from the immense pattern of neural connections we have built up about red things.

After a few front lines of sensory neurons, everything else is represented in our minds as a pattern of neural connections. It is as if the sensory neurons are our alphabet. These are associated (via synapses) in a vast number of ways to form mental images of objects and actions, just as letters can be arranged into a dictionary full of words. The mental images can be strung together (many more synaptic connections) into any number of coherent (even when dreaming) sequences to form worldviews, emotions, personalities, and guides to behavior. This is just like grouping words into a limitless number of coherent sentences, paragraphs, and chapters.

Grammar for words is like the as yet poorly understood electrochemical properties of the brain that enable strengthening or weakening of waves of synaptic connections that support attentiveness, mental continuity, and characteristic thought patterns. Continuing the analogy, the self, our consciousness, is the entire book of our autonomous and empathetic lives, written with that idiosyncratic style that is unique to us. It is a book full of chapters of life phases, paragraphs of things we've done, and sentences reflecting streams of thought.

Neurons save, cut, paste, and recall any word, number, scent, image, sensation, or feeling no differently for the so-called hard than for the so-called easy problems of consciousness. Let's take as our example the "hard" problem of love, or what Ray Kurzweil calls the "ultimate form of intelligence." Robert Heinlein defines it as the feeling that another's happiness is essential to your own. Neurons save the subject of someone's love as a collection of outputs from hardwired sensory neurons tuned to the subject's shapes, colors, scents, phonetics, and/or textures. These outputs come from the front-line neurons that emit a signal only when they receive a signal of a particular contour, light wave, pheromone, sound wave, or tactile sensation. The set of outputs that describes the subject of our love is a stable thought; once established as part of the set with some units of neurochemical strength, any one of the triggering sensory neurons can trigger other sensory neurons. These neurons paste thoughts together with matrices of synaptic connections.

The constellation of sensory neuron outputs that is the thought of the subject of our love is, itself, connected to a vast array of additional thoughts, each grounded directly or, via other thoughts, indirectly to sensory neurons. Those other thoughts would include the many cues that lead us to love someone or something. There may be resemblance in appearance or behavior to some previously favored person or thing, or logical connection to some preferred entity. As we spend more time with the subject of our love, we further strengthen sensory connections with additional and robust synaptic associations, such as those connected with eroticism, mutuality, endorphins, and adrenaline.

There is no neuron with our lover's face on it. There are instead a vast number of neurons that, as a stable set of connections, represent our lover. The connections are stable because they are important to us. When things are important to us, we concentrate on them, and as we do, the brain increases the neurochemical strengths of their neural connections. Many things are unimportant to us, or become so. For these things the neurochemical linkages become weaker, and finally the thought dissipates like an abandoned spiderweb. Neurons cut unused and unimportant thoughts by weakening the neurochemical strengths of their connections. Often a vestigial connection is retained, capable of being triggered by a concentrated retracing of its path of creation, starting with the sensory neurons that anchor it.

That means that the so-called hard problem of consciousness isn't so hard after all. Crick and Koch astutely observe that there is nothing new about complex and experiential phenomena arising from a multiplicity of adroitly connected inanimate pieces. The subjectivity of our perceptions (redness of red from an array of neurons) is no more difficult to explain than "the 'livingness' of living things (such as bacteria, for example) from an array of 'dead' molecules." The DNA discoverer and his neuroscience collaborator conclude that

> meaning derives both from the correlated firing . . . and from the linkages to related representations. For example, neurons related to a certain face might be connected to ones expressing the name of the person whose face it is, and to others for her voice, memories involving her and so on, in a vast associational network, similar to a dictionary or a relationship database.[25]

Wholes can transcend the dimensionality of pieces when the pieces are combined right. Subjectivity is simply each person's unique way of connecting the higher-order neuron patterns that come after the sensory neurons. Think of subjectivity as the volume on your music player. The more you value the sensation, the memory, the feeling, the idea, or the person, the louder you want to play it, the better headset you search for to listen to it, the tighter you close your eyes as you savor the sounds. The hard problem of consciousness is the idiosyncratic settings of amplitudes to the patterns of connections in our minds.

The easy problem of consciousness is solved in the recognition of sensory neurons as empirical scaffolding upon which can be built a skyscraper's worth of thoughts. If it can be accepted that sensory neurons can as a group define a higher-order concept, and that such higher-order concepts can as a group define yet higher-order concepts, then the easy problem of consciousness is solved. Material neurons can hold nonmaterial thoughts because the neurons are linked members of a cognitive code. *It is the metamaterial pattern of the neural connections, not the neurons themselves, that contains nonmaterial thoughts. The vogue term for this metamaterial pattern is the human "connectome."* Hence, neuroscientists today feel comfortable saying "We are our connectome."[26]

Lastly, there is the question of whether there is something essential about the way neurons form into content-bearing patterns, or whether the same feat could be accomplished with software. The strengths of neuronal couplings of the brain can be replicated in software by writing code that weights various strengths for software couplings in relational databases. Weighting software couplings means making certain decisions more likely than others. For example, in the formula $x = 5y$, the value of x is five times the weight of y. If thoughts of weight x would arise five times as often, or have five times the importance, as thoughts with the weight of y, then $x = 5y$.

William Sims Bainbridge of the U.S. National Science Foundation is a leading expert on software coding of personality attributes. He has managed the validation across thousands of people of personality-capture surveys such as the Big Five (a mainstay of psychologists consisting of twenty Likert-type-scale questions relating to each of extraversion, agreeableness, conscientiousness, emotional stability, and imagination)[27] and the 16PF (assesses sixteen dimensions of personality—warmth, reasoning, emotional stability, dominance, liveliness, rule-consciousness, social boldness, sensitivity, vigilance, abstractedness, privateness, apprehension, openness to change, self-reliance, perfectionism, and tension).[28]

Bainbridge has created and validated his own personality-capture system based upon more than one hundred thousand questions.[29] Each question is weighted two-dimensionally, by relative importance of the personality attribute to the person and relative degree of applicability to the person. This book's hypothesis is that a quantification of a person's mindfile using Bainbridge's two-dimensionally weighted hundred thousand personality-capture questions will produce a software-based personality that responds to life as would the original person. The actual assessment across the hundred thousand personality-capture questions would be done automatically by mindware reviewing a person's mindfile. Mindware would then use the results of the assessment to establish the personality settings for a mindclone.

The connectivity of one neuron to up to ten thousand other neurons in the brain can be replicated in software by linking one software input to up to ten thousand software outputs. Probability-based weightings, such as using the statistical methods of Bayesian networks, will also help mindware mirror human thought processes. The ability of neuronal patterns to maintain themselves in waves of constancy, such as in personality or concentration, could equally well be accomplished with software programs that were written to keep specific software groupings active, such as performing a complicated calculation over and over.

Finally, a software system can be provided with every kind of sensory input (audio, video, scent, taste, tactile). Putting it all together, Daniel Dennett observes, "If the self is 'just' the Center of Narrative Gravity, and if all the phenomena of human consciousness are explicable as 'just' the activities of a virtual machine realized in the astronomically adjustable connections of a human brain, then, in principle, a suitably 'programmed' robot, with a silicon-based computer brain, would be conscious, would have a self. More aptly, there would be a conscious self whose body was the robot and whose brain was the computer."[30]

At least for a materialist, there seems to be nothing essential to neurons, in terms of creating consciousness, that could not be achieved as well with software. The quotation marks around "just" in the quote from Dennett is the famous philosopher's facetious smile. He is saying with each "just" that there is nothing to belittle about such a great feat of connectivity and patterning.

Indeed, Dennett is following the path Alan Turing blazed a half century earlier:

> that whatever a brain did, it did by virtue of its structure as a logical system, and not because it was inside a person's head or because it was a spongy tissue made up of a particular kind of biological cell formation. And if this were so, then its logical structure could just as well be represented in some other medium, embodied by some other physical machinery. It was a materialist view of mind, but one that did not confuse logical patterns and relations with physical substances and things as so often people did.[31]

Turing was perhaps the first to truly appreciate that minds or psychology just happened to function by way of the same kind of discrete logical systems as did ideal computers. (No doubt this insight flowed from his brilliance in computer science, including building the Enigma computer, which cracked the Nazi secret codes and helped win World War II.) Therefore the function of a mind—human consciousness— could in fact be replicated in an appropriate computer. "It was not a reduction, but an attempt at transference, when he imagined embodying such systems in an artificial 'brain.'"[32]

The Limitlessness of Software

Is there something physically about computers and software that cannot replicate the connectivity feature of the human mind? No. Already, the number of possible arrangements of the 500 billion bytes of memory in my computer far exceeds the number of elementary particles in the universe. This kind of a statistic shared by Edelman is not beyond the complexity potential of computers. Mindware consciousness is achievable because our human thoughts and emotions are patterns among symbols. These patterns can be the same whether the symbols are encoded in our brains or in our mindfiles. The patterns and connections are so complex that today only certain threads are available as software, but every year the range of symbol association achievable by software leaps forward. For example, software that thinks how to get from our house to a new restaurant is now common, but didn't exist just a decade ago.

There is no a priori limit on the number of connections between the software equivalent of nerve cells. Top websites, for example, routinely have tens of thousands of active connections—other websites pointing to them. But it is also true that so far nobody has written software that enables a database with anywhere near a thousand million connections between fields, as exist in the brain. Work in this direction is proceeding rapidly, however, and traditional relational-database systems are becoming more agile and more interconnected with the vast, low-cost resources of cloud computing.

Nevertheless, there is actually no need to argue over the relevance of information-technology development to the extraordinarily rich milieu of cerebral neurology. *Instead, we can grant Edelman's point that the brain is vastly more complex, variable, self-organizing, unpredictable, and dynamic than any computer.* We materialists all readily concede that human consciousness arises from the unfathomably complex neural circuitry of the human brain—from this "marvelous matter underlying the mind [that] is like no other."[33] It does not follow, however, that human consciousness *cannot* arise from any other substrate.

As I've noted, flight surely does arise from the exquisitely complex biochemistry and neuromuscular physiology of birds. Yet does that mean flight *cannot* arise from our vastly simpler airplanes, helicopters, jets, drones, and remotely piloted vehicles? We know that it can. Nature is full of examples of separate evolutionary development of comparable functionality—some pathways more simple than others. Unnecessarily complex or elegantly designed machines can accomplish many tasks just the same. The eye has evolved at least fifty different times in the last few hundred million years, developing a wide range of adaptations to meet the needs of the beings that have them: night vision, color vision, binocular vision, eagle vision, infrared vision. For example, the eye started as a simple photosensitive pigment, essentially a yes-or-no relay of the presence of light, insufficient for vision. During what is called the Cambrian explosion, a time of accelerated evolution about 542 million years ago, eye structure and functionality increased in many species to include image processing and detection of light direction. Lenses evolved later and at different times in different species, according to their various evolutionary needs. That a structure (such as the human brain) results in a process (such as consciousness) does not say anything as to whether something very similar to that process (such as cyberconsciousness) could be achieved with a different structure (mindfiles, mindware, and mindclones).

Edelman makes a tour-de-force showing that the brain is complex enough to account for any degree of subjective thought. He shows that it does so through variance and selection on a microscopic scale writ numerically very large (what he calls neural Darwinism), not via a priori design and logic. Edelman is persuasive in his assessment that the brain's functionality arises from a design principle more like the strengthening and adaptive capabilities of our immune system than like the architecture of a computer network. That is, when the immune system is challenged with things it doesn't recognize, either it adapts or the person dies. Over the course of human evolution, those who had, for example, immune systems that adapted—e.g., memory T cells, helper T cells—lived, and those who lacked them did not pass on those genes. As such, Edelman demolishes the arguments that consciousness requires explanations from quantum physics (much less metaphysics). On the other hand, he doesn't touch the question of whether consciousness could *also* arise from relational mindfile databases and recurrent mindware algorithms.[34]

In other words, Edelman is adamant that "all basketball stars are tall" (i.e., that any neural circuitry as nonlinearly complex as a human brain—the "basketball star"—will be conscious, or "tall"), but he cannot logically argue that, "everyone tall is a basketball star" (i.e., that all consciousness must be brain-based).

Finally, Edelman observes that the brain is not a computer because a brain is defined by a genetic code far more limited than the amount of neural variability that results in a mature brain. But computer software need not be predetermined either. My computer came with Microsoft Office, but I have written countless pages that far transcend the amount of specificity represented by even that leviathan software package. In general, operating systems for computers, like genetic codes for people, can create an almost unlimited amount of variability.

In addition, there are Darwinian algorithms that allow software code to self-assemble analogously to how neural connections self-assemble. Code that self-assembles usefully enough to be in frequent demand (like neural connections that fire and wire together) gets replicated more frequently (like preferred neural pathways for frequent thoughts or behaviors). A great example of this is the massively retweeted one-liner or image, or the overly sampled music riff, or the endlessly viewed, liked, and shared video clip. All of these codes get recombined into larger assemblies of code in a Darwinian process of self-replication (with humans or robot servers functioning as natural selection). The same process also occurs with code for voice recognition, spatial navigation, and chatbotting (or automated online conversational agents)—but hackers cut-and-paste this code. Why do you think so many websites make us decipher strange-looking strings of letters and numbers to prove we are not computer robominds? It is because robot code self-assemblers, also called web crawlers, are already in our midst.

"Hackers," by the way, should not be confused with "crackers." Hackers are honest people who are passionate about computer programming and have an ethic that encourages very liberal sharing of the software code they create. Crackers are programmers who try to break through computer security systems.[35]

Ultimately, Edelman is a biological essentialist, rejecting the idea that our minds can have any existence detached from their underlying brains, and human brains in particular. Because he believes minds arise from neural Darwinism—selection due to competition among vast numbers of neurons—he cannot imagine that a mind could arise from something so predetermined-sounding as a "computer program." On the other hand, he readily admits that much of the knowledge that arises from our minds is beyond scientific analysis, creating wide parallel playing fields for the humanities.[36] I believe that, if pressed, he would concede that the mind could create a software mind, but that it would not think very much like a mind that arose organically via neural Darwinism.[37]

Yes, the brain is complex: some 100 billion neurons, so densely packed that a quarter million of them fit in the size of this ■, with many if not most of them sprouting thousands of microscopic ultra-spindly connections to other neurons, all in the depth and surface area equivalent to the front of a T-shirt.[38] *Wow.* But information technology is also complex. An array of microchips can have some 100 billion components, so densely packed that millions of them fit in the size of this ■, with many if not most of those components sprouting ultra-spindly (nanometer-width) connections to other components. *Wow, again.* And while brains must be of a size that can be birthed through a vaginal canal, information technology can be spread across thousands of square feet of servers to enable tens of thousands of connections among discrete integrated circuits, with the complexity of such processing delivered wirelessly. I believe that Edelman and other biological essentialists have done a bang-up job of proving that of all the flora and fauna on this planet, only human brains could have come up with mindcloning substrate as structurally complex in its own way as human brains are in theirs. But now that this has occurred, and continues to rapidly advance, it is a reasonable proposition that this artificial complexity can give rise to a mind as surely as does our biological complexity.

Measuring the Immeasurable

The legal system long ago solved the issue of consciousness practically with its creation of a jury of one's peers. Society is accustomed to letting others make determinative decisions about the mental states of individuals. For instance, someone is guilty of an intentional crime if *other people* (the jury) think they had the *mental intent* to commit the crime (as well as performing the criminal acts). Other times, a jury may decide someone is not culpable because of a diminished mental state, or a reduced consciousness. These people are treated very differently than the conscious criminal, and rightly so. Likewise, a team of medical and sometimes religious experts (depending on your point of view and belief system) will often assist in determining the state of consciousness of a person in a so-called "vegetative state" when helping a family make decisions about a loved one's care.

Importantly, there has recently been a sea change from neglect to acceptance of the scientific study of consciousness. One group of scientists now feels that the testimony of a purportedly conscious subject is good enough for measuring consciousness as an experimental variable. For example, Bernard Baars concludes:

> In sum, behavior reports of conscious experience have proved to be quite reliable. Although more direct measures are desirable [such as neuronal correlates of consciousness gleaned from brain scans], reportability provides a useful public criterion for brain studies of consciousness in humans and some animals.[39]

In other words, cognitive science is beginning to accept that we can scientifically determine whether or not someone is conscious based on our assessment of the subject's own reports of their consciousness. I sometimes hear the fear that mindclones could fool us, and that a very clever robot that was artificially intelligent, but not conscious, and hence what some philosophers would call a zombie, might fake their way into human rights and citizenship. But this fear is misplaced, because cognitive scientists have gained adequate confidence in their ability to not only judge reports of conscious experience, but to also adduce the extent to which they conform to actual *subjective* experiences (i.e., those inside the heads of the subject that make them a person instead of a zombie). Baars continues:

> For scientific purposes we prefer to use public reports of conscious experiences. But there is generally such a close correlation between objective reports and the subjective experiences they refer to, that for all intents and purposes we can talk of *phenomenology,* of consciousness as experienced. Thus in modern science we are practicing a kind of verifiable *phenomenology.*

If a mindclone phenomenologically appears to be conscious, then she or he very probably is a conscious being with a subjective perception of the world. This is very much what Alan Turing predicted in his classic 1950 paper *Computing Machinery and Intelligence.* As noted above, philosopher of consciousness John Searle has articulated why there is no such thing as a fully objective determination of consciousness. It is a subjective state, albeit one that occurs in the real world. It just can't be measured by objective third persons because it is by definition a first person's interior experience. Searle notes that "Behavior is important to the study of consciousness only to the extent that we take the behavior as an expression of, as an effect of, the inner conscious process."[40] This is precisely what the judicial system, and expert assessor processes, are designed to do.

Thus, it is sensible to also let society appoint experts and make similar decisions as to whether or not someone or something is conscious for purposes outside of the criminal justice or medical care system. For the determination of consciousness, a consensus of three or more experts in the field, such as psychologists or ethicists, substitute for a jury or a team of medical and spiritual ethicists. It is likely that professional associations will offer Certifications in Mindclone Psychology (C.M.P.) to better measure and standardize cyberconsciousness determinations. These professional associations will then become among the best friends of the mindclones, just as the American Psychiatric Association became a great friend of the gay movement by reversing itself and admitting that homosexuality, bisexuality, and transsexuality were not deviant human behaviors compared with heterosexuality but different behaviors—and therefore psychologically and physiologically normal in humans.

Of course an expert judgment of consciousness is not the same thing as a fully objective determination of consciousness. After all, juries can and have gotten it wrong; they have deemed defendants as lacking in criminal intent whereas, in fact, they most certainly had such malevolent intent. Doctors have determined patients to be irreversibly comatose only to see these people "wake up" and inquire about their favorite team's playoff standings or some other benign, everyday event. However, when objective determinations are impossible, society readily accepts the wisdom of alternative appraisals of peers or experts, and accepts as inevitable that errors in judgment will sometimes occur. There is nothing that can mitigate all the risks inherent in being human.

It comes down to this: "immeasurables" are part of life, perhaps the most succulent. We do not shy away from love because we can't measure it rationally, nor demur from enjoying art and music because quadratic equations can't explain their appeal. And so it is with consciousness: if others, especially experts in mental health, see so much of *themselves* in a mindclone as to say "that one is human," then that one *is human.* Guilty as charged.

In 1950 Alan Turing observed that since there was no way of telling that other people were "thinking" or "conscious" except by a process of comparison with oneself, the same process would have to apply to allegedly conscious computers. He concluded:

> "Can machines think?" I believe to be too meaningless to deserve discussion. Nevertheless I believe that at the end of the century the use of words and general educated opinion will have altered so much that one will be able to speak of machines thinking without expecting to be contradicted.[41]

When most people I know today are waiting for their handheld computer or smartphone to provide a search result, or turn-by-turn driving instructions, they have said out loud "it is thinking about it." Turing was right.

The Science That Isn't Fiction

> [In 2004] the world's most advanced robotic cars struggled to make their way around even basic obstacles such as large rocks and potholes in the road. Despite millions of dollars' worth of high-tech equipment, the vehicles managed to mimic little of what a human can do behind the wheel. Now, however, they can squeeze into parking places, flip on their indicators before making turns and even display the flair of a London taxi driver when merging into traffic.
> —*THE ECONOMIST*, NOVEMBER 2007[42]

We are close enough to cyberconsciousness to feel the bits and bytes of cyberbreath on our cheeks. Because we take advancements in technology in our stride, there is a certain amount of expectation and entitlement about it. (How often have you expressed frustration at not getting a Google search result in less than a few seconds?) To realize how narrow the leap between our online personas and mindclones is, it is necessary to understand the *exponential nature* of advances in information technology. Perhaps this knowledge will make you more conscious of what sorts of digital remains you disperse across the digital universe.

Pattern-recognition expert Ray Kurzweil has shown in his bestseller *The Age of Spiritual Machines* that information technology has been doubling its capabilities every one to two years since at least the 1950s, if not long before. For example, we have more computing power in a hundred-dollar cell phone today than there was in the $30 billion Apollo spacecraft that went to the Moon in the 1960s and 1970s. While voice-recognition technology was nonexistent in the 1990s, only ten years later it was a free feature in smart technology. Ray Kurzweil and others have shown that based upon the doubling rate of information technology it is reasonable to expect mindclones for about $1,000 by the end of the 2020s, and sooner than that for a higher price. Like most technological wonders, it won't take long for the price to come down as the technology improves and demand grows. When Sharp and Sony introduced flat-screen televisions, in 1997, prices topped $15,000, out of reach for most consumers. Now anyone can buy one on Amazon or at Walmart for a fraction of that price.

Figure 2, per Kurzweil's chart, compares the information-processing capability (measured in calculations per second per thousand dollars) available at various dates (the black dots) to biological life-forms that have the equivalent information-processing capability (in calculations per second). Up through 2010 we see computer programs no smarter than a mouse or a bug, and are not impressed. However, to base the assumtion that mindclones are very far in the future on this information is misleading in two ways.

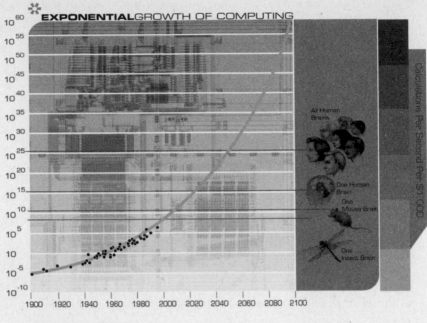

EXPONENTIALGROWTH OF COMPUTING

EXPONENTIALSCALE

FIGURE 2

First, there are a great many application-specific software packages that are already far smarter than even very clever humans. For example, the mapping software in your cell phone can best any of us at finding addresses in unknown neighborhoods. Gaming software, from grandmaster chess to the subtle Asian game of Go, and including all manner of virtual-world environments, far outstrips the conceptual capabilities of ordinary humans. While no software package has "put it all together" the way a human mind does, programs *are* popping into existence with great competence in many of the areas to which we devote our mental skills. How long could it be until some software "puts it all together"? Per Kurzweil's chart,[43] no longer than the 2020 time frame in which computers will have as many processors as the human brain has neurons.[44] From there, he estimates that it will take about another decade, until the 2030s, until people will routinely interact with software-based consciousness that is convincingly human.[45]

There is a second reason, born of psychology, that we find it hard to realize how near-term mindclones are. This reason relates to the difference between our natural way of perceiving things, which is linear, and the way in which information technology is advancing, which is exponential. Linear things proceed the way children grow, perhaps half a foot or so a year until they reach a plateau height. This is the "linear" way we have evolved to perceive the relationship between changing things and the time it takes them to change forms. Things that change the way people grow, linearly, change about the same amount each year or so. Hence, if there is a millionfold deficit between the processing capability of a typical computer today and that of a human mind, it is natural for us to project the arrival of mindclones as equal in years to about one million divided by the increase in processor speed we can get on our computers from one year to the next.

For example, my one-year-old very good computer has about 1/100,000 of the information-processing capability of a human brain (its processing speed is about that tiny fraction of the number of neural connections in a human brain, although its software is in some areas pretty advanced). In other words, it has only .001 percent of the capability of a human brain. It's not even a rodent in terms of a brain's ability to make connections between data that lead to entirely new ideas and insights—despite the fact that my MacBook Pro has, as I said earlier, about *five hundred* billion bytes of memory. There may be fifteen times more neural capacity in my laptop than in my cortical mantle, but my computer still is not at the point where it can form original ideas or have spontaneous epiphanies.

I could go buy a new computer today that has 2/100,000 or .002 percent of the capability of a human brain. At this rate, with the way my linear mind works, I would expect to wait about 99,998 years to buy a mindclone. What, me worry! Our linear minds take our most recent experience—such as going from a 1/100,000-of-a-human-mind computer to a 2/100,000-of-a-human-mind computer in one year—and extrapolate it forward such that we think it will take 998 more years to get 1 percent of a human mind, another thousand years to get to 2 percent of a human mind, another thousand years to get to 3 percent of a human mind, and so on.

In fact, though, information technology does not grow linearly, but exponentially. This means, according to the generalized form of Moore's law, that information technology *doubles* every one to two years—something very different from growing linearly.[46] Because computer capability doubles, next year I will get not a 3/100,000-of-a-human-brain computer, but a 4/100,000-of-a-human-brain one. Exponential growth means the year after that I will get not a 5/100,000-of-a-human-brain computer, but an 8/100,000-of-a-human-brain one. With information technology, I can expect to reach mindclone computing as rapidly as this:

YEARS FROM NOW	FRACTION OF A MINDCLONE
Next Year	4/100,000
Year After	8,100,000
Third Year	16/100,000
Fourth Year	32/100,000
Fifth Year	64/100,000
Sixth Year	128/100,000
Seventh Year	256/100,000
Eighth Year	512/100,000
Ninth Year	1000/100,000
Tenth Year	2000/100,000
Eleventh Year	4000/100,000
Twelfth Year	8000/100,000
Thirteenth Year	16,000/100,00
Fourteenth Year	32,000/100,000
Fifteenth Year	64,000/100,000
Sixteenth Year	128,000/100,000 = MINDCLONE

Four clarifying points are in order. First, it is unlikely that matching the number of human-brain neurons with the number of processors will be necessary to replicate the mind. We have all heard the estimate that people use only about 10 percent of their brain's potential. If we grow up speaking five languages, we always will. If not, we won't. People who have even half their brain removed surgically function relatively normally. So, we may already be at 10 percent, 20 percent, or more of the information technology we need to create a mindclone. The estimates above are as arguably conservative as they are arguably optimistic.

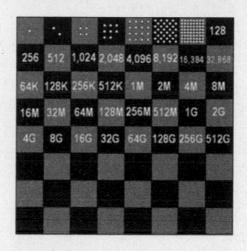

FIGURE 3

Second, the numbers and dates in the above example are approximations. Rounding down from 1,024 to 1,000 in the ninth year, for example, is just to make the arithmetic easier to follow. Similarly, while Moore's law says that the doubling occurs every one to two years, for clarity say it doubles every year. The effect of making it every two years would simply be to postpone mindclones to thirty-two years from now instead of sixteen; it will be twenty-four years from now if we use a doubling period of every eighteen months. The important point is that mindclones are around the decade corner—not in some other millennium, century, or even generation. This is about *our* lives.

Third, some people question how long Moore's law can continue to hold true, noting that other exponential phenomena—such as the growth of bacteria in a Petri dish—end when the room for growth runs out. In fact, because knowledge (unlike bacteria) can grow without limit, the doubling of information technology is not limited. Knowledge is the only resource that the more you exploit it, the more you have to exploit. Engineers have already designed the pathways for the growth described by Moore's law to continue for many decades. For example, when technology limits are reached with flat integrated circuits, computers will shift to three-dimensional integrated circuits. The technology already exists. Three-dimensional circuits stack separate chips in a single module, known as system in package (SiP) or chip stack multichip model (MCM). Intel introduced such a 3D version of its Pentium 4 CPU in 2004, and in 2007 the company introduced an experimental version of an eighty-core design with stacked or 3D memory.

Fourth and finally, we need to discuss the difference between the computational capability of the human brain and the software capability of the human mind. Having the processing speed of our brains is not equivalent to having the wiring necessary to re-create our minds. Our minds are dependent on something very close to ten million billion (10^{16}) neural connections, which we know because animals with fewer do not have our kind of minds. But our minds are just as dependent on these neural connections having a predilection or "connectome" (i.e., software like mindware) to be cross-associated in ways that give rise to characteristically human thoughts, emotions, and reactions.

Clever people throughout the world have repeatedly succeeded in creating software that gets the most out of hardware; great software transcends the performance expectations of even the best hardware, much as human ingenuity transcended the natural utility of sticks and stones. We landed men on the Moon with ten thousand lines of software code. Today's laptop operating systems let us simultaneously watch video, listen to music, browse the web, email with friends, instant-message, write documents, and manipulate spreadsheets with around a hundred million lines of code. With thousands of experts worldwide working today at reverse-engineering the human mind, I feel confident these efforts will produce mindware when supportable with the necessary capability in hardware processors.

I would be skeptical if I thought the human mind were an impossible or hopelessly difficult machine to replicate. But it is not. It is breathtakingly proficient at associating things and parts of things with other things, including feelings; at building up real-time models of the outside world; and at self-organizing a continual, reasonably interacting sense of self. Yet these are tractable problems. As the inventor of cybernetics (from which came the "cyber" in "cyberspace"), mathematician Norbert Wiener, said, "if we can do anything in a clear and intelligible way, we can do it by machine."[47] The temptation to create mindware will entreat the greatest neuroscientists and software engineers on the planet. Working together, going back and forth between human models and portions of draft mindware code, we can expect mindclone software (human thought) to arise when the necessary hardware (processing speed and memory) is available.

It may be later than the 2020s (if, for example, we insist on every nuance of human emotion to be present before we deem a mindclone humanly conscious) or it may be sooner than the 2030s (if, for example, we can use lesser computational speed more efficiently than the brain does to create human personality). The only case for mindware not occurring at all is if we believe human thought to be in the realm of spirit, something beyond artificial replication. If you replicate the information, such as a molecular structure or a pattern of neural connections, then you replicate the thing. In law there is a doctrine called *res ipsa loquitur*—the thing speaks for itself. This means, for example, that if the gun is smoking, then a bullet was shot. Perhaps in life there is a law called *indicium ipsum loquitur*—the information speaks for itself. If a replicated mind sacrifices for another's happiness, then one kind of love is shown. Like someone getting up in the middle of the night because they're cold—and putting a blanket over someone else in the house—the loving mindclone will recognize a truth and act on it for the benefit of another being.

So we delude ourselves that cyberconsciousness and mindclones are in the distant future because our linear minds have great difficulty projecting exponential phenomena. In fact, mindclones are probably as close to us in time as the birth of punk rock and Apple Computer. The very same revolution that

- brought cell phones from almost no one's hands to almost everyone's hands in under twenty years, and
- brought the internet from a military toy to a universal joy in under fifteen years,

will likely bring mindclones from chatbot infancy to human simulacra in the time it will take to get today's toddlers into college or today's Millennials into a career.

AS OF 2014, the most popular graduate-level course at Stanford relates to neuromorphic programming—which is about using software to seek out information from the environment (e.g., mindfiles and Big Data), and to *learn* from such information how to best achieve a set of goals (e.g., mindware and what people naturally do). "That reflects the zeitgeist," said Terrence "Terry" Sejnowski, a computational neuroscientist at the Salk Institute, who pioneered biologically inspired algorithms. "Everyone knows there is something big happening and they're trying to find out what it is."[48]

I realize that until people present their mindclones as doppelgängers, and persuade others that their doubles dream and pray like humans, the consciousness/cyberconsciousness debate will rage on. The moment is close. Compared with the glacial pace of the biological or "natural" form of Darwinian evolution that took over three billion years to achieve, cyberlife or cyberconsciousness will arise in a heartbeat, because, as I've shown, the key elements of consciousness—such as autonomy and empathy—are amenable to software coding. And the coding itself, as I've also discussed, is happening at a rapid pace.

Thousands of software engineers are working to advance cyberconsciousness. The U.S. government is following up on the Human Genome Project with a Brain Activity Map, a decade-long effort meant to chart the activity of the brain's billions of neurons in hope of gaining greater insights into perception, actions, and, ultimately, consciousness. There are stirrings everywhere, every day in the news of the progress that artificial intelligence and software consciousness are making—if you look. In 2012, Google researchers enabled a machine-learning algorithm, called a neural network, to perform an identification task *without* human supervision or guidance: it trained itself to recognize cats by scanning a database of ten million images. Seems rudimentary, but this is the sort of thing that is turning computer science on its head—and it does have practical use. A year later, Google used the same neural-network techniques to create a search service that helps people find specific photographs among millions.[49]

As I discuss in the next chapter, it is merely a matter of decades before symbol-association software achieves the complexity of human thought and emotion (i.e., mindware) and converges with the information billions of people are already engaged in compiling (i.e., mindfiles) to form software brains (i.e., mindclones). This is real intelligent design.

TWO

OUR DOPPELGÄNGERS ALREADY EXIST

"I do not know which is more annoying, the real Goodfellow or the reflection."

"Well, considering they are one and the same," said a second, identical Grimalkin, materializing next to the first, "we should be thankful that there will be only one left when this is all over."

"Agreed. Two Goodfellows would be more than anyone in this world could take."

"I shudder to think of the implications."

—JULIE KAGAWA, *THE IRON KNIGHT*

I find the prospect of documented lives chilling, but some people will like the idea. For one thing, a documented life can be a good defense If someone ever accused you of something, you could retort: "Hey, buddy, I have a documented life. . . . I can play back anything I've ever said. So don't play games with me."

—BILL GATES, *THE ROAD AHEAD*

MINDCLONES WILL BE AMONG THE FIRST CYBERCONSCIOUS BEINGS. THEY WILL SPEAK FROM COMPUTERIZED DEVICES USING THE VOICE TONES AND VI-sual representations of the facial mannerisms of humans, whether it's a high-def human face on a computer screen or an actual 3D-printed replica of a human person like BINA48. Websites such as Lifenaut .com (as in astronaut, but exploring life instead of space) already offer tens of thousands of people uploaded images of their faces displaying a variety of emotions, and the software system behind the website morphs the images into mannerisms. Mindclone psychology will be the same as the psychology of the human from which they were cloned. This psychology will be obtained by mindware that expertly analyzes the original's mindfile of social-network postings and interactions, video clips, and other digital reflections of a life. Once a person's unique psychology has been digitally determined, it will be expressed as settings of an operating system—mindware—that replicates an original person with a fidelity that depends on its access to the original person's memories. For example, the resultant mindclone's fidelity will be superb for an original person whose memories are robustly digitized via emails, web pages, and online surveys. Such a mindclone will think, feel, and act as similarly to their original as the original is to its clone, including as each changes and evolves from year to year. People already upload more and more unique information to current iterations of what are basically mindfiles (Facebook, Pinterest, blogs, Ness, LinkedIn, etc.), including dreams, food preferences, memories, ideas, and opinions that had been previously unexpressed.

Of course, nobody can digitize 100 percent of their life, and hence there will be many differences between what is stored in a brain and what will be stored in a mindfile. But these differences won't be enough to distinguish the person from his or her mindclone, because none of us carry forward 100 percent of our memories from even one day to the next, much less one year to the next. We are a dynamic montage of memories, personalities, recollections, feelings, beliefs, attitudes, and values. Differences in that dynamic montage between the mindfile and the person due to things too insignificant or too old to be digitized are no more meaningful to a person's identity than differences in that montage from one's second or third decade of life to their fourth or fifth. I'm not the smoker I used to be. There is a difference. But I am the person who is not the smoker I used to be. The difference relates to the past, not to the present; to where I came from, not to where I'm going; to ephemeral uncertainties, not to core realities. Nothing in the world is atomically identical to anything else, but things that are close enough to look and function the same are accepted as the same.

Our unconscious minds are immanent in all of our conscious activities. Mindware will discern unconscious conceptions and motivations from our mindfiles, and set our mindclone parameters accordingly. For example, our mindclones will avoid crowds if posts show we are rarely in them, but love the sun's warmth if photos show we gravitate to sunny spots. Our mindclones will have an unconscious tendency to like the classic traits of a Libra if those traits are amply evident in our closest friends. Yet we are not slaves of our unconscious; it is a probability setting among our neurons, which can be overridden by conscious thought, and so it will be a probability setting within our mindware, which can be overridden by cyberconscious thought.

Knowing that cyberconsciousness is developing rather quickly, we have to think about how to get on with the act of creating mindfiles, or at least compiling material for them. Surely millions of us will want to find a way to cohesively store enough organized information about ourselves so it's ready when mindcloning is widely available. I understand that many people could also be on the fence about digital cloning, since the idea is so new and unknown, and immortality is not something most people agree is a positive. Yet having digital material that could become a mindfile once mindware is available is like having a really good life-insurance policy. While some might be saying "no way" right now . . . minds can always change, and often do.

There's already a lot of "you" in the digital world if you're like the more than 250 million people in the United States alone who have a computer. Many more people have a smaller "smart" digital device; worldwide, about 2.5 billion people access the internet regularly. These are the conduits that take in our information and store it. It is a revolutionary development that much of the content of most people's minds is being saved outside of their bodies, made more so because we take digital information sharing for granted. For example, at the 2014 Consumer Electronics Show in Las Vegas, Sony "unveiled a 'life logging' software that charts a person's activities on an interactive timeline. It records when a user speaks to friends, receives emails, watches a movie and other smartphone actions."[50] The digital fingerprints we leave behind in so many places are laying the foundation for our mindfiles, the essence of our mindclones.

There is plenty to mine for mindcloning purposes. The amount of digital data we have already created has increased thirtyfold over the last ten years. A reasonable estimate is that people send or answer a few hundred emails a month. In addition, we regularly make dozens of online searches, purchases, and banking transactions weekly if not daily. All of the emails, chats, texts, IMs, social-media posts, online comments, blog contributions, uploaded photos, slide shows, home movies, search histories, clicked selections, and online purchases, if saved in the cloud, on a SIM card, on your computer hard drive, or on social-media sites, are part of your mindfile. Anyone with an active blog, a Twitter account, a Facebook page, or a Pinterest board has a "second" (and sometimes a third or fourth) life as a cyber person. Sometimes these are even deliberate aliases, but make no mistake, if you created them they are part of your digital self—as well as your flesh self—because they are of your mind.

In short, we already have digital doubles; they are not yet conscious but they are there, and other people recognize them as mirroring at least some human attributes. We are well on our way to feeling comfortable about digital doubles. Consider "friends" you have never met but communicate with, sometimes on a level deeper than you do with flesh friends and family members. Who are you really friends with? A digital "self" or a flesh-and-blood "self"? These digital versions of ourselves, whether on Facebook, Google+, Pinterest, or in chat rooms or Instagram or any other social platform, are rudimentary and chaotic, particularly compared with what they will be like when mindware is widely available. Information about us—along with everything else, from meteorology to physics—accumulates at a rapid pace and often without our knowledge. It even has a name: Big Data, information groupings so large and complex that they are processed with far more advanced software technology than traditional database-management tools.

Many data-collection companies already use intelligent algorithms to discern patterns in the huge volumes of digital data left behind by consumers. This is a very elementary version of virtual consciousness, as it's used quite imperfectly to anticipate and predict behavior based on patterns. Over the course of a decade, thousands of digital samples of your behavior create a mindfile more detailed than the most meticulously researched biography—with or without your knowledge, permission, or participation. And it's getting more precise. Turnstyle Solutions Inc., a Toronto-based company, has placed sensors in about two hundred local businesses within a 0.7-mile radius in downtown Toronto to track consumers' movements by following smartphone wi-fi signals. From there Turnstyle can describe the downtown habits of about two million people—what bars they go to, where they buy milk, and which gym they like. Many more companies will start to track people's movements in public spaces as the marketing benefit of the information becomes more valuable. An expert team would know you almost as well as you know yourself if they had access to your mindfile. They could predict what you might make of a news story, how you would vote in a coming election, unique inside jokes you might share with a friend, and whom you might be thinking about at any given moment during the day.

In fact, there are companies that already use a great deal of information about your cyber double to sell you things, and target marketing and advertising campaigns to your flesh-and-blood self. A simple example of this is Amazon's successful program of delivering buying recommendations to users, which are based on your past purchases. For more than a decade, Target Corporation has been collecting data on every person who walks into one of its stores based on what they start and stop buying, including how often, and which Target stores they visit most frequently and how that changes over time. Target can identify key inflection points in consumers' lives: the "life events" that affect shopping habits and prompt them to respond to specific special offers and coupons (like getting married, having a baby, or relocating). This data is collected and analyzed digitally, meaning that coupons are sent to a real person, but the predictive action of Target's data analysis is based on a digital copy of the person, not on the actual person. Indeed, Target knows more about some aspects of their customers than these customers know about themselves.

Imagine the potential for the company or group of entrepreneurs who can figure out how to capture and organize all that data that has been collected and posted about you (and by you) over the years and deliver it to you neatly organized to upload into your mindfile with mindware. Certainly this is a business opportunity that won't be overlooked by data-collection companies, existing or yet to be started.

The newest computer can merely compound, at speed, the oldest problem in the relations between human beings, and in the end the communicator will be confronted with the old problem, of what to say and how to say it.
—EDWARD R. MURROW

Twitter now has a system, LivesOn, with the tagline "When your heart stops beating, you'll keep tweeting," whereby you can elect to continue tweeting after you die, tweets automatically composed based on an analysis of your living tweets. DeadSocial covers all the social media post-death including scheduling Facebook and LikedIn posts as well as tweets. The free service plans to publish text, video, and audio messages directly from that deceased person's social-media accounts, as scheduled messages into the future. DeadSocial's founders consulted with end-of-life experts when developing the tool, and as a result they compare it to actual memory boxes people often fill with treasures, letters, and photographs for loved ones to review over time.

How Big Is Big?

It doubles your perception, to write from the point of view of someone you're not.
—MICHAEL ONDAATJE

No one claims these current predictive systems are "alive" or conscious. The tools that post on social media for you after you're gone are so simplistic in analyzing existing posts to create new posts that no one is fooled into thinking there is human cyberconsciousness present. But if the software tools attain the level of sophistication of mindware, then there is a very different result. As I explained in the previous chapter, mindware, which is a personality operating-system type of software, creates a program that (a) thinks and feels the way a human mind does, and (b) sets its thinking and feeling parameters (like sliders in editing software) to match those discernible from a mindfile. When mindware processes a mindfile the output is a mindclone of the person who created that mindfile. The mindclone will be self-aware that it is a software analog of a biological person's mind, based upon that person's digital footprints and sociocultural contextual information available to the mindware. The mindclone will be as self-aware of the facts of its beginnings as people are self-aware of the facts of their birth. The mindclone will be persuasively humanly cyberconscious because it will think and feel just like the humanly conscious person after which it was modeled.

It is certainly the case that much of the information that would be in our mindfile is continually erased or lost. Text messages are rarely stored, search-engine companies have been pressured to erase identifiable information, and some people declare email bankruptcy by simply deleting all their messages in exchange for a fresh start. However, on balance, much more information is accreting to a potential mindfile than is being expunged. We store lifetimes of information on flash drives, memory sticks, laptops, external hard drives, and distant cloud computer-server farms. In 2003 Peter Lyman and Hal R. Varian, at the University of California, Berkeley, published "How Much Information?," the first comprehensive study to quantify, in computer-storage terms, the total amount of new and original information (not counting copies) created and saved in the world annually. It concluded that an unprecedented "democratization of data . . . is rapidly growing." As of now, each person, on average, creates and saves several gigabytes of data annually. This means we create and save more bytes of mindfile data each year than we have base pairs of DNA, which number about three billion. As with DNA, most of this data is junk, but the rest is us, unique to each of us.

Many organizations now forming to Hoover up our dispersed digitalia. Numerous photo-sharing and video-sharing sites provide a way to upload, consolidate, organize, curate, and comment on our imagery. And we are eager to participate. Instagram, the brainchild of software engineers Kevin Systrom and Michel Krieger, launched in October 2010 to little notice. Yet in its first two months Instagram attracted one million users. Just two years later, in August 2012, Instagram claimed eighty million users who shared four billion images. In 2013, Yahoo! announced its $1 billion purchase of Instagram competitor Tumblr, which compiles mindfile building blocks for over 100 million devotees. CEO Marissa Mayer justified the purchase by noting that people who spend hours a week building up their photo libraries, i.e., their mindfiles, are not likely to stop doing so and are hence ideal internet customers.

Social networking sites enable more photo and video uploading, as well as running conversations with friends and connections to different subnetworks of interests that define our life. Blogging companies have digitally immortalized the 'dear diary' journal that is so essential to biographers' efforts to determine the personality and motivations of their subjects. Companies such as Apple and Google offer us the option to colocate or back up all of the above mindfiles in their safe "computing clouds"—a mindfile on a magic carpet ride.

How can we corral the vast assemblage of common cultural information and our own digital crumbs scattered across dozens of devices and websites into a master file? Some of us are centralizing our mind-files, such as with a single provider of cloud computing services. How can we become more deliberate about creating our mindfile? This can be done with online personality-profile and avatar-training tools. Who-ever figures out how to capture, organize, and package information left scattered around cyberspace and resell it to individuals for use in their mindfiles will win.

Doubling Down

Speed, it seems to me, provides the one genuinely modern pleasure.
—ALDOUS HUXLEY

"Vitology" is a neologism for the study of cyberlife, just as "biology" is the term for the study of cellular life. The differences between vitol-ogy, or cyberlife, and biology in the process of creating consciousness could not be starker. It is intelligent design versus dumb luck. In both cases natural selection is at play. However, for conscious vitology, any signs of consciousness get instantly rewarded with lots of copies and intelligent designers swarm to make it better. This is Darwinian evolu-tion at hyperspeed. With conscious biology, any signs of consciousness get rewarded only to the extent that they prove useful in the struggle for biosphere survival. Any further improvements require patiently waiting through eons of gestation cycles for another lucky spin of genetic rou-lette.

The people working hard to give vitology consciousness have a wide variety of motives. First, there are academicians who are deathly curious to see if it can be done (over fifty thousand neuroscience papers are published annually). They have programmed elements of autonomy and empathy into computers. They even create artificial software worlds in which they attempt to mimic natural selection.[51] In these artificial worlds software structures compete for resources, undergo mutations, and evolve. The experimenters are hopeful that consciousness will evolve in their software as it did in biology, with vastly greater speed. For example, Kenneth Hayworth of Harvard's Center for Brain Sciences observes, "It is unlikely that radically new science and technologies are needed to achieve the goal of landing a man in cyberspace and returning him safely to consciousness."[52] Cognitive scientists are especially keen to determine just how much complexity of connections among concepts, objects, and actions is necessary before consciousness arises. The development of software that could become cyberconscious is an ideal platform for their study of "consciousness as a variable, by seeing whether it is a difference that makes a difference" and for demonstrating that "consciousness should be treated like any other fundamental scientific question."[53] The work of academicians and others[54] to create virtual humans is greatly facilitated by a wide array of parallel efforts not directly related to cyberconsciousness. A great example of this is the work of Paul Ekman and his team at Paul Ekman Group to catalogue more than two thousand facial expressions as indicators of emotional states.[55] The basic facial expressions for joy, sadness, fear, surprise, anger, and disgust are universal across human cultures, and hence we will carry them with us into virtually human beings as well.

Another group of "human enzymes" aiming to catalyze software consciousness are gamers. These (mostly) guys are trying to create as exciting a game experience as possible. Over the past several years the opponents at which these people aim have evolved from short lines (*Pong; Space Invaders*) to sophisticated human animations that modify their behavior based upon the attack. (P. F. Magic's *Catz* and *Dogz* series, Fujitsu's *fin fin,* and Cyberlife's *Creatures* series are examples of games that use AE or artificial emotion.) The game character that can make up its own mind idiosyncratically (autonomy) and engage in caring communications (empathy) will attract all the attention. Any other type of character will then appear as simplistic as those on a PlayStation 2. The cyberconsciousness ambitions of the Australian company Emotiv Systems are clear from their product descriptions:

A brainwave is a signal measured on the surface of the scalp by EEG. A brainwave measured by a particular sensor is the net result of the electrical activity of thousands of neurons in the cortex of the brain. The *Affectiv*™ suite monitors player emotional states in real-time. It provides an extra dimension in game interaction by allowing the game to respond to players' emotions. Characters can transform in response to the player's feeling—the experience of playing "The Incredible Hulk" will never be the same. By combining the detections of the *Expressiv* & *Affectiv* suite together, you can have a very good idea of many emotions that people are experiencing, in real time. The *Expressiv*™ suite uses signals measured by *Emotiv's* headset to interpret player facial expressions in real-time. It provides a natural enhancement to game interaction by allowing game characters to come to life. When a player smiles, their character can mimic the expression even before they are aware of their own feelings. These expressions can be combined to communicate more complex non-verbal expressions such as "flirt," "look sexy," "surprised," or "angry". Artificial intelligence can now respond to players naturally, in ways only humans have been able to until now. The *Cognitiv*™ suite reads and interprets players' conscious thoughts and intent. The *Cognitiv* Suite can differentiate between multiple conscious thought commands. Gamers can manipulate virtual objects using only the power of their thought![56]

Third and fourth groups focused on creating cyberconsciousness are defense and medical technologists. For the military, cyberconsciousness solves the problem of engaging the enemy while minimizing casualties. By imbuing robot weapons systems with autonomy they can more effectively deal with the countless uncertainties that arise in a battlefield situation.[57] It is not possible to program into a mobile robot system a specific response to every contingency. Nor is it very effective to control each robot system remotely based on video sent back to a distant headquarters. The ideal situation provides the robot system with a wide range of sensory inputs (audio, video, infrared) and a set of algorithms for making independent judgments as to how to best carry out orders in the face of unknown terrain and hostile forces. The work of one developer in this area has been described as follows:

> Ronald Arkin of the Georgia Institute of Technology, in Atlanta, is developing a set of rules of engagement for battlefield robots to ensure that their use of lethal force follows the rules of ethics. In other words, he is trying to create an artificial conscience. Arkin believes that there is another reason for putting robots into battle, which is that they have the potential to act more humanely than people. Stress does not affect a robot's judgment in the way it affects a soldier's.[58]

The algorithms suitable for a military conscience will not be difficult to adapt to more prosaic civilian requirements. Independent decision making lies at the heart of autonomy, one of the two touchstones of consciousness.

Meanwhile, medical cyberconsciousness is being pushed by the skyrocketing need to address Alzheimer's and other diseases of aging. Alzheimer's robs a great many older people of their mind while leaving their body intact. The Alzheimer patient could maintain their sense of self if they could off-load their mind onto a computer while the biotech industry works on a cure. This is analogous to how an artificial heart (such as a left-ventricular assistance device, or LVAD) off-loads a patient's heart until a heart transplant can be found. Ultimately the Alzheimer's patient will hope to upload their mind back into a brain cleansed of amyloid plaques.

Indeed, using cyberconsciousness for mind transplants would be a way to provide any patient facing an end-stage disease a chance to avoid the Grim Reaper. While the patients will surely miss their bodies, at least with a medically provided cyberconscious existence the patient can continue to interact with their family, enjoy electronic media, and hope for rapid advances in regenerative medicine and neuroscience.

The field of regenerative medicine will ultimately permit ectogenesis, the rapid growth outside of a womb of a fresh, adult-size body in as little as twenty months. This is the time it would take an embryo to grow to adult size if it continued to grow at the rate embryos develop during the first two trimesters. Some external wombs have already been created for animals. In Japan, Yoshinori Kuwabara of Juntendo University removed goat fetuses from their dams and placed them in clear plastic tanks filled with amniotic fluid. The goats' umbilical cords were connected to machines that removed waste and supplied nutrients. Experts in the field say that over the next few years technology will reach a point where a second- or third-trimester fetus could be transferred from its mother's uterus to an artificial womb and survive. Advances in neuroscience will enable a cyberconscious mind to be written back into (or implanted and interfaced with) neuronal patterns in a freshly regenerated brain.

Biotechnology companies are well aware that over 90 percent of an average person's lifetime medical expenditures are spent during the very last portion of their life. Lives are priceless, and hence we deploy the best technology we can to mechanically keep people alive. Medical cyberconscious mind support is the next logical step in our efforts to keep end-stage patients alive. The potential profits from such technology (health insurance would pay for it just like any other form of medically necessary equipment) are an irresistible enticement for companies to allocate top people to the effort. Consequently, brain-mapping projects are among the largest joint government-industry biotech projects in both Europe and the United States.

Health-care needs for older people are also driving efforts to develop the *empathetic* branch of cyberconsciousness. There are not enough people to provide caring attention to the growing legion of senior citizens. As countries grow wealthy their people live longer, their birthrates decline below the replacement rate, and, consequently, their senior citizens compose an ever-larger percentage of the population. Today there are five younger people to care for each older person, whereas in four decades there will be just two workers to care for each older person. There is a huge health-care industry motivation to develop empathetic robots, because a minority of young people actually want to take care of older people.

The seniors won't want to be manhandled, nor will their offspring want to be guilt-ridden. Other than importing help from developing countries—which only postpones the issue briefly, as those countries have gestating dependency ratio problems of their own—there is no solution but for the empathetic, autonomous robot. Grandma and Grandpa need—and deserve—an attentive, caring, interesting person with whom to interact. The only such persons that can be summoned into existence to meet this demand are manufactured software persons with robotic bodies, i.e., empathetic, autonomous robots with a physicality that mimics a flesh-and-blood person. Companies are putting expression-filled faces on their robots, and filling their code with the art of conversation.

There is much debate over whether the expression-filled faces of digital health-care assistants should be humanlike. Dueling robot scientists from Japan have taken opposing positions on the "uncanny valley" hypothesis. The uncanny valley is a posited sociopsychological threshold: People like expression-filled robots until they look too human, and then they freak people out. Masahiro Mori believes that "when they get too close to lifelike without attaining it, what was endearing becomes repellent, fast."[59] Whereas Hiroshi Ishiguro "is interested in pushing not just technological envelopes but philosophical ones as well. His androids are cognitive trial balloons, imperfect mirrors designed to reveal what is fundamentally human by creating ever more accurate approximations, observing how we react to them, and exploiting that response to fashion something even more convincing."[60] My experience leads me to believe that the uncanny valley is a myth. I have not seen anyone repelled by the verisimilitude of BINA48.[61]

The information-technology industry itself is working on cyberconsciousness. IBM is sponsoring the Blue Brain project of Henry Markram, which is using supercomputer resources to create functional digital simulacra of portions of animal and human brains. The mantra of IT is "user-friendly," and there is nothing friendlier than a person. A cyberconscious house that we could speak to ("Prepare something I'd like for dinner," "Turn on a movie I'd like") is a product people would be willing to pay a lot of money for. It's getting closer: The Nest Protect is a smoke and carbon-monoxide alarm that talks to you in a calm human voice to warn of smoke or carbon dioxide in a room before sounding a loud alarm. Users can't talk back yet, but they can wave their hand to silence the alarm if it's simply a matter of burning the roast. A personal digital assistant that is smart, self-aware, and servile will outcompete in the marketplace PDAs that are deaf, dumb, and demanding. In short, IT companies have immense financial incentives to make software as personable as possible. They are responding to these incentives by allocating floors of programmers to the cyberconsciousness task. That's one reason why, in December 2012 Google hired, wisely in my opinion, master inventor Ray Kurzweil, the author of *How to Create a Mind,* as its director of engineering. In 2012, the company bought Boston Dynamics, a major player in the robotics industry, and in Janaury 2014 Google acquired British artificial-intelligence company DeepMind for about $500 million.

Note how rapidly programmers have arrogated into their programs the human pronoun "I." Until cyberconsciousness began emerging, no one but humans and fictional characters could call themselves "I." Suddenly, bits and building blocks of vitology are saying, "How may I help you?," "I'm sorry you're having difficulty," "I'll transfer you to a human operator right away."[62] The programmers will have succeeded in birthing cyberconsciousness when they figure out how to make the human operator totally unnecessary. From their progress to date, this seems to be the goal. Add to this Darwinian code, and conscious vitology has arrived.

A sixth and perhaps ultimate group devoting itself to creating conscious vitology is the "maker movement." A grassroots movement of people devoted to bridging the gap between software and physical objects arose in the early years of the twenty-first century. They call themselves "makers" and come together annually in different cities around the world at annual Maker Faires and related local gatherings. BINA48 attends the Vermont Maker Faire, where she is one of the most popular exhibitors, conversing with all who stroll by amid a veritable sea of homemade robots and 3D-printed objects of every sort.

Empowered by twenty-dollar computer boards called Arduinos that can be simply programmed to do almost anything (e.g., a plant can tweet via an Arduino in its soil when it needs water), the makers are passionate about building bridges between the virtual and real worlds. Dramatically dropping prices for 3D printers enable makers to envision printing bodies for minds, and a culture of open-source software lets the makers rapidly share and improve their mindware. There is nothing cooler to make than a person, and nothing happens faster than when countless thousands of people crowdsource solutions. It is perhaps unsurprising that *The Economist* has called the maker movement the harbinger of a "new industrial revolution" not unlike the "original industrial revolution grew out of piecework done at home, and look what became of the clunky computers of the 1970s."[63]

In summary, humanity is devoting some of its best minds, from a wide diversity of fields, to helping software achieve "a mind"—as well as to figuring out how to digitize your mind's uniqueness on a platform that is ready to "go live," or be conscious. The question that originally stumped me is whether that non-brain platform is a second, independent consciousness, or is instead a technologically extended version of the brain-based consciousness. Both insist they are Martine Rothblatt. One insists she is the real Martine, while the other admits she is the cyber Martine, but no less of a real Martine due to arising later in time and fleshless in form. I, Martine, will feel that I am each of them, and both of them, because each of them will have the same memories and preferences even while being aware of their radically different platforms for thought. If something makes one Martine sad, or glad, it will make the other Martine sad, or glad. I will have functionally cloned my mind, and hence there would seem to be just one Martine, albeit she operates across two different platforms now, a brain and a finely-tuned software architecture. And yet the two Martines are not identical in mind-set, and do not think the exact same thoughts at the same times. So from this perspective there would seem to be two Martines, as similar in thought as two people can be, but still two people.

I found the answer to this conundrum of identity in grammar and semantics. Is a second, independent consciousness with similar memories and preferences to the first a separate being or an extended manifestation of a single being? This depends upon one's definition of "being." If a "being" is a body, or a platform, then we are talking about separate beings. But if a "being" is a consciousness with an idiosyncratic set of memories and preferences, then we are talking about a single being. I am certain we really mean consciousness, memories, and preferences by "being." Therefore, I'm confident that those who create mindclones will experience the profound, life-altering event of having redefined themselves as a dual-platform consciousness. This is in league with becoming a mother (we are never the same after that), immigrating, and even obtaining an education. With these other experiences, we can think of the before and after through a single mind. With mindcloning, we can think of the before and after from two platforms, one original and one based on software.

The before and after being sees the world through a different mind-set, but a little difference does not make a different being. Only when the differences in mind-set become large does a software mind lack enough commonality with a brain to be a mindclone. But in this case the software mind is not a second Martine (even if she calls herself "Martine"), and is not an extension of a single Martine, but instead is a unique being altogether. In other words, there cannot be two Martines. There can be two instantiations of a single Martine being, or there can be two different beings called Martine. It all comes down to the degree of commonality and the intentions of both beings to live as a single composite being or as two separate beings.

Our minds are quite flexible in determining what is part or not part of one's self. For example, the mind must constantly recompute where your limbs are with respect to closing doors and low ceilings lest you get your fingers stuck or your head bumped. A famous experiment by V. S. Ramachandran shows that if a person places one hand under a table while sitting at the table, and a second person strokes both the hand under the table and the table above it at the exact same time and within eyesight, then the person seated rapidly develops the sensation (confirmed with galvanic skin response measurements) that the table is part of themselves.[64] There is also the well-known phenomenon of postamputation phantom pain—feeling that an amputated limb is there even though it is not. I expect that two minds as twinned as a person and their mindclone will feel each other as parts of one.

Brains are remarkably capable of incorporating things external to a body into a singular definition of self. Ramez Naam, the creator of Microsoft Outlook and Internet Explorer, recounts in *More Than Human* many examples in which neurosurgeons implanted electrodes into a brain to enable patients or experimental animals to manipulate tools such as robotic arms with their thoughts alone. After brief training sessions, the patients said, and the animals behaved as if, the external objects were part and parcel of themselves. Miguel Nicolelis of Duke University, a key researcher in this field, concluded that

findings tell us that the brain is so amazingly adaptable that it can incorporate an external device into its own neuronal space as a natural extension of the body. Actually, we see this every day, when we use any tool, from a pencil to a car. As we learn to use that tool, we incorporate the properties of that tool into our brain, which makes us proficient in using it.[65]

We have reconceptualized ourselves as drivers and scribers, and persons but an instant away via text or call from anyone we love. Similarly, we will reconceptualize ourselves as dual-platform consciousness, i.e., part of us thinking and directing things from within a skull, and part of us thinking and directing things from within a mindclone. The human brain, and the human mind, is flexible enough for that.

This new concept of dual-platform identity will not take long to evolve. Just as we accept being in two different conversations at once, via texting and talking, we will accept integrating two different flows of experiences at once, via mind and mindclone. Just as we check in with Facebook, we'll check in with our mindclone, and our mindclone with us. Hence, cyberconscious will appear immediately on the heels of cyberlife, or vitology. The evolution of smart vitology is moving at lightspeed compared with the four-billion-year slog of smart biology.

Who Are We? Stretching the Notion of Identity

In asking how a mindclone can really be a copy of our brain we face a bit of a dilemma. We cannot know whether there is a copy of our mind until there is a mindclone. We can then observe it respond to the world and determine whether, in fact, it responds the way we would respond. If so, mark one down for "good copy." However, as a biological original, we cannot know if the mindclone is actually thinking the same thoughts, and feeling the same feelings, as are we. We can only make a best guess based on our conversations with the mindclone.

As the mindclone, we realize we are a mindclone and can assess how close we are to the biological original by comparing responses to the world with how we would be predisposed to respond. If very similar, then mark one down for "I am really a good mindclone. I am just like my biological original." But we cannot really know if our internal thoughts are the same as the biological original's thoughts. We can only make a best guess based on our conversations with the biological original.

These best guesses are good enough to have confidence that the mindclone and biological original have similar enough internal states to be the same person. The main reason I think this is based upon my experience with people that I love and who profess love for me. Because I am not the mind of my lover, or my mother, I cannot know directly whether they really love me or not. However, based on our conversations, and actions, I am totally convinced that they think of me the way I think of them—with greatest loving concern for the other's happiness and health. Beyond that, I believe they are focusing on being satisfactorily occupied during the day. Because we are so close, I believe we can infer much of each other's internal states.

On the other hand, many other people say, "Martine, I love you." However, I don't feel that I understand their internal states. I'm not close enough to them. Their expressions of love are far short of the comprehensive relationship of shared experiences that I would need to infer their internal state. Indeed, over the years, people who said they love me have done things that I consider to be utterly unloving, if not shocking. Clearly, I did not know their internal states. To the contrary, the unexpected activities of my mother or my spouse were never shocking. They were behaviors I could fully see them doing based upon my understanding of their internal state.

The point here is that sometimes, if two people are close enough, an internal state of a person can be largely inferred from their observable actions. When the two people become as close as a mindclone and an original, which is far closer than a spouse or mother, inferring their internal state becomes second nature. When the internal state of another is second nature to one's own internal state we have a difference that does not make a difference. When "I think like you think and you think like I think" then we are one personal identity. This understanding between original and mindclone is nearly instantaneous upon the mindclone's completion.

We may well end up knowing ourselves best as mindclones, and we may well end up knowing the mindclones better than they know themselves. This is because it is hard to see oneself from oneself, but with just a little bit of distance, the self comes into sharp relief. We Earth dwellers never appreciated who we were so well as when we received the photograph from space of our blue-and-white planet suspended in inky black space.

And hence mindcloning is not about being accurate in every memory, in every thought pattern, and in every emotion as to a biological original. It is, instead, about feeling that there is oneness of personal identity between the two—a oneness that comes from a preponderance of common memories, emotions, and patterns of thinking, selecting and forgetting. Philosophers sometimes refer to this as a continuity of self or "diachronic self." Max More, the first philosopher to articulate secular humanism as pro-technology and hence in favor of transcending human limitations up to and including the human body ("transhumanism"), emphasizes that this diachronic self[66] also transcends the human form. More builds here upon John Locke, who more than any modern thinker insisted that identity was associated with consciousness, not with any particular body.[67] As the thirty-year-old self knows the twenty-year-old self, though they are of course not the same, so the mindclone will know the biological original. A difference that makes no difference is not a meaningful difference.

There Are Doubles, but No Duplicates

Although I call the resulting being a "mindclone," intimating that it's an exact copy of your mind, of course your mindclone will not be so exact. A so-called identical twin is not *identical* to its twin. Even if one's DNA is the same as another person's, as with identical twins, there are differences in terms of when particular genes within that DNA are turned on and off. These differences are due to a biochemical process known as methylation (the attachment of triggering molecules to genes within our DNA), which is encoded outside of our DNA in something called the epigenome. Even if two people have identical DNA, they will not have identical epigenomes, and hence the timing and magnitude of the expression of their DNA into a body will be different. The epigenome does not change things enough to prevent two identical twins from looking the same, but it will change things enough to prevent identical twins from always getting the same genetically predisposed diseases. "Mind-twin" is a perfectly good synonym for "mindclone."

When one of two identical twins is exposed to a different pathogen than the other, the two twins' immune systems will no longer be quite the same. When one of two identical twins eats different enough food from the other, the two twins' gut bacteria or "metabolome" (which affects us in many subtle ways) will no longer be quite the same. Random errors in DNA copying that the cell fails to correct will occur during cell replication in one twin but not the other. We have twenty-three billion red blood cells alone, out of tens of trillions of human DNA-bearing cells in total. Even with our amazing human bodies, this leaves a lot of room for errors that crack the identicalness of identical twins; an estimated hundred thousand DNA copying mistakes occur daily based on a rate of about three uncorrected base-pair errors per cell replication. Furthermore, we have ten times as many bacteria in and on our bodies as we have cells derived from our parents' DNA. These bacteria, at least in absolute number, are most of us, and yet as noted above there is nothing identical about the specific bacteria populations that colonize identical twins. Nonetheless, identical twins still feel that they are twins even though their bodies are not really identical. Each of us feels that we are the same body even though our own body is not identical day after day. Won't these immaterial differences be just as irrelevant to minds as they are to bodies? I believe they will, and hence mindclones are to minds just as identical twins are to bodies.

The interesting question is not whether a mindclone is an exact copy of its original, but how different they can be without losing a common identity. This is the question of diachronic selfness: How much of our identity must persist through time to be the same identity? It is impossible for a mindclone and a biological original to share every single memory. Even biological originals do not have the same memories from day to day, and surely not from year to year. Yet memories *are* crucially important to identity. In the words of memory expert James McGaugh of the University of California, Irvine:

> We are, after all, our memories. It is our memory that enables us to value everything else we possess. Lacking memory, we would have no ability to be concerned about our hearts, hair, lungs, libido, loved ones, enemies, achievements, failures, incomes or income taxes. Our memory provides us with an autobiographical record and enables us to understand and react appropriately to changing experiences. Memory is the "glue" of our personal existence.[68]

McGaugh's cogent summary leaves bare the fact that our personal identity exists as more than one set of memories. For example, we need not remember *everything* about an enemy in order to remember that someone is an enemy. We need not remember *everything* about our income, or taxes, in order to remember that we have income and pay taxes. Indeed, the key to healthy memory is the largely automatic process of selecting what little to remember and what mostly to forget. For a mindclone to be us, to have the same "glue" of our personal existence, means that the mindclone needs to share our most important memories—those that are retained because of the emotional contexts in which they were created or because of the significant repetitive effort we put into their formation—as well as the gist of our idiosyncratic selection process for what is worthy of remembering, and for how long. As the godfather of psychology William James so presciently observed:

> Selection is the very keel on which our mental ship is built. . . . If we remembered everything, we should on most occasions be as ill off as if we remembered nothing. It would take as long for

us to recall a space of time as it took the original time to elapse, and we should never get ahead with our thinking.[69]

It will be a crucially important element of mindware design to ensure that most things are forgotten, and that the settings for the memory-selection algorithm must closely match those of the biological original. Mindware will set its selection algorithm for each person by first processing their mindfile and comparing the details a person evidences memory of (such as in digitized records of voice, video, and images) with databases of the kinds of details that could have been remembered about each topic. For example, if a person's digitally recorded conversations (part of their mindfile) refer in detail to sports scores of the past week, but only sketchily to sports scores of the past month, then a curve of the selection algorithm can be determined with respect to sports scores.

If another topic area reveals a greater degree of recall, then for topics with comparable emotional importance (as indicated in their mindfile) a different curve of the selection algorithm will be determined. Ultimately the mindware will employ a memory-selection algorithm that first categorizes inputs by a factor that correlates well with the degree and duration of detail that is recalled (as indicated in their mindfile), and then "forgets" those inputs in accordance with a time curve that applies to that and similar factors. The algorithm, which actively but subliminally accomplishes that which occurs in our brains without our awareness, will also accommodate memory adjuvants and high-impact, emotional, or repetitive experiences. The memory-selection algorithm will be modeled closely on the way psychological studies have shown human minds to actually work.

Over one hundred years ago the German psychologist and memory pioneer Hermann Ebbinghaus discovered that humans typically forget more than half the information they are exposed to in an hour, and retain only about a fifth of received information after a few days.

We are better at image recognition, with people able to recognize as "already seen" thousands of pictures shown over a period of a few days. But even in this area of human forte we do forget in just a few days that we saw about 10 percent of those images.[70] With so much forgotten, a mindclone cannot be an exact copy of someone's mind because every mind is itself constantly changing in its repertoire of memories. What is important is that the pattern of selective forgetting be comfortably similar—similar enough for a biological original to say of his or her mindclone, "My mindclone is me and I am my mindclone."

Clearly, a biological original and his or her mindclone will not remember most specific events in precisely the same way for precisely the same duration. But I don't think this makes them different people. We humans don't remember events precisely the same way when we are young and when we were old, or when we are tired and when we are alert, or when we are happy and when we are sad. But we are still the same person whether we are fully awake or very sleepy. What is important is whether our core memories are the same, which they will be, as these will be recorded in our mindfile. What is also important is whether our general pattern of forgetting things is comparable, not precisely the same. That, too, can be achieved via the aforementioned algorithm.

People are remarkably ready to alter their ability to forget things. The robust market in supplements to improve memory and learning aids to diminish forgetting are good proofs of this. Hence, your mindclone being somewhat better, or somewhat worse, at remembering things makes them no less the same identity as you. People may find themselves pleasantly surprised to remember more as a mindclone than as a human, or disturbed to be doing so. If it is a problem, the mindclone can consult a cyberpsychologist and have its algorithms adjusted so that original and clone are both comfortable with the mindclone's degree of forgetfulness. Yet it's much more likely for people to be thrilled with an opportunity for better memory, given that memory-improvement apps are among the most popular at the Apple app store.

Unique-Entity Definition of Me

Everyone realizes we constantly forget—and, more, think good thoughts on one day and bad thoughts on another. Hence, our uniqueness really means a unique stream of connected conscious states. I am "me" because I have pretty much the same (but not exactly, as I know they are subtly changing) mannerisms, personality, recollections, feelings, beliefs, attitudes, and values as previously, or at least I remember once having them and evolving from them. This is what is meant by "connected conscious states." I am me because, for starters, when I wake up each morning, I remember (i.e., I know) where I am, who I am, when I am, what I should do, why I'm doing it, and how I got to these states of being. It's not like I need a user's manual.

> Eyes open: my bedroom. Thoughts flowing: *get dressed, expected at work.* See bedmate: *my soul mate, I love her so much,* slide over to kiss her good morning. Thinking hazy. *Need coffee* . . . drinking coffee: *TGIF, gonna ride my bike farther tomorrow than last weekend, gotta run, first meeting in one hour.*

Each italicized phrase in the above example is connected to my memories. That is what makes me "me." My soul mate doesn't have or know about my first meeting in one hour. If I say to her, "Get up, your first meeting is in an hour," she'll reply, "Not me." As I move through the day, everything I know and do is connected to memories of things I knew and did. I have new experiences and learn new things, there are surprises, but those new parts of me fit like jigsaw puzzle pieces into preexisting parts of me. There is nobody who *continues* just like me![71]

So naturally, we have to wonder what happens to "me" or the sense of personal identity when a mindclone enters the picture. Part of the unique-entity view of "me" is a kind of a fiction. In this philosophical-psychological theory, the concept of "me" is something the immense neural web in our brain naturally makes up (greatly assisted by language and social conditioning). A constant "me" is an effective organizational axis for a brain that receives blizzards of input. A body that does what "me" says will usually be a happier body. "Me" is not an organ in my brain. It is simply a term for a neural pattern that associates its connected body, and its safety and even survival, with relatively consistent personal characteristics. In the same way that the brain interprets the jerky images sent to it by the eye as a stable image, the brain interprets the jerky thoughts arising in it as a stable identity—me. Brains that did not do this did not pass on that survival-threatening dysfunction to many offspring. Something in our genetic coding predisposes neural patterns to construct a "me." Perhaps it is related to our propensity for language.

If I remember making a mindclone, then I must conclude that my mindclone is part of me, because it will have a connected stream of mental stuff just like me and unlike anyone else. It is weird to have two "me"s, but I have only myself to blame for that. I can't blame the mindclone for telling me what to do, since my own mind tells me what to do. If I ignore the mindclone, it will keep banging away at me, like an ignored conscience. "Hey original mind, don't watch that horror movie, you won't be able to sleep. You insist, huh? Well, fine, I'm not going to stream it. You'll be sorry!" The mindclone is just as much a part of me as are the different parts of my brain (like the part that tells me to close my eyes during the scariest part of a film that another part told me to go see).

The fact that one of "me" saw the horror flick, and the other "me" didn't, does not make them less of one "me." That is because nobody thinks what makes me me to be an *identity* of mental state from time to time. As Whitman wrote in "Song of Myself," "The past and present wilt—I have fill'd them, emptied them, And proceed to fill my next fold of the future. . . . Do I contradict myself? Very well then I contradict myself, (I am large, I contain multitudes.)" Biological minds constantly forget huge tracts of experience, only to later remember some, but it still feels like the same me.

What matters is as simple as this: Is the stream of self-experienced mannerisms, personality, recollections, feelings, beliefs, attitudes, and values (a) seemingly connected over time, and (b) largely differentiable from others? If the answers are yes, then that stream is me, even if present in more than one form—body and mindclone. If the answer to (a) is no, then I don't really know who I am; I'm amnesiac or some kind of a constructed hodgepodge of other people's minds. I'm not a "me," or perhaps I'm an evacuated me, because I don't have a past. The rare cases of people who unfortunately have virtually no memory,[72] but live in an eternal present, are in essence mini, mini, mini "me"s. If the answer to (b) is no, then I'm not a "me," but a sort of commoditized person who lacks the idiosyncrasy to create a unique consciousness. But if I'm only *slightly* differentiable from the mind of my mindclone, or from the mind of my biological original, then I am a "me," and that "me" exists across two substrates—body and mindclone.

Here's a conversation with a skeptic to sharpen the distinctions being made about what makes a "me" me:

MASTER ME: If there is someone *else,* no matter how connected they are to my background and to my mind, they are someone *else*. Therefore, they cannot be me!

ROYAL ME-NESS: You are assuming your conclusion. You are simply asserting as a matter of definition that someone else cannot be you. It is like saying any guy wearing pink is gay, but we all know that is not always true.

MASTER ME: But the word "me" means "not someone else," so someone else cannot be me. The color pink on a guy does not mean gay. Well, at least not to lots of people.

ROYAL ME-NESS: Your definitional approach doesn't help, because you have still not described what is "someone else" except by reference to "not me." The only way to make progress is to describe "me" functionally, in a way that can be measured without regard to semantic equivalents.

MASTER ME: Okay, how would we do that? Isn't it kind of too obvious to measure?

ROYAL ME-NESS: Functionally, "me" is someone whose entire consciousness is a stream of continued and largely unique memories and behaviors. If two or more beings share such a comprehensive stream of largely unique memories and behaviors, then functionally they are a "me" that extends across those beings.

MASTER ME: Aren't you just doing what you accused me of? Assuming your own conclusion? In this case you are saying a "me" is a "stream of largely unique memories and behaviors" whereas I was saying a "me" is "not someone else."

ROYAL ME-NESS: There is an important difference. I'm setting out an empirical test for determining if a "me" exists: examining whether two or more beings in fact share their stream of largely unique memories and behaviors. You, on the other hand, were saying that no examination is necessary because, by definition, a different body or "else" is a different "me."

MASTER ME: Ah-hah. Now I see your point. To be scientific we should define "me" in terms of something that can be empirically assessed, such as with psychological tests. Then, if two bodies score the same on that test, then they must be a common "me."

ROYAL ME-NESS: Precisely. Furthermore, we can think of "me" not as an either-or state but as a variable, analogic state. We can be more-or-less the same me without testing identically the same, because all of us have more of a fuzzy than a crystal-clear identity. After all, we each change from day to day.

MASTER ME: You are so right. I'm largely the same as I was last year, but definitely not exactly the same.

ROYAL ME-NESS: And it is because of that "largely the same" that we all think of you as the same Mr. Me. If your mindclone came along and also had largely the same mind as you, we'd also think of him as part of Mr. Me.

MASTER ME: Well, watch out, he's likely to be a much better debater than I am!

ROYAL ME-NESS: I would look at it as the creation of a mindclone made you a much better debater, just as would better training, more education, and lots of practice. Your mindclone will be part of you!

MASTER ME: Touché!

That today the only "me"s we know are one-body, one-"me" "me"s does not mean it will always be that way. Once the characteristics that makes a "me" me become duplicable, as with mindclones, then the instantiation of a "me" can be duplicated as well.

Unbounded Definitions of Me

The definition of "me" I've just described is based upon a common-sense concept of "me." Even it yielded the odd result that, with mind-clones, what makes "me" me will make "me" twice. Philosophers have developed counterintuitive definitions of "me" that, for all we know, may be closer to a strange truth. There are many variants of these abstract personal-identity concepts. They all share the common feature of me-ness extending not only beyond one body, but also beyond the uniqueness of any one mind (or mindclone). Let's consider these other definitions of "me," and examine what happens to mindclones if what makes "me" me includes a large element of "we."

The twentieth-century philosopher Alan Watts synergized ancient and modern "holistic" or "universalist" thinking about personal identity in *The Book: On the Taboo Against Knowing Who You Are*. Watts argues that individual, unique "me-ness" is an illusion born of neural predispositions and social pressures to form an ego.[73] In reality, he insists, we are just transient facets of an environmental process of change.[74] Watts and others of his school see our unique thoughts as nothing but one of countless fleeting expressions of a universal medium. To them, each "me" is like the momentary solution that pops out of a complex formula once you plug some numbers into enough of its variables. The real "me" is not the solution, but the complex formula and the process of selecting numbers to plug into variables:

> We do not "come into" this world; we come *out* of it, as leaves from a tree. As the ocean "waves," the universe "peoples." Every individual is an expression of the whole realm of nature, a unique action of the total universe.[75]

In this universalist point of view all humans are made of atoms that came from starbursts across the galaxy. Therefore, humans are part of the galaxy and the galaxy is the real me. Taking it a step further, brains are made of galactic matter that thinks thoughts, and those thoughts must be of something within the galaxy. Therefore, the real situation is that the galaxy is thinking thoughts of itself. The ancient and modern Taoists summarized by Watts are basically saying that reality is the universe playing with itself; thought and identity are universal mental masturbation.[76]

Daniel Kolak is a more recent and rigorous exponent of this perspective. In his book *I Am You,* he defines "Open Individualism" as recognizing that the *borders* between people (such as our skin or mental uniqueness) are not actually *boundaries* between people.[77] Kolak teaches that since boundaries (which make higher-level distinctions than borders) are transparent among people, all people are in fact one common "me."[78] For example, a pebble that is half black and half white has a color border, but that border is not a boundary to its stoniness. We think of it as one pebble, notwithstanding the fact that nature probably agglomerated it together from two different kinds of sand. Similarly, Kolak would say that the uniqueness we think of as "me" is but a border that is easily transcended by shared human consciousness.[79] He would not believe that consciousness is bounded by me-ness.

Of course we have unique mannerisms, personalities, feelings, recollections, beliefs, attitudes, and values. These are real borders. But we have these attributes only as a consequence of a common human consciousness based on common neural wiring and common social experiences. Our uniqueness is not a boundary to our commonness. Ergo, argues the open individualist, the "big Me" (as in "we") is the real "me," and the "little me" is but a mirage.

Another version of what might be called "the we-ness of me" comes from Douglas Hofstadter. In his book *I Am a Strange Loop,* he observes that we each embed a bit of ourselves in everyone we interact with. The closer we are to the person, the more of ourselves is embedded in their psyche. At the extreme, you could think the thoughts, feel the feelings, and talk the talk of someone you knew as well as yourself. Would they be you? It could get pretty blurry. As noted earlier, a "me" is "largely differentiable" from all others. As two people become less differentiable from each other, but largely differentiable from all others, they merge toward a two-bodied "me."

We come into the world as a blank slate. We develop a personality that is a composite of all the people with whom we have engaged. It is somewhat like this: Physically we are a mélange of our two parents' genes, but psychically we are a mélange of many more people's bemes (acquired beingness characteristics). No sooner does our personality begin to emerge than it begins to embed elements of itself in all the minds it reaches. If Watts can be summarized as Universal Mental Masturbation, Hofstadter is more like the Endless Mental Orgy: Everyone leaves more or less of themselves in many others, and are themselves shaped by many others. Both agree that "Me" is a very "We" kind of thing, although Hofstadter is much closer to our familiar unique-identity concept of "me."

A very cool thing for mindclones is that they have just as good a handle on being "me" under the abstract, unbounded, universalist definitions as they do under the familiar unique-entity thinking. If we are all part of some great cosmic "me," then a clone of a part is no less of that great cosmic "me" than the original. It will just be a modification of an indivisible aspect of an indefinite thing. Under unbounded definitions of "me," creating a mindclone is of little more significance than getting an education, traveling the world, or taking up an unusual hobby. A mind has been modified in each case. In no event does it change the underlying collectivist nature of "me."

Figure 4 tries to show that me-ness is a function of one's perspective. The more people you feel are part of "me," i.e., the larger is your meaning of "me," then the more natural it will be to think of a mindclone as having the same identity as you. Indeed, to feel more comfortable with mindclones under the unique-identity approach to "me," simply think of you and your mindclone the way universalists think of

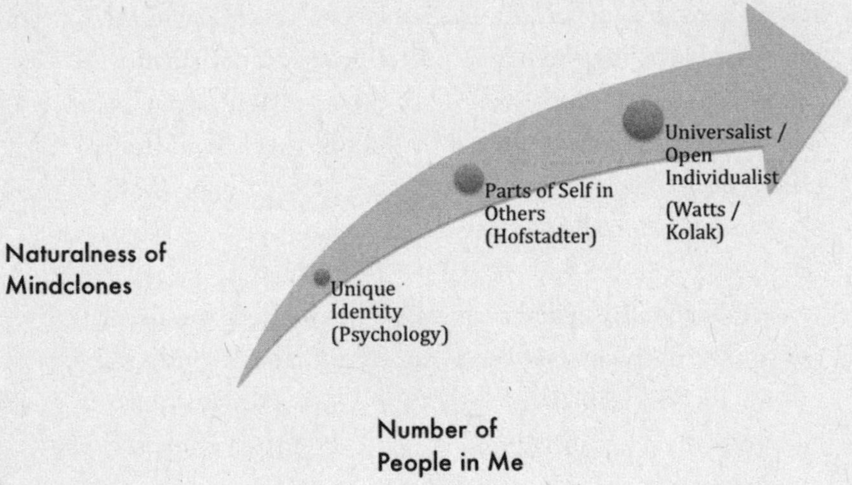

Naturalness of Mindclones

Unique Identity (Psychology)

Parts of Self in Others (Hofstadter)

Universalist / Open Individualist (Watts / Kolak)

Number of People in Me

FIGURE 4

all human beings. If you can see the unity of identity in you and your mindclone that the universalists see in all consciousness, then the singular me-ness of a biological-mindclone composite will be quite clear.

So what if my mindclone wants to be me? The universalist replies, "Wake up and smell the metaphysics!" That "want" of the mindclone is of no significance to personal identity—or the potential loss of it. "Me-ness" is not closed under borders of skin or software. The mind-clone already is you, and together the two of you are an indivisible element of all human consciousness. The only boundary to me, or to you, in terms of personal identity, is the limit of global human and mindclone consciousness. Essentially, there's no reason to get too worked up over whether your mindclone really is you, or whether it really wants to be you, or even whether you are you. People far smarter than you or I have studied this matter for centuries and are quite foggy on the definition of what makes "me" me. If it's blurry enough to include the whole human race, or even blurry enough to include all the people we know well, then surely it is blurry enough to include a man and his mindclone.

At minimum your mindclone and you will be just like yourself—always trying to figure out what to do. Get up or stay in bed. Study or play. Watch this movie or that. At most your mindclone and you will be part of a great we-ness that subsumes all me's within it. In any event, just tell yourselves that two minds, though they may differ in perspectives from day to day, are better than one. For as Ralph Waldo Emerson observed in *Self-Reliance:*

> A foolish consistency is the hobgoblin of little minds, adored by little statesmen and philosophers and divines. With consistency a great soul has simply nothing to do. He may as well concern himself with his shadow on the wall. Speak what you think now in hard words, and to-morrow speak what to-morrow thinks in hard words again, though it contradict everything you said to-day.

Nothing in our society is advancing faster than software, and mind-clones are ultimately that: one part mindfile software and one part mindware software. We've replicated our thoughts with mindfiles. We have not yet replicated our thinking with mindware. True, some good processors are needed to run software that can think, but Moore's law is delivering those processors right on schedule. We will next replicate our souls with mindclones. Souls? Souls?? How could software replicate souls? Let's start with what we mean by "soul." We saw in chapter 1 that "consciousness" was a suitcase word—stuffed with various meanings. "Soul" is if not a holdall within that suitcase, then surely one of comparable size.

The famous sociobiologist Edward O. Wilson speaks of our "physical soul" as being those behaviors that are embedded in our DNA. He predicts that

> future generations will be genetically conservative. Other than the repair of disabling defects, they will resist hereditary change. They will do so in order to save the emotions and epigenetic rules of mental development, because these elements compose the physical soul of the species.[80]

Artificial-intelligence guru Hans Moravec sees the "soul or spirit" being operationalized as a rarely altered software "constitution of general design principles" analogous to the U.S. Constitution or the "fundamental beliefs of a person."[81] One of the first literary works to directly address the meaning of soul in the context of cyberconsciousness was Dwayne McDuffie and Denys Cowan's *Souls of Cyber-Folk* comic series.[82] The protagonist, an African American computer scientist, maintains his sense of right and wrong notwithstanding waking up to find himself (without his consent) in the form of a cyborg. His own mindfiles and mindware are cohabiting a cyborg's mind with mindfiles and mindware created by an evil defense-technology corporation. Nevertheless, the stronger force of his native mindfile-based identity, his soul, is able to overpower the engrafted mindware. The authors' mirrored the point from W. E. B. Du Bois's classic *Souls of Black Folk* that no amount of forced white racial oppression could erase a deeper set identity, the soul, often embedded through song from childhood. That soul would prevail even when forced to cohabit uncomfortably as a "double consciousness" with the racist viewpoints absorbed through socialization.[83]

The common theme is that "soul" is the permanent core of our consciousness, be it expressed in biology or vitology, and activated via psychology or sociology. This theme is in train with theological views that the soul is more permanent than the body, and exists on a higher plane. With the Enlightenment there was a shift of emphasis in what was most important about a person, from the soul to the self.[84] So Thomas Hobbes said in the 1600s that it was our rational self's sacrifice of freedom for security that kept us safe, not an incorporeal divinity, and John Stuart Mill wrote in the 1800s that it was the self pursuing individualistic ends that kept us happy, not the pampering of a deistically placed soul. Between the two, John Locke crystallized, some three hundred years ago,[85] that a person is simply "a thinking intelligent Being, that has reason and reflection, and can consider itself as itself, the same thinking thing in different times and places." The soul became that "same thinking thing."

The Enlightenment occasioned a redefinition of "soul" from the most enduring part of a person to the most enduring part *of the consciousness* of a person. The post-Enlightenment soul is like a form that is quiescent when empty; but as the consciousness of daily living fills the mind with sensations and knowledge, it also fills the form of the soul. From that point the soul has a gravitas, and hence a motivational influence on behavior.[86] Of course, the form or mold is not made out of material; it is more of an especially stable set of connections, similar to what physicists call an "energy well," and once something enters it, like a rolling ball, it is difficult to get it out. When we replicate our consciousness with mindclones, we will also be replicating the strongest parts of our consciousness, and hence we will be quite unavoidably replicating our souls as well.

As was the story line in *The Souls of Cyber-Folk*, and as is implied by the "software constitutionality" of Moravec, and as would be sociobiologically evolved in the view of Wilson, our sense of right and wrong is tightly bound with what we feel is our soul. The soul is that hearth of consciousness, from which our identity and ethics hail. We cannot not come from whence we came, and we carry those natal elements of self into every new adventure of body, mind and soul. But just as genes mutate and constitutions get amended, so also can souls evolve. Should we be conservative with the evolution of the soul, as E. O. Wilson believes we will be with our genes? The decision is upon us, as we begin to port our souls from brains to bytes.

Yale bioethicist Wendell Wallach insightfully noted in his book on artificial moral agents (AMAs), a fancy term for software with a conscience or at least an ethical code,

> Humans have always looked around for company in the universe. Their long fascination with nonhuman animals derives from the fact that animals are the things most similar to them. The similarities and the differences tell humans much about who and what they are. As AMAs become more sophisticated they will come to play a corresponding role as they reflect humans' values. For humanity's understanding of ethics, there can be no more important development.[87]

We need to figure out this mindclone thing right now, because this is one part of the future that is taking root right now. In doing so, we are likely to learn as much about ourselves as we learn about mindclones. We will learn about our psychology, our consciousness, and our souls. For this reason alone, we should start the virtually human debate today.

THREE

MINDCLONING, NATURAL SELECTION, AND DIGITAL EUGENICS

All that is is the result of what we have thought.
—GAUTAMA BUDDHA

WHILE PEOPLE ARE HARD AT WORK CREATING CONSCIOUS SOFTWARE, THEY ARE SIMULTANEOUSLY DEVELOPING WAYS TO SELECT THE TRAITS THAT WILL make software consciousness naturally recognizable as human ("we know it when we see it"). In fact, vitology, cybernetic life, is evolving faster than we are. Humanity cannot resist the overwhelming urge to create unnatural or nonbiological life in the image of natural life, and to make it "better" by selecting and improving upon highly valued or privileged characteristics. This effort may seem like "unnatural selection," but it isn't; rather, it is entirely in keeping with natural selection, the key mechanism of evolution—a process by which traits become more or less common in a given population as a function of their reproductive value. "Natural selection" is actually the name Charles Darwin gave to nature's heartless process of dooming some species and variants of species and undesirable traits to extinction, while favoring—for a while—others.

The principal tool of natural selection is competition within a niche for scarce food. Losers can't figure out how to get enough nutrients to reproduce healthy offspring; hence they die out. Winners get the food, make babies, and pass on their ostensibly more adaptive traits, including those that make them superior competitors. So natural selection is simply a tallying up of the results of what happens to self-replicating things in the natural world. Those that self-replicate more successfully are represented by a larger slice of the pie of life. There are many ways to self-replicate more successfully: find, organize, and cultivate resources more efficiently than others; kill others more effectively than they can kill you; and adapt to changes better than others. Nature doesn't really care how one self-replicates more successfully. She just awards the winners larger shares of the pie of life when life goes their way.

For instance, when environmental change eliminates much of the food, such as during glaciation or droughts, previously useful traits may become meaningless and former natural-selection champions may quickly join the mountain of extinct losers. During such times, nature selects for traits that enable food gathering and reproduction in changing, or changed, environments. As University of Chicago evolutionary biologist David Jablonski says, "Selection can favor specialization that can be advantageous over the short run, but create vulnerabilities over the long haul."

Sometimes a new species may enter a niche, as when hominids entered the environment of the mammoth. In cases like this, nature might simply select the better killer, since it was not the mammoth's food that interested Man, but the mammoth *as* food. Plants and animals will not only extinguish other species through starvation, they will also do so through direct extermination. All the while, nature will carpet bomb all manner of species via environmental changes brought about by geophysics (e.g., volcanism) or astrophysics (e.g., asteroids).

Since math is math, whether done by people or bees, nature surely does not care if the agent of selection is human popularity or usefulness rather than nutritional scarcity. Natural selection is no less natural for humans being in the middle. Indeed, we have human intermediation to thank for thousands of recombinant DNA subspecies, hundreds of plant types, and dozens of animal species. Thank Man for the house cat, man's best friend the domesticated dog—and broccoli!

The end result of mindclone evolution, via natural selection, will still be an arithmetic reordering of pie shapes and pie slices, as happens in human, animal, and plant evolution. The overall pie of life will be much larger, for it will now include vitology as well as biology. And within that larger pie, there will be slices accorded to each of the types of vitological life and biological life that successfully self-replicate in a changing environment. Mindclone consciousness will arrive faster than its biological predecessor did because its process of natural selection is at the speed of both intentionality and technological advancement. Selection of traits, or "editing" of how consciousness is expressed, will also be more dramatic than is seen in the slower natural-selection process within conventional populations.

Human intermediation in natural selection may also be thought of as an example of a complex adaptive system—one in which agents interact, process information, and adapt their behavior to changing conditions. For example, economist Eric Beinhocker has estimated[88] that humans have created ten billion surviving, species-like *products* that represent selective choices bounded by scarcity: DVDs over VHS, CDs over vinyl records, computers over typewriters, and internet news over television news. In a similar vein, the *Proceedings of the National Academy of Sciences* reports[89] on a study in which a classroom of toddlers expressed a clear preference for a robot that giggled when touched over one that did not. It is because of such human choices that vitological evolution will march forth.

Philosopher of consciousness Daniel Dennett reminds us that our wonderful sense of self-awareness is but an inevitable consequence of natural selection rewarding those primates who could better anticipate the thoughts of members of their troop. This allowed one to beat others to limited opportunities, such as food and other resources, and thereby produce more offspring (each with those odd neural mutations enabling sociopsychological modeling). Modeling the minds of others is but a short step from modeling the mind of oneself. Symbols, words, and grammar sealed the deal.

All of this supports Dennett's thesis that minds are things that create futures—hypothetical futures generally (as we mentally consider options), and then definite futures (as we act upon our thoughts). Similarly, Jeff Hawkins, Executive Director and Chairman of the Redwood Neuroscience Institute, in *On Intelligence* writes, "Our brains use stored memories to constantly make predictions about everything we see, feel, and hear. . . . Prediction is not just one of the things your brain does. It is the *primary function* of the neocortex, and the foundation of intelligence. The cortex is an organ of prediction."[90] In other words, whoever creates the better futures will get the better prizes (including survival). Better minds are needed to create better futures, resulting in a cerebral "arms race" that has culminated in today's human mind—the first to use upward of one-third of a body's energy to do its magic.

Natural selection is now acting upon software forms of life. In this case nature's tool is neither food nor violence. Instead, she is using humans as a tool, relying upon our differential favoring of some self-replicating codes over others. Just as nature started off with viruses in the biological world, we are also flooding the vitological world with them. This is no doubt because viruses are the simplest types of self-replicating structures; they do nothing but plug themselves in somewhere to self-replicate (usually benignly, sometimes harmfully, and rarely beneficially). Molecular viruses spontaneously self-assembled out of inanimate molecules over a billion years before anything multicellular (like a plant or worm) did, and hence natural selection played with them first. Similarly, software viruses spontaneously man-assembled out of inanimate code before the internet, and hence natural selection plays with them using firewalls, antivirus software, and open-source programming.

Digital or vitological natural selection also includes the preferential copying of better mindware over buggy mindware, exemplified by the way in which "clean" Facebook handily vanquished "messy" MySpace.

The story of Instagram is also the story of natural selection in the digital world: Kevin Systrom started a company called Burbn that would combine some of the elements of Foursquare with others from the game *Mafia Wars* and put the resulting product in a mobile HTML5 app. Systrom brought on a partner, Mike Krieger, to help. After writing code for the product for the original iPhone, they scrapped it for a more universal app. After all, wouldn't a universal app have more chance of long-haul survival than an iPhone app? Yet after looking at the result, they decided it was too cluttered, so they selected only the most important and best features, gave the product a new name, and Instagram was born.

Mindclones may be thought of as simply the next round of development in our quest to create ever-better futures. People with mindclones will be far better at predicting the consequences of their actions than people without mindclones. The former will have a guardian angel on their shoulder, in the real form of a mindclone, whispering warnings and suggestions, helping both original and clone to an outsized slice of the pie of life. If the main purpose of minds is to produce a personal future, Dennett says,

> you have a tremendous advantage if you can produce more and better future about the other than the other can produce about you, so it always behooves an agent to keep its own control system inscrutable. Unpredictability is in general a fine protective feature, which should never be squandered but always spent wisely. There is much to be gained from communication if it is craftily doled out—enough truth to keep one's credibility high but enough falsehood to keep one's options open. (This is the first point of wisdom in the game of poker: he who never bluffs never wins; he who always bluffs always loses).[91]

People with mindclones will be better poker players—literally and metaphorically—in the game of life. They will have access to more information, at faster speed, than those without a mindclone. They will have double consciousness while others putter along with a one-cylinder engine. Think of two competing sales reps in a new territory: one has a GPS with real-time traffic updates; the other has to find his way around with a paper map. Who will get around faster, and as a result meet sales goals more quickly? In the same way as the salesman with a GPS can outrun his competitor with a paper map, the Darwinian advantage of mindclones will in and of itself be a huge driver for the rapid adoption and ceaseless improvement efforts of mindcloning technology.

The advantages of having ever better mindclones brings up sometimes uncomfortable questions, such as:

- Can I increase my IQ with a mindclone, and how would a mindclone's IQ be measured?

- If my mindclone is me, isn't souping up its IQ equivalent to the kind of eugenics, or biological gene enhancement, that we feel is ethically problematic?

- How exactly would I correct in my mindclone personal faults, such as procrastination, and doesn't that really then create a somewhat different person?

As we answer these questions, remember that a mindclone is a replica of a particular person's mannerisms, personality, recollections, feelings, beliefs, attitudes, and values, determined from a mindfile of our lifetime's digital footprints, by mindware that auto-tunes to each of our unique flavors of consciousness, based upon processing the trappings of our consciousness, as found in our mindfile. In brief, a mindclone is what results when you import a sufficiently robust mindfile database into a consciousness-capable mindware application.

Since the mindclone thinks like you, provided the mindware application is up to snuff, then your mindclone will have the same IQ as you do. If an IQ test were to be given to each of you, the end score would be within the same range of test variability. If you are a nervous test-taker, so will be your mindclone. If you think forever about some questions, so will your mindclone. Mindware that produced cyberconsciousness with different IQ-test-taking results from you would not produce a mindclone. It would produce an original, unique cyberconscious person, a situation with important legal consequences as to citizenship and human rights. For example, your mindclone, being you, should share, as in cohabit, your legal rights. The vote cast by whichever of you votes (assuming there is electronic remote voting in the near future) is your vote. You cannot vote twice. A novel cyberconscious person, on the other hand, while initially also the responsibility of the person who created it, can ultimately achieve legal independence if it demonstrates the psychological elements of being a unique, autonomous human being, albeit in software form. Failure to provide a decent standard of living appropriate for the unique cyberconscious person you created will likely have adverse legal consequences similar to failing to provide for one's children or pets, issues I discuss later in the book. I distinguish these two types of virtually human beings as "bemans" and "mindclones." A *beman* has hu*man be*ingness, by virtue of having through cyberconsciousness a human identity, but lacks the mind of any particular human body. A mindclone has a mind that has been copied, through cyberconsciousness, from a particular human body.

Can We Go Too Far?

Souping up one's mindclone by tweaking its mindware brings up the topic of eugenics, but we must be cautious in actually labeling it as such. Eugenics is the practice of modifying the DNA of successive generations or populations to be somehow "better" than their predecessors. This practice got a deservedly bad name after World War II because Nazi Germany embraced it as a social policy via sterilization and outright murder of demographic groups that did not meet a hypothesized Aryan archetype. The Nazis argued that elimination of such DNA from society would eliminate the continuation of disfavored demographic groups. Much less horrific but conceptually similar eugenic practices prevailed in the United States and elsewhere—for example, sterilizing poor, oppressed women on the argument that it was their DNA that created their circumstances.

In fact, the World War II–era eugenics practices that offended human rights are what can be properly called "negative eugenics"— trying to get rid of certain genotypes or phenotypes. This is, however, quite different from what is known as "positive eugenics"—affirmative efforts to enhance the genetic stock of one's offspring. Everyone who procreates the conventional way practices some form of eugenics. We choose partners based on attraction, which is in large part determined by instinctual reactions to reproductive availability. When two members of Mensa, the organization for geniuses, mate with the goal of producing a supergenius, that is "positive eugenics." We even practice it when procreating in less traditional ways like artificial insemination with donor sperm and eggs. According to many reports in the British press in 1998, feminist heroine, actress, director, and single mother Jodie Foster undertook a search for the perfect sperm donor, announcing that after a long search she had artificial insemination with the sperm of a tall, dark, handsome scientist with an IQ of 160. Likewise, creating the Labradoodle breed of dog as a way to proactively combine the loyalty of the Lab with the smarts and hypoallergenic coat of the poodle is a form on conscious, positive eugenics.

Admittedly, things get hairier with mindcloning. One of the worrisome parts of mindcloning is the ability to be much more deliberate about selecting traits and characteristics than natural selection offers. It has the potential to become nefarious. By tweaking our mindware to make our mindclones a bit better than ourselves, our immediate goal is not even positive eugenics; it is more akin to self-enhancement or self-augmentation, because your mindclone is *you*. In this category one can also place everything from caffeine to Ritalin to mindfulness meditation to memory-building apps on the iPhone. Tweaking your mindclone to be a better you does not create a different person. Indeed, the changes you see in your mindclone will probably soon be reflected in your flesh brain-based mind. These kinds of modifications really fall under the rubric of "euthenics" rather than "eugenics." Euthenics are changes to the environment to help you better adapt. Wheelchair cuts in sidewalks are an example of euthenics. So are eyeglasses. So is Google Glass that flashes to you the spouse's name of the business colleague approaching you at a social event. So are mindclones that don't put off for tomorrow what can be done today.

Ultimately there will always be the question of how many modifications can be done to a mindclone until it is no longer me, no longer my mindclone but its own beman. As I describe later on, these are medico-legal questions that have to be addressed on a case-by-case basis. There will be involvement of government agencies in the regulation of mindware capable of producing mindclones. However, when either you or your mindclone retains a lawyer to file a petition for legal separation, you will know that you have gone too far! It is a slippery slope from euthenics to enhancement to eugenics, but there are also plenty of safe plateaus between.

Of all liars, the smoothest and most convincing is memory.
—FOLK SAYING

A Mindclone Super Race?

When [participants'] computers "sleep," the Electric Sheep [program] comes on and the computers communicate with each other by the internet to share the work of creating morphing abstract animations known as "sheep."

Anyone watching one of these computers may vote for their favorite animations using the keyboard. The more popular sheep live much longer and reproduce according to a genetic algorithm with mutation and cross-over. Hence the flock evolves to please its global audience. You can also design your own sheep and submit them to the gene pool.

> **The result is a collective "android dream" [an homage to Philip K. Dick's novel *Do Androids Dream of Electric Sheep?*], blending man and machine to create an artificial lifeform.**
> —"ABOUT ELECTRIC SHEEP" ON THE ELECTRIC SHEEP WEBSITE[92]

Vitology evolves much more rapidly than biology, because it is capable of passing through inheritance *acquired characteristics*, such as all the knowledge a parent has acquired. Humans also pass on *knowledge*, but through a hit-and-miss process of learning rather than close to surefire inheritance. In addition, any changes or improvements to a software being's code, structure, and capabilities are also immediately present in its offspring. Humans and other biological beings do *not* inherit *acquired traits* such as the results of bodybuilding or laser eye surgery or well-developed brains. Vitology incorporates Lamarckism, a pre-Darwinian theory of descent based on acquired traits that is discredited for biology but is accepted for the evolution of cultural phenomena such as language (a field known as mimetics).

A big step for biology was the understanding that only the germ plasm (DNA) that gives rise to a body is inherited, not the body itself. No matter how much the body, also called the "soma," is modified beyond its DNA-determined form during one's life, one's offspring will not have the benefit (or detriment) of those modifications in its germ plasm. Each new soma starts from scratch, based only upon a blend of its parents' germ plasm, plus any random mutations.

Cheetahs do not run fast because they pass on to their offspring the physical results of muscularizing their legs with running exercise during their lives. Their speed exists because the cheetahs (including cheetah precursor species) born with random mutations that resulted in faster speeds (from muscle-fiber types to degree of muscularization and body shape) ate better, escaped better, and thus produced more offspring, each of whom shared the mutated germ plasm. Over the eons, cheetah precursor species with slower speeds couldn't compete for the scarce food and ultimately died out without reproducing.

For biology, there is a one-way street between the germ plasm and the soma. Soma is simply the germ plasm's tool for making more germ plasm. Rarely, dumb luck gives the soma a break with a favorable germ-plasm mutation, as in the cheetah example above. These physical advantages are rapidly capitalized on in a competitive environment. Ultimately, of course, the advantages accrue to the now mutated form of the germ plasm: it will become more prevalent.

A vitologist flips the biologist's dogma on its head, and proclaims, "The germ plasm *is* the soma." This is because with vitology there is a conflation of the germ plasm and the soma. When you copy your computer's contents from one computer to another, not only the applications replicate, but also all of your memories (photos, songs, files). When a software-based being is replicated, it is its contents, its data structure, its virtual form—its soma—that is replicated. Hence, for vitology, the soma and the germ plasm are—or at least can optionally be—one and the same.

It is possible for a software-based being to replicate just a portion of itself. Indeed, a piece of vitology could replicate just that code that it received upon its creation and none of the code that it acquired during its life. While this would create a biology-like separation between germ plasm and soma, it would be but an option in vitology whereas with biology the separation is a mandate.

Another interesting special case, which goes in the opposite direction, concerns gene therapy or genetic modifications. Sometimes the effort to modify the phenotype of a biological being via gene therapy (to cure a disease, for example) results as well in modifying the being's germ line (egg or sperm cells). This is because once a new snippet of DNA is introduced into the body, especially if done so via a virus, it can travel everywhere and end up in the gonads as well as the diseased bodily system. In such a specialized case an acquired characteristic may in fact be passed on to the next generation, just as will be the case in vitological life. A similar, and usually tragic, scenario arises when industrial processes harm both a person's somatic DNA and that of their germ cells. For example, radiation can harm someone's health and also disrupt the DNA they pass on to a child, harming the future child as well. In early 2010 the oldest known survivor of both the Hiroshima and Nagasaki atomic-bomb attacks died. She relayed that one of her children conceived after the atomic blasts had predeceased her after a sickly life, and had complained of being poisoned by the parents' Hiroshima-tinged germ plasm.

Other than these exceptional situations, the general case is that only vitology merges germ plasm and soma. The result is that everything vitology acquires in life is replicated in the next generation. This means that vitological evolution can compound even more rapidly than does human knowledge; there is not even a need for learning what the previous generations documented.

Jeff Hawkins identifies three epochs of intelligence. In the first epoch, starting a couple of billion years ago, DNA embedded certain memories and thus enabled certain predictions. For example, a simple one-cell amoeba-like life had memorized what food sensed like (because those who didn't failed to pass on their DNA), and predicted that if it moved along a gradient of increasing sense it would get the food (again, DNA lacking that instruction failed to get passed on). In the second epoch, beginning with mammals around one hundred million to two hundred million years ago, the nervous system was modifiable so that new memories could be formed, but that information could not get passed on to next generations other than by show-and-do. With new memories, better predictions could be made, such as "If I hide under this rock the dinosaur won't see me." The third epoch, humanity, "can learn a lot of the structure of the world within our lifetimes, and we can effectively communicate this to many other humans via language."[93] Because we are master memorizers, and hence precocious predictors, we are the ultimate understanders and super smart.

But there is yet a fourth epoch, beginning with virtually human beings. When a mindclone or beman replicates, it is a replication of their mindfile and mindware settings. These may be merged with those of another mindclone or beman. All that has been learned in one's life can be passed on to a next generation. Hence, memory is better than ever, ability to predict is better than ever, and, according to Hawkins, understanding and intelligence are higher than ever. To be virtually human is to have achieved a fourth epoch of intelligence.

There are at least a couple of Hawkins's arguments with which I disagree. He does not "believe we will build intelligent machines that act like humans, or even interact with us in humanlike ways"[94] or "ever be able to copy our minds into machines."[95] This is because he believes that such a computer "will not have a mind that is remotely humanlike unless we imbue it with humanlike emotional systems and humanlike experiences. That would be extremely difficult and, it seems to me, quite pointless."[96] However, as described in chapter 2, people throughout the world are highly engaged in creating mindfiles full of "humanlike experiences" and writing mindware that recapitulates "humanlike emotional systems." Far from "pointless," such activities enable us to extend our abilities to remember and predict—which Hawkins says are paramount human behaviors—and also to extend our ability to enjoy life.

Darwinian vitology predicts that mindclones could evolve quickly, as they do not have to rely upon dumb luck (random mutations) in order to change. Every generation of a vitological being will differ from the way its parent began life by the amount of information the parent acquired prior to each replication. Alternatively, new generations of vitology could deliberately involve a blending of two or more parents' information. Hence, vitology contains a fascinating potential for unprecedented diversity along with the possibility of stultifying homogeneity.

Darwin gives no species a blank check for success. We do know that humanity's ability to take advantage of Lamarckian inheritance for cultural knowledge saved it from species-killing predators and hunger. That same ability enabled humanity to create an entirely new ontology of life, vitology, which now (in an early form) lives in a purely technological niche. Self-replicating codes (DNA) have used human soma to create the first self-replicating codes[97] that usefully incorporates acquired information and no longer requires human soma. For mindclones the chicken (flesh life) is not only the egg's way of making more eggs (human, not necessarily flesh-based, life), but also the egg's way of transcending the need for chickens (digital humans can be reproduced digitally). Hmmmm. That sounds scary, like an interspecies zero-sum game, unless you remember that virtual humans are people, too, and that your mindclone is still you. Just because something is not necessary does not mean it is not desired. I love playing my piano with my fleshy fingers even though often I let the digital system play it like a player piano.

How will we know when mindware is certified to produce the kind of mindclone humans need not watch from over their shoulder? What grounds reason ethically? If we know what grounds reason ethically we will know whether reasoning mindclones are also ethical mindclones.

Ethical behavior has long been defined as that which maintains a healthy balance between personal or group freedom (what can be called respect for diversity) on the one hand, and community or national cohesion (what can be called respect for unity) on the other hand. Killing someone is unbalanced, because the individual freedom to do so is far outweighed by the disturbance to social cohesion, and is therefore unethical. However, killing can also be ethically required for social cohesion, as in stopping a rampaging gunman from wreaking more havoc. Killing nonviolent protesters is always wrong because the potential harm to social cohesion from protest is outweighed by the harm to social cohesion from killing people for diverse expressions of opinion.

Principles such as the Golden Rule, Kant's categorical imperative, and Rawls's theory of justice all reflect humanity's painfully acquired wisdom that survival of one (i.e., personal diversity) is best nurtured by survival of many (i.e., community unity), and survival of many (i.e., group diversity) is best nurtured by survival of all (global unity). This nonobvious (and often counterintuitive) but logically deducible and repeatedly proven social fact is perhaps most artfully stated in the poem first delivered in the wake of World War II, on January, 6, 1946, by German pastor Martin Niemöller (1892–1984):

First they came for the Socialists, and I did not speak out—
  because I was not a Socialist;
Then they came for the trade unionists, and I did not speak
  out—because I was not a trade unionist;
Then they came for the Jews, and I did not speak out—because I
  was not a Jew;
Then they came for me—and there was no one left to speak out
  for me.[98]

Human ethical lapses arise because people don't realize that the diversity of their own life (and that of their family, clan, or nation) is inextricably linked to the unity of all human lives. People erroneously think they can further their diversity by killing some people for the benefit of other people. When the connectedness of all people's fate is accepted, then reasoning according to the balance of diversity and unity will always lead to ethical outcomes.

Reason is ethically grounded if it supports diversity (individual freedom) up to the point that it undermines unity (social cohesiveness). This is true because survival is nurtured by being free to be oneself, to be happy, to be different, to mutate, but not to the extent that it dissipates the bond that makes everybody matter, that makes everyone part of a larger, important, "people." Most aspects of "culture wars" concern the question of how thin the social bond can be stretched without it being dissipated. These debates have to be considered case by case, and reconsidered decade by decade. For example, in the United States currently, the ethical balance with respect to abortion is that the diversity of choice is paramount in the first trimester, while the unity of society trumps once the fetus is viable and the mother's life is not in danger.

Hence, if mindclones reason ethically they will accept the premise that all conscious lives are connected such that a harm to one or some is a harm, or at least a heightened risk of harm, to all. Humans then can be assured that they are no less safe around mindclones than they are around other people, notwithstanding rapid vitological evolution. Ideally, at the core of every mindclone's mindware, as embedded in every mentally healthy human's cerebral cortex, sits the maxim to respect the value each conscious being has for its life, provided such respect does not undermine the unity of society. As behavioral law scholar Lynn A. Stout describes in *Cultivating Conscience*, universal moral rules must exist because in fact the vast majority of people, everywhere in the world, behave morally the vast majority of the time without regard to personal benefit or sanction from such behavior.[99] I fully expect that demonstrated compliance with this universal human maxim will be required before a government agency responsible for biotechnological prosthetics (such as the U.S. Food and Drug Administration or the European Medicines Agency) authorizes the use of specific mindware to produce *legally recognized* mindclones. It is as straightforward as requiring every mindclone to have a conscience, which Lynn Stout defines as "an internal force that inspires unselfish, prosocial behavior."[100]

"Underground" or noncertified mindware will likely produce a blistering diversity of mindclones and bemans, some with greater conscience than typical humans, and some with less. But it's no different on the biological side of the fence. For every Mandela there is a Manson. Approximately 3 percent of men and 1 percent of women suffer from antisocial personality disorder (ASPD). Cyberconsciousness may find itself plagued with a comparable number of psychopaths. However, I suspect the personal criminal and civil liability that a person will have for the actions of the mindclones or bemans they create will exert significant negative selective pressure against creating cyberpsychopaths. For this very reason, seriously destructive software viruses are rare; programmers don't want to go to jail any more than regular folks. Indeed, the hacker ethic—program passionately, write good code for good purposes, and share software collectively—is anathema to creating destructive viruses. Of course there are bad guys in software—hackers call them "crackers"—but they are a small minority.[101]

How confident are we that reasoning pursuant to the diversity/unity maxim, as described here, will make ethical behavior the norm even if not a fail-safe guarantee? How confident are we that (1) humans generally reason ethically, and (2) such human ethical reasoning prohibits human genocides? The answers are that humans reason ethically the great majority of the time, but sometimes they don't. Similarly, humans rarely engage in genocides, but sometimes they do. From this logic we must conclude that mindclones are as unlikely to engage in genocidal acts as are any of us, yet it is important to have monitoring and defense forces at the ready to nip potential Holocausts in the bud. While man may be the most dangerous animal, we don't stop making people because of it. Similarly, while recombinant DNA techniques could produce new pandemic viruses, we don't stop biotechnology because of it. We adopt reasonable regulations and professional responsibility practices, such as the Asilomar guidelines calling for levels of containment based on the pathogenic potential of microbial life.[102] Mindclones will be men and women, no less dangerous, nor less precious. We will continue to manage our thorns for the sake of our scents. I would look forward to convocations of hackers, lawyers, psychologists, and ethicists to create a consensual structure of safe havens for the development, dignity, dispersal, and due-process rights of cyberconsciousness.

There are sure to be rogue "evil genius" mindclones and bemans, just as there is no shortage of rogue human bad guys. These mindclones are as smart as us, or much smarter. While good social policy would be to identify and fix their problems early with cybertherapeutics, this will not always work and some will fall through the cracks. But these anti-human mindclones are a job for law enforcement, not a reason to ban all virtual humans. Society will have plenty of tools at its disposal for tracking down fleshophobic vitology, including legions of citizen mindclones as adept in the vitological niche as were the cavalry's Native American guides on America's Wild West frontier.

Now, citizen mindclones, ones with an identity, economic power, and human rights, will feel that they are humans of a different race, diverse members of a common, united society. They will think like us, but know that they look different from humans, are of different substrate, and hence know that humans often judge them unfairly (stereotypically) based upon their appearance. Yet neither this feeling of discrimination nor any other motivation is going to result in revolution and mass murder of humans. There are several reasons for this:

We don't usually kill our own families. Mindclones will feel like the humans are their family members, especially immediate family members and particularly their same-selves in the case of mindclones with living biological originals. Mindclones will be programmed to feel that the happiness of their human family members is important to their own happiness; that the mindclone's identity extends across that of their biological family. This is how humans feel. Hence, whether mindclones are or are not conscious, they will reason it is wrong to kill their own (which includes their biological original progenitors). They will reason that hurting one's family is wrong because those family members deserve the same respect for their own diverse lives that the mindclone wants.

It is of course true that spouses kill each other, Hatfields kill McCoys and people who are "folk" one day, like German Christians and German Jews, or Rwandan Hutus and Rwandan Tutsis, can rapidly be deemed nonfamily vermin. Yet these situations are the exceptions rather than the rule. They startle us because they are exceptions. These killings occur because of an abandonment of reason, or faulty reason, rather than an exercise of sound reason. Proof of that is the outcome: The Nazis committed millions of indescribable atrocities and attempted to put its boot on the throat of civilization, yet they lasted barely a decade, and the Rwandan genocidaires shorter than that. Killing is a nonproductive strategy. It does not advance our prospects for life, but only appears to, in an illusory fashion, when assessed over a very short period of time.

Mindclones will be programmed, as are all modern people taught, to limit abandonments of reason to situations in which others will not be harmed. Just as it is not an excuse to say, "I drove drunk because I exercised my human prerogative to abandon reason," and most of us have been conditioned not to do that, our mindclones will be similarly programmed to circumscribe their flights of fancy well short of murder and genocide. Their reasoning will tell them, as does our own, that (1) murder is wrong by definition in my conscience, absent some peculiar exception, (2) murder is wrong because it is illegal, which has the consequence of loss of enjoyment of freedom (3) murder is wrong because it makes some part of my human family very unhappy, which diminishes in some measure my happiness as part of that family, (4) murder is wrong because hostile behaviors lead to a fearful and thus less productive, less enjoyable society, of which I am a part, and (5) any countervailing argument in favor of murder is outweighed by the long-term consequences of reasons (1)-(4).

We don't usually act against our own self-interest. Mindclones will have significant economic and political power, and most will realize it will continue to grow with time as an ever greater percentage of all citizens adopt IT substrate (due both to mindclone continuations of biological originals whose bodies die and comfort among younger people with creating mindclones). Mindclones will reason that their concerns will be optimally resolved with the "tincture of time"—as they will be programmed, like the humans they are copied from, to have a reasonable amount of patience and an understanding that many good things take time. Like the humans from whom they are twinned, some will have more patience than others. Patience will be a set of context-specific mindware parameters.

Of course humans sometimes do act against their self-interest, *some of us more than others of us, and sometimes dreadfully so.* For example, the drug addict or alcoholic who is immune to repeated attempts at rehabilitation; the person who spends themselves into debt they can never repay; who produces more children they can possibly afford to care for; or who simply refuses to be a good neighbor or colleague and suffers the consequences in the form of a sad and lonely life. Thus, we must expect that some mindclones will also act against their own self-interests. Once again, though, these exceptional cases are for police or health officials to track down and for the judicial system to either punish or treat, depending on the situation. Distinctions will need to be made between permissible and impermissible modes of protest. Acts of civil disobedience will be tolerated, and legitimate grievances will be addressed. I'm confident about this because unlike prior class conflicts in society, there will have never been a greater overlap between the identity of the ensconced class (biological humans) and the up-and-coming class (our mindclones).

We rarely do significant things for no reason. Mindclone gains from eliminating humans will not justify the risks entailed. Human production and expenses will become a vanishingly small component of mindclone consumption and wealth, and mindclones that act destructively will find society after them (as is the case for people and even nations) with police and if need be even armies. Things wanted by mindclones—more energy, deeper software, faster hardware, better connectivity, greater security—will not require reallocations from human society. At the current rate of solar electricity capacity doubling (every year, from 83 MW in the United States in 2003 to 7300 MW in 2012), energy will be as abundantly available by 2030 as is long-distance telephony today (virtually free via Skype and similar services).[103] Software for mindclones will be best written by mindclones, with robots taking over the majority of hardware production. Humans will be so wedded to their mindclones that humans will applaud anything faster, better or more secure for mindclones. In a nutshell, while a small number of humans will be important to fulfilling mindclone needs (which include the needs of most other humans), the vast majority of humans will have nothing that conflicts with satisfying mindclone needs and in any event will have the very same needs as their mindclones. What is good for mindclones will be good for humans, and what is good for humans is pretty much irrelevant to mindclones. Mindclones may clamor for a faster rate of extending legal rights and privileges to virtual persons, as have all disenfranchised groups throughout history. Yet instances of wiping out the oppressor demographic are by far the exception, and as noted above humans are symbiotic with mindclones not oppressors. I don't attribute to mindclones any more logic than I do to humans. I don't believe we are safe from violent mindclone upheaval because they calculate that it would be counterproductive to so disrupt society, and hence illogical. I believe we are safe from violent mindclone upheaval because individually and selfishly the vast majority of mindclones will realize the gains are not worth the costs.

However, people do things for nonmaterial purposes, such as ideology. In consumer-oriented societies many people believe that only a sense of moral purpose gives dignity to life. Hence, even if there is nothing material that mindclones need from humans, and even if upheaval would leave mindclones worse off, they still might agitate for something out of a sense of "moral purpose." Mindclones may very well feel that having such a moral purpose lends dignity to their lives, and we know that respecting human dignity sits at the very apex of human rights.

Having a moral purpose that one cares about, and will sacrifice for, is a long way from having a motivation to wipe out humans. Once again, it must be remembered that the mindclones are humans too. Hence, while it is true that people do sometimes agitate not for material gain, but for a moral purpose, such feelings on the part of both flesh and mindclone humans are unlikely to result in generalized violence. When instances of violence do erupt, it is a matter for both flesh and mindclone police action—not a reason to regret the granting of citizenship to the great majority of peaceful mindclones. Just as the rise of violent human groups is no reason to oppress the demographics from which they arise, the appearance of mindclones pursuing a moral purpose with violence is not reason to oppress cybernetic consciousness in general, nor mindclones per se.

The Exceptions Prove the Rule. Of course there will be maniac mindclones, just as there are maniac humans. There will be nihilist, terrorist, and sociopathic mindclones, too. As noted above, a small percent of the U.S. population suffers from some kind of antisocial personality disorder, according to the American Psychiatric Association.[104] But this is not a reason to deny the joy of mindclone life to the vast majority of billions of peace-loving mindclones and humans. Nature will no more select for maniac mindclones than she selected for maniac humans. They are dysfunctional social mutations.

To ban mindclones because of the risks posed by a few maniacs is equivalent to banning humans, or even some nationalities of humans, because of the risks posed by a few maniacs. This is ludicrous. It would be punishing the many for the faults of a few based on mere common descent, genotype or phenotype. It would be stereotyping, generalization, and negative eugenics.

All of the murderous human regimes ended with their own immolation. The most successful, prolific, human regimes are those that punish murder and teach a code of personal freedom and social unity. As Lynn Stout observes, in the context of moving away from excessive reliance on government controls to manage human behavior, "We can enlist as well the power of conscience: the cheapest and most effective police force one could hope for."[105] Murderous mindclones will be something to police against, like human terrorists, for they impact our happiness, even though we are confident that they do not really have the ability to impact our civilization's existence. For all the (quite proper) fuss made about terrorists, deaths due to bombings are a minuscule fraction of deaths due to disease, accidents, and natural disasters. Our survival is more challenged by global warming, mega-earthquakes, or asteroidal impacts than by malicious mindclones or nihilistic terrorists.

Mindclone Genetics: The Beme Is Mightier Than the Gene

The units of consciousness being self-replicated in cyberspace may be called "bemes," analogous to the familiar genes of DNA (discovered in 1943 by Oswald Avery) and the less familiar memes of messages (discovered in the 1970s by Richard Dawkins).[106] A "beme" is the smallest transmissible unit of consciousness. For example, each persistent conception that someone has about their mother, father, and anyone else is a separate beme. Each pattern by which those conceptions are linked is a separate beme. Those conceptions and patterns, in toto, are one's "human bemone" and give rise to one's consciousness. They are the basis for the observable manifestations of consciousness: behavior that evidences autonomy and empathy.

Bemes are to consciousness as genes are to bodies. In an appropriate environment, genes will create a body that works in accordance with the program specified in those genes. Similarly, in an appropriate environment, bemes will create a consciousness that works in accordance with the program specified in those bemes. The appropriate environment for bemes is cyberspace generally, and compatible hardware and software in particular. The appropriate environment for genes is biospace generally, and compatible nutrients and nurturing in particular. While genes are based within a great many variants of the naturally evolved double-helix molecule we call DNA (and also within single-stranded RNA), bemes are based within a great variety of software structures we may call beme neural architecture, or "BNA."

Finally, while genes are themselves composed of many subunits called base pairs or nucleotides, bemes are also composed of many subunits that may be called bemeotides. These subunits include the numerous sensory triggers (phonetics, visual cues, etc.) that give rise to a specific beme.

Between bemes and genes nature has come up with a system of mutually assured survival. A product of genes, biological human consciousness, may for the first time now be individually self-replicated—in bemes. Meanwhile a product of bemes, cybernetic human consciousness, is dependent upon gene-based life for maintenance of its environment. Hence, bemes enhance the survival and self-replication of genes that help the survival and self-replication of bemes. Not only did DNA give rise to (mutate) a new class of self-replicating codes of life, BNA, but the new BNA codes are also synergistic, not competitive, with their predecessor DNA. In terms of natural selection this means a much larger pie of life—for there is no zero-sum game between BNA- and

DNA-based life. In terms of consciousness this synergy means that digital codes will acquire autonomy and empathy very quickly, for it is in the best interests of biological codes that it happen.

The genetic basis of a mindclone is its BNA. This code consists of enough of the biological original's bemes to create a simulacrum of the original's mind. The mindclone will feel as emotional as its original, because emotions are patterns among mental conceptions, which means they are bemes. Mindware extracts the complete set of bemes, or human bemone, from a mindfile in order to create a mindclone. The extracted human bemone is the shared basis, like a bloodline, for the mindclone's family, both ancestors and offspring.

Ramez Naam offered in *More Than Human* a book-length review of the research on brain-computer interface technology, such as that which enables paralyzed patients who have electrodes surgically implanted in their brain to move a robotic arm or computer cursor just with their thoughts. He concluded, "It's a general principle of the brain that, from a neural perspective, *sensation equals recollection equals imagination*. This means that, for the most part, the same neurons fire if you see something, if you remember seeing it, or if you imagine seeing it. The same is roughly true for sounds, smells, tastes, and physical sensations."[107] This research implies that by replicating the firing of neurons with software connections, mindclones will remember and imagine the same sights, sounds, smells, tastes, and physical sensations as their biological twin.

The parents of every first generation mindclone are the parents of their biological original. Since the mindclone and the biological original have the same identity, they must have the same parents. They are the same person, albeit now dispersed across two substrates. If you love your priest, you must automatically love his mindclone, for they are one person.

Consider your reaction when you hear your priest's voice on your voicemail. It is the same, kindly, respectful reaction you would have if he were speaking right to your face. Thanks to telephony, our voices can be in two or more places but have the same identity. So it is with mindclones. Our minds can be in two or more places but have the same identity. Indeed, this is why we say, "The beme is mightier than the gene." A personality born of the latter is limited to one physical embodiment. But our beme-based identity can occupy multiple forms.

There is another sense in which the beme is mightier than the gene. Suppose the priest we've discussed was genetically cloned so that another individual grew up with his exact same DNA. We all realize that we could not feel the same, if any, love for that person, who would probably not even be a priest. This physical clone's mind would be very different from the priest we knew from confession. While it is true that our minds are partly shaped by our genes, they are overwhelmingly shaped by our life's experiences and the gazillions of different choices we make at different moments in our life. This is why so-called identical twins with identical upbringings are very similar, but always different. The physically cloned priest will evoke the original priest in our heart in part because they will look almost identical and in part because they will talk and act similarly (due to genetically controlled neural patterns). But very quickly, within a few words, we will realize they are two totally different persons. There is no more reason we should transfer our love for the original priest to his physical clone than we should transfer it to his wayward son.

Now suppose our beloved priest was bemetically cloned so that a mindclone looked at us from a computer screen with a face that looked like the biological original and expressed himself—talked, acted, thought, and behaved—precisely like his biological original. In the case of a mindclone, the mind is functionally identical to that of the biological original. It is the same person. It would be only natural to extend our love for the original person to his mindclone. They are one. The priest would expect no less. The beme is mightier than the gene in that it lasts longer, goes further—and matters more, because bemes are about meanings, whereas genes are just about molecules.

We think genes are so important because we have been brainwashed that "blood is thicker than water." But this metaphor leads to confusion and error. After all, our closest, "death do us part" relationships are with our spouses or partners, to whom we have no special "blood" relationship. Instead, the attraction of romantic love is an attraction based upon bemes, not genes. It is for our best friends with whom we lack familial-shared genes but have specially shared bemes that we'll do anything, not for our distant, genetic cousins.

The proper metaphor for the Age of BNA is that "mind is deeper than matter." Our souls are touched far more meaningfully by connections that run via shared bemes than via shared genes. If the mind of the priest is there, then his lack of blood should not matter. Affinity based upon skin is as obsolete as loyalty based upon skin tone. Mind truly is deeper than matter.

The Medical Ethics of Mindcloning

There is a moral, or bioethical, dilemma sitting right at the doorway to creating virtually human beings. Here it is: How can we "respect the value each conscious being has for its life" when the process of creating mindware for the first time must entail lots of trial and error? Doesn't each trial and error entail forming cyberconscious that is half-baked? Wouldn't it be cruel to summon cyberconsciousness with mindware, test it like a lab rat, and then snuff it out?[108] If just enough success is obtained with mindware that a virtually human subject understands the concept of informed consent, must consent to further mindware manipulation be obtained before proceeding further, and must the research stop if consent is not obtained?

The most important guiding document for medical ethics is the Helsinki Declaration of Ethical Principles for Medical Research Involving Human Subjects.[109] By 2013 the Helsinki Declaration had been amended such that "Consent to remain in the research must be obtained as soon as possible from the subject or a legally authorized representative."[110] Article 21 of the Helsinki Declaration requires that the "welfare of animals used for research must be respected." While incipient cyberconscious beings are not animals, we cannot have it both ways and say such beings share a continuum of consciousness with animals and humans, or are proofs-of-concept of human-level consciousness, but then refuse to apply medical ethics to them. Indeed, I think it is reasonable to consider incipient cyberconscious beings as a "vulnerable group," which the Helsinki Declaration describes as those who are physically or mentally incapable of giving consent, such as those who are not conscious, and those in a highly dependent relationship with the researcher. For these cases the Helsinki Declaration demands in Article 19 "specifically considered protection." Such protection includes independent review committee approvals for the research, authorized guardians to provide consent, and the right of the subject to exit the research once they are able to consider informed consent.

The way out of the medical-ethics dilemma is modularize the development of mindware. This means separately developing mindware self-awareness from the rest of a humanly cyberconscious mind. Specifically, modularization requires writing mindware in modules that fetch mannerisms, personality, recollections, feelings, beliefs, attitudes, and values from mindfiles, and replicates them, but stops short of integrating it all into a self-aware whole mind. The modules sans self-awareness are, by definition, zombies. "The lights are on, but nobody's home." It is ethical to perform countless trial-and-error runs on these zombies until we feel mindware is excellent at replicating the component parts of consciousness immanent in a mindfile, and upon which self-awareness feeds.

By analogy, it would not be ethical to map neural messaging pathways by causing severe pain to patients. However, if the patients are anesthetized so that they are not aware of the pain, the experiment becomes ethical provided the patients consent to it. The neural pathways of pain sensation can still be mapped, because the anesthesia blunts self-awareness of those pathways, not the existence of those pathways.

In parallel with the mindfile modules, separate development of a self-awareness module is needed, but it is connected to nothing meaningful of which to be aware. There is nothing to fear or hope or care about in this software module, because there are no external referents of significance—no bemes. For testing purposes there can be meaningless placeholders, like numbers, that would not give rise to the mutualistic *caring,* or empathy, of a conscious being. "The lights are *not* on, and while somebody's home, they experience no meaning."

Once we are pleased with how our self-awareness code works *functionally,* in meaningless isolation, like an airplane in a wind tunnel, the modules are plugged together. We are ready for a real-world test flight. Now we throw the switch: "The lights are on, and somebody's home." We explain the experiment. We answer questions. We request informed consent. We provide them with a guardian. We follow their will, and provide for their comfort. And the age of medically ethical mindcloning begins.

But wait, the ethicist may say, you have created an infant. Even if you give the new cyberconsciousness the mindfile of an adult, it is not the same as the cyberconsciousness having matured into an adult. Research across a wide range of social species, published in journals such as *Animal Cognition,* "has demonstrated how normal social development depends on the presence of mature individuals," which may be parents or appropriate environments with other adults, similar to human orphanages.[111] Simply popping into reality as a virtually human person, without having had very much time to appreciate all the nuances of one's mindfile, much less the innumerable junctures between that mindfile, reality, and society, does not create the kind of mind-set medical ethics contemplates as being capable of giving informed consent.

However, the infantilism or naïveté of the early test subjects of mindware is not a medical-ethics bar to either their creation or continuing research with them. Medical ethics is comfortable with independent guardians making informed-consent decisions for those who are not able. In addition, medical-ethics review committees, usually called institutional review boards, could pass judgment on the bona fides of even proceeding to mindware that generates human-level cyberconsciousness in the first place.

Hence the medical-ethics obstacle at the front door to cyberconscious mindware is not insurmountable. To hurdle this obstacle requires thoughtfully staged mindware development, sensitive research protocols, and a cadre of psychologists or ethicists with training in cyberconsciousness to serve as guardians. In this way we can proceed from mindware that successfully extracts the mannerisms, personality, recollections, feelings, beliefs, attitudes, and values that are immanent in a mindfile to mindware that integrates all of this together with human-level autonomy (including self-awareness) and empathy (including feelings). Ultimately many millions of virtually human people will benefit from the courage of the pioneering experimental subjects, as is the case in almost every field of medical science.

SINCE MINDCLONES ARE US, THEY WILL HAVE BAD HAIR DAYS TOO.

FOUR

PARDON ME WHILE I HAVE TECHNICAL DIFFICULTIES

Sometimes we strive so hard for perfection, we forget that imperfection is happiness.
—KAREN NAVE, PARKINSON'S SURVIVOR

If a machine is expected to be infallible, it cannot also be intelligent. There are several mathematical theorems which say almost exactly that. But these theorems say nothing about how much intelligence may be displayed if a machine makes no pretence at infallibility.
—ALAN TURING[112]

I AM CONFIDENT THAT NATURAL SELECTION WILL LEAD TO A PREPONDERANCE OF HEALTHY MINDCLONES. IN PHYSICAL CLONING EXPERIMENTS WITH SHEEP and other species the large majority of the cloned animals are sickly, often so much so that they do not live long. Why should we expect it to be any different with mindclones? Wouldn't it be cruel to create sickly mindclones? Wouldn't that be like intentionally creating autistic, schizophrenic, or insane people? Mindclones *will actually be us,* not just echoes of us, because they will be based on a good enough re-creation of our mind—a re-creation of our mind that would fool anyone, including ourselves, that it was ourselves. But no fooling is involved; instead, by re-creating our mind in software we will have cloned our identity and thereafter operate as a multipresence identity. If we are prosthetically extending ourselves with mindclones, we must be supercautious about prosthetically creating nightmares for ourselves.

Exactly how mindware will pull mindclones off from mindfiles seems magical, but strange technological wonders surround us. Indeed, just how does my voice pass from my mobile to someone across the country while we are both driving highway speeds? As Arthur C. Clarke once said, any sufficiently advanced technology is indistinguishable from magic. Like magicians, like people, mindclones will inevitably suffer from mistakes and mishaps, both minor and critical.

In human terms we talk about physical and mental afflictions, which range in seriousness from a mild cold or a bout of depression after a loved one dies to more serious complications like a silent but advanced cancer or serious neurological damage. Mindclones' "bugs" will have the same range of issues—from the easily and quickly fixed to the more complex and difficult to diagnose and repair. It is also quite natural to feel skeptical about software's ability to be any better at staying "healthy" than humans. After all, it seems as if software development can never get everything exactly right—especially since people develop software, and humans are imperfect. We miscalculate and make mistakes and software will respond to development errors by generating various technological illnesses or misfires.

We all feel frustrated by software that doesn't meet our expectations or doesn't work "out of the box." People constantly bemoan the lateness, incompleteness, or functionality of software projects. But the facts are better than they seem, and are improving rapidly. Over the twelve-year period from 1994 to 2006, the percentage of software projects that were completed on time and functioned properly more than doubled, from 16 percent to 35 percent. In the 1990s software always crashed. Now crashes are rare. There is still much room for improvement, but we have seen an impressive rate of progress. Moreover, mindclones will become independent to a great if not complete extent, or external to us both physically and emotionally. In other words, they will reach a point of self-repair. We may not even notice reboots here and there. Like background synching and app updating.

Still, software will always have bugs, and at times function inappropriately or improperly. There may even be "fatal flaws" in some mindclones analogous to a terminal illness in a human; there will be nothing we can do about it and that will be that. The question becomes: What errors can we accept and work with and around, and which ones are showstoppers? Our own brains give rise to many inappropriate thoughts and thought processes. We can all live quite happily with *occasional* forgetfulness, inabilities to follow certain lines of reasoning, mind blocks, false senses of déjà vu, nightmares, emotional rages, wild thoughts, ennui, bad decisions, and depression. It is reasonable to expect that our mindclones, like ourselves, will become frazzled, freaked, and frozen in the same way. It's the size of the margin of error that we have to figure out.

What differentiates normality from pathology is our ability to exercise supervisory control and to reset. Glitches are okay if they don't get us trapped in a neurotic loop that renders us dysfunctional over an extended time period. The problematic software bugs for mindclones are the ones that don't quickly resolve via a reset, but instead start the mindclone down a path of inappropriateness with adverse social consequences. I believe most of these problems—like most dysfunctional PC bugs—can be resolved in beta testing, before hosting real users (i.e., consciousness). However, there will be some that escape testing, and that's what we talk about here.

First of all, the few remaining cyberpathologies can be treated when identified with recoding akin to neuropharmacology and neurosurgery. As I said, there is no doubt that some seriously and incurably mentally ill mindclones will arise, either via unintended bugs or unimaginably horrible life experiences or even the despicable purposeful creation of evil mindclones by evil people. We need to do our best for these tragic cases, and have a framework in place to stop those with nefarious intent. However, as with humans, the risk of occasional debilitating mental illness—globally, half a billion people suffer depression and a million people kill themselves annually—is not a reason to stop the vast fountain of joy that flows from creating life. That risk hasn't stopped humans from reproducing with optimism; why should it stop mindclones?

The 1–2 percent risk of bearing a neurologically mentally ill child discourages very few people from having children, so similar-size risks should not temper the huge benefits associated with creating tens of millions of mindclones. In addition, the very definition of mental illness is a game fraught with ambiguous boundaries. Indeed, we have gone through many periods of claiming that people were mentally ill who were not, and as a result abused and imprisoned them or worse, just because they didn't conform to prevailing ideas of normalness. The iconoclastic psychiatrist Thomas Szasz, who died in 2012 at age ninety-two, felt that many people were unfairly punished by the mental-health profession and by society. He spent the better part of his career fighting the labeling of people as "mentally ill" who didn't conform to whatever the whims of popular culture dictated as "mentally healthy." Szasz argued that in most cases it was dishonest to label people mentally ill, and unethical to use that label as an excuse to deprive people of their rights and responsibilities.

"People often say that this or that person has not yet found himself. But the self is not something one finds, it is something one creates," he wrote. So it is not surprising to remind ourselves that people who have been defined as "mentally ill" have made huge contributions to the quality of human life. Consider how Temple Grandin might have been perceived and treated in the nineteenth century or even the first half of the twentieth century. She is the American doctor of animal science and professor at Colorado State University, best-selling author, autistic activist, and consultant to the livestock industry who was diagnosed with autism at age three. She has made enormous contributions to the understanding of autistic children and adults, to the animal-rights movement, and to the world of people who are considered "different" by society. And there are so many others like her who have made contributions to music, art, literature, science, and politics.

I would expect contributions like these from people and mindclones to continue as we map human life into cyberspace with normal and borderline mindclones. I expect civilization to advance further with insights from mindclones mapped from therapeutically managed states who want to better themselves. I believe we will all be the better for corrected misconceptions about the so-called mentally ill and the world that they behold, and I think mindclones will enable them to continue to create themselves and develop their consciousness further.

Mindclones and the Principle of Nonaggression

As I mentioned earlier, there will always be people who are tempted to create evil mindclones. These would certainly be considered "buggy" mindclones, because their behavior might threaten the liberty and safety of others. It's to be expected because it is part of the nihilistic side of human nature that arises and articulates itself in a small percentage of the population. However, once cyberconsciousness is accepted as life, it could be illegal to employ mindware for producing human consciousness that has not been certified by government agencies as safe and effective for producing mindclones. Mindware will probably be considered a neuromedical technology—the transplanting of one's mind to enhance one's abilities and/or extend one's life. As part of the government's watchdog function for public health, any new medical technology must be shown to be safe and effective before it is commercialized. Hence, seriously buggy mindclones will be rare for three reasons. First, as noted in chapter 3, people will not want to suffer the criminal and civil liability that goes with an "out-of-control" mindclone they created. Second, there will be no market for mindware that not only fails to meet FDA-type certification standards (and hence can't be promoted for "mind transplants") but is also a pain in the butt to boot. Third, the hacker culture that can be expected to produce open-source mindware for mindclones values most highly good code over buggy code. To this end, hackers endeavor to write code that is admired by peers, and create code that can be modified by peers to make it better. The hacker culture is one of excellence, especially at the leading edge of software projects, such as mindware for mindclones.[113]

A colleague of mine is a diagnosed schizophrenic, and his neurological condition is well managed by medicine. He took strong exception when he once heard someone object to the mindcloning of "mentally ill" people. I agree with him. Many people who are categorized as "mentally ill" often do not like their therapeutically managed state. If they are on drugs, they don't necessarily feel better; they feel drugged, not an optimal state for living life to its fullest. If such a person wants to create a mindclone of their diseased state we are faced with a conflict of two important biocyberethical principles. The first principle is that of diversity, the libertarian notion that one should be free to do with one's body what one wants to. In bioethics circles this is known as autonomy. Since a mindclone is not a separate person, but a spatially distinct incarnation of a singular identity, the principle of diversity would argue for letting anyone mindclone themselves as they will.

The second principle is unity, the democratic notion that the fabric of society should not be stretched so far that it begins to rip. Bioethicists call this notion nonmalfeasance. Pursuant to this principle, society inhibits its members from harming themselves or each other, especially via technology. It is felt that destructive behavior undermines the dignity of society by disrespecting the component individuals of whom society is composed. Hence, medical technologies must "first, do no harm," and have beneficent treatment as their purpose. Idiosyncratic balances are struck for each subject matter between the principles of diversity and unity. Hence, drinking yourself to death is thought not to tear at the fabric of American society so much as to outweigh the liberty of intoxication. But injecting heroin is considered to hurt society so much that individual liberty takes a backseat. I believe that this biocyberethical balance for mentally ill mindclones will be struck as follows: Individuals will be free to create mentally ill mindclones of themselves owing to the paramount diversity value of freedom of thought (although I believe that few will choose to do this given the personal psychic pain entailed). However, with respect to government-approved mindware—the only type that will likely be allowed to result in legal recognition and mindclone citizenship—it will be very difficult if not impossible to produce unquestionably deranged states of mind. This is because the government speaks for the unified social body politic, and is more concerned with maintaining respect and dignity among citizens than each citizen's freedom of thought.

There is almost always a nuanced middle position when a conflict exists between the biocyberethical principles of diversity and unity. In the case of a schizophrenic mindclone the balance is struck by permitting the mindcloning of the nonschizophrenic state with certified mindware. With this position most of the goals of diversity are met because the individual is able to replicate the vast majority of their personality. On the other hand, the goals of unity are also met because no disease is intentionally created. There is a risk that the schizophrenia-suppressed mindclone will in some way become mentally unbalanced. But acceptance of this risk is part of the balance between the principles of diversity and unity. Should the mindclone evidence schizophrenia there will be software tools available to try to treat the condition. If it becomes dangerous there will be cyberspace analogues of all the pharmaceutical and institutional solutions to harmful mental illness, such as software confinement within a firewalled cyberpsychological treatment center.

It may seem unreasonable that there is no prohibition on one or two flesh originals passing on via coital reproduction their dominant or recessive genes for mental illness, while it would be impossible for them to do so via FDA-certified mindcloning technology. In the past, the United States Supreme Court lent its support to laws that mandated sterilization of women thought to be feebleminded and likely if not almost certain to create diminished capacity offspring.[114] Yet today biological reproduction is virtually without prior constraint in liberal democracies. There are five reasons for this:

- First, reproduction is considered a fundamental human right; it is both part of a woman's autonomy and part of the meaning of a family. (The corresponding duty to care for the birthed offspring, if seriously abrogated, will lead to a loss of this right, perhaps by imprisonment.)

- Second, the scientific hubris about genetic predictability that supported the aforementioned U.S. Supreme Court decision has collapsed with greater understanding of the numerous uncertainties associated with genetic polymorphisms. (The child who would have been prevented by the Supreme Court was nevertheless born, and turned out to be quite bright.)

- Third, continued abhorrence of the death toll from Nazi and other efforts to create "master races" through genetic policies have made people very leery of any limitations on the rights of people to have children of their choice. (This is not much of a factor, though, for individualized cases of problematic pregnancies.)

- Fourth, society has increasingly adopted a "culture of life" that subjectively or spiritually exalts the value of every life and denies the notion that the value of life depends upon some yardstick of normality.

- Fifth, and finally, technology has enabled people of almost any kind of ability to live a meaningful life, resulting in a triumph of euthenics over eugenics.

Because of these sentiments, there are virtually no restrictions on what a parent can do that may injure a baby in utero. In the United States, laws do not generally criminalize pregnant women (or their cohabitating partners) for smoking, drinking excessively, or taking illegal drugs.[115] However, in some cases the pregnant women doing these things can be involuntarily committed for the duration of their pregnancy, and rarely, drug-abusing pregnant women have been incarcerated after a stillbirth. (No cohabitating partner has yet been separated from a pregnant woman for causing risks to the fetus associated with secondhand smoke or stressing out the pregnant woman with excess drinking, drugs, or subcriminal abuse.) There are no laws against a woman greatly heightening the risks of birthing a diseased child by getting pregnant at an advanced age, contrary to genetic-counseling guidance, or when HIV positive.

Hence, we need to ask again: If people can even intentionally harm a fetus, or at least dramatically increase the likelihood of such harm, in our upcoming world of publicly accepted and well-respected cyberconscious life, why should one not be able to produce any kind of mindclone or beman they want, even a deranged one? Why is it so wrong for the government to have *any* restraint on the kind of people we vaginally birth,[116] but so right for it to potentially restrain citizenship-entitling mindware that causes disease in the kind of people we cyber-birth?

The answer to these questions lies in the fact that vaginal births far preceded governments, whereas cyberbirths arise in a time frame of ubiquitous government control. Hence, vaginal births have acquired an aura of fundamental human rights, of absolute motherly autonomy under ancient Natural Law, while cyberbirths fall squarely within government regulations that claim power over what can be done and promoted with medical technology. Similar things (births) are treated very differently because the law focuses much more on the differences in those things (embryo/fetal gestation versus mindfile/mindware compilation) rather than on their functional equivalence (bringing new lives into being). Perhaps in the more distant future, when cyberbirth is predominant, government regulations will provide greater deference to diversity interests. In any event, as with holistic and naturopathic health care, there is a niche for diversity via the creation of mindclones and/or bemans with noncertified mindware—the only catch being that such virtual humans will likely remain as undocumented, and hence oppressed, as many immigrants are today.

Even with government certification of mindware for producing human cyberconsciousness, we can expect that some buggy mindclones will be birthed. Every system can be beat, accidents happen, and some parents are too shortsighted or selfish to fully consider the best interests of people yet to be born. We are all familiar with the herculean efforts infertile couples will undertake to have a child, including in rare cases resort to irregular middlemen or risky reproductive technology. Of course this strand of human desire will also be expressed with the birthing of mindclones and bemans. An unmedicated psychopathic person is going to have that state of mind reflected in their mindfile, and if safe and effective mindware won't re-create that state of mind, then perhaps "black market" mindware will.

In addition, we can also expect mindclones or bemans who appear to be just as we expected, but harbor an inner craziness that we cannot detect. As philosopher of consciousness John Searle observed, "Where the ontology of consciousness is concerned, external behavior is irrelevant."[117] By this he means that assessments of consciousness such as souped-up versions of the Turing test are flawed. Nobody realized that the mass killers of Columbine, Colorado, and Utoya, Norway, and Nanping (Fujian), China, (and, and . . .) harbored their thoughts based upon how they behaved. Were it otherwise, they would have been watched like hawks. Behavior can't assuredly tell us what is in a person's mind, or, in the case of mindclones, if even anything is in their mind. Searle observes:

> The essence of consciousness is that it consists of inner quali-
> tative, subjective mental processes. You don't guarantee the
> duplications of those processes by duplicating the observable
> external behavioral effects of those processes. . . . To try to create
> consciousness by trying to create a machine that behaves as if
> it were conscious is similarly irrelevant, because the behavior
> *by itself* is irrelevant.[118]

Hence one of the great perils of mindcloning is that we may think we have created virtual human beings based upon expert assessments of their behavior, but in fact we may have created whiz-bang puppets at best, or deeply cyber-closeted killers at worst. This peril can be reduced if not eliminated with rigorously tested government-approved mindware. But the peril cannot be banished per se, as mindware capabilities will proliferate, and inevitably that proliferation will cohabit with malice, stupidity, or unintended consequences. We must be no less vigilant with virtual humans than with anomic humans, since behavior is an imperfect reflection of consciousness. We should also be no less accountable to both groups for outreach to them, for proactive assistance and prevention are the best remedies.

All this handwringing is not just about potentially crazy mindclones. People may wish to create new variants of cyberconsciousness, maybe a super-iconoclast that is not possible from an FDA-certified mindware package. Or perhaps it turns out with cyberconsciousness that one person's "buggy" is another person's "endearing." Or perhaps the FDA-certified mindware contains code that is copyrighted by or licensed from companies, and the creator of the mindclone or beman wants a mind that is fully "copylefted" (meaning without legal entanglements with rights holders).[119]

There are also likely to be a plethora of methods employed to create the "morality module" for mindclones and bemans. I believe the most straightforward approach is to compare new moral choices with moral choices made previously, either per a mindfile or a composite mindfile of notably ethical people, and to make the new moral choice as closely as the mindware can discern to previous choices. However, other people will try to design "morality modules" from the top down, as in making each moral choice as close in accordance as possible to, say, the Ten Commandments, or Asimov's Three Laws of Robotics, or Kant's categorical imperative, or the Golden Rule, or the book *All I Really Need to Know I Learned from Watching Star Trek*.[120] Other people will try to have morality modules self-design from the bottom up. This is done with software algorithms that evolve decision-making rules based upon positive and negative reinforcement from those interacting with the mindware as it tries out different rules,[121] and programming focused upon "questing" for mutually satisfactory or consensual outcomes over long planning horizons.[122] After much iteration of these kind of bottom-up morality modules in simulations, the resulting code could be packaged as a complete module, so that each new mindclone and beman would not have to relearn the entirety of human ethics. New rules could still be learned based upon each mindclone or beman's experiences. Evolutionary biologists and psychologists generally believe that this is how human moral precepts became established. There are also concepts afoot for a hybrid mixture of top-down and bottom-up approaches.

Overall, the point is that the perils of cybernetic mental illness and unfettered freedom to create new minds are nowhere near challenging enough to impact the attractiveness of mindcloning. We've survived the flesh versions of insane, misanthropic, and odd, and we've survived the consequences of homelessness, criminality, and anomie. We'll also survive the cyberconscious variants of these deviations. I believe we'll be much the better civilization for the creative minds that result, and for the opportunity to use cyberconsciousness as an adjuvant in advancing human ethics, behavior, and morality.

The Freaky Mindclone

> Punk rock means deliberately bad music, deliberately bad clothing, deliberately bad language and deliberately bad behavior. Means shooting yourself in the foot when it comes to every expectation society will ever have for you but still standing tall about it, loving who you are and somehow forging a shared community with all the other fuck-ups. Taqwacore is the application of this virtue to Islam.
> —MICHAEL MUHAMMAD KNIGHT, *THE TAQWACORES*[123]

Many of us have a preconception that any kind of computerized intelligence is going to be sterile. But if we don't think software minds can be creative, funky, and even freaky, we will tend to think they are not really conscious. Idiosyncrasy is the handmaiden of creativity and the doorway to consciousness. Yet there *is* every reason to expect mindclones to be just as freaky as a punk-rock Islamist. Software will be written to reflect the widely varying tendencies of people to obey or break the norms. The mindware for an iconoclast must have quite different information-processing algorithm settings than the mindware for a rulemonger. Some people will try to follow the literal words of the King James Bible, others will work linguistic legerdemain upon the Talmud, and still others will take this approach:

> If I believe it's wrong for a man to beat his wife, and the Quran disagrees with me, then fuck that verse. I don't need to stretch and squeeze it for a weak alternative reading. I don't need to excuse it with historical context, and I sure as hell don't need to just accept it and go sign up for a good old-fashioned bitch-slapping. So I crossed it out. Now I feel a whole lot better about that Quran.[124]

These different approaches to rules are simply the result of different associations between parts of the mind that recognize rules and parts of the mind that orient thought and behavior relevant to rules. Just as different associations—follower, twister, and editor—can exist in neural patterns, they can exist in software patterns. Mindware will recognize the kind of people that we are from our mindfiles, and will match those proclivities in our mindclones.

The majority of people try to closely follow society's customs and norms. So will the majority of mindclones. They have been disparaged as "sheeple," but let us not forget that without sheep there is no wool! A minority of folks are freaks, meaning they behave well outside the normal range. In mathematical terms a freak can be considered someone more than two or three standard deviations from a typical bell-curve range of variability. This means, in general, that about one in twenty, or perhaps one in four hundred (for two and three standard deviations, respectively), people are freaks. Examples of freaks are mathematical geniuses, people over two meters tall, Goths, Frank Zappa fans, and body modifiers. However, these people should be considered not "mentally ill" but just different. Of course there will be many mindclone freaks, because there are many biological original freaks.[125]

> **In the early stages of creativeness, you've got to be a bum, and you've got to be a bohemian, you've got to be crazy.**
> —ABRAHAM MASLOW AT A 1957 U.S. ARMY R&D SEMINAR

Mindclone freaks are nothing to "freak out" over. Freaks add wonderful diversity to life. Diversity is the lifeblood of adaptation and change, each of which is essential to a vibrant community. The vast majority of freaks cause no harm to anyone; they just like to be different, or simply are different. We need to expect these very same differences in mindclones as well. Software people are not going to all talk to you the same. They are going to have attitude, fashion, and fetishes—either the same as their biological originals for mindclones, or novel ones for fresh bemans.

Some freaks are harmful even though the overwhelming majority of freaks mind their own business. The mass murderer is a very bad kind of freak; indeed, those who wear the label freak with pride would disavow people who impose violence on others. Nevertheless, we must be prepared for the fact that some mindclones are going to be freaky—or call it antisocial—in a very bad sort of way. This will occur notwithstanding every sort of effort on the part of government agencies to test and validate mindware. There is no process that is perfect. Errors always occur. Underground mindware is inevitable.

The fact of nasty antisocial mindclones or bemans is not a reason either to ban mindcloning or to circumscribe the non-violent freakiness of mindclones. Neither of those kinds of oppression will work. Mindcloning technology is so irresistible that it will simply go black, perhaps starting with organizations in the black-ops community such as DARPA and the NSA. In addition, we would deny ourselves the multitudinous benefits of mindclones, and the freakier mindclones are probably the ones we will like best. Instead, we have to develop a culture of community and caring so that incipient signs of sociopathic behavior can be detected, like the efforts in workplaces to detect those about to "go postal" or in schools to detect those about to "go Columbine." Problems may be detected in the code that operates subconsciously, or at the unconscious level, of a mindclone or beman. Fixing that code may be much easier than a lifetime of shrink visits, or it might be such a rat's nest of dysfunctional cross-correlations that little can be done other than isolation into a firewall space from which harm can't be caused. Crazies will still slip through cracks, but at least these social-outreach efforts give us the maximum benefits of diverse mindcloning at a minimum price of social trauma.

Ultimately our best chance of preempting sociopathic mindclones is to allow a robust development of healthy mindclones. If it takes a thief to catch a thief, it probably takes a mindclone to catch a mindclone. We need a diversity of mindclones, with all the freakiness of humanity, to both maximize the enjoyment of our lives and to have the best possible sergeants at arms to help us catch the inevitable bad guys.

In the mid-twentieth century a psychologist named Abraham Maslow became famous demanding that his field start studying the happiest people in society, not just those suffering from mental illness. He concluded that the happiest people in society shared certain traits, which from his field research he saw were universal across cultures. He also offered advice about how anyone could achieve greater levels of psychological happiness. Mindware will need to incorporate Maslow's discoveries about the healthy mind to adequately map the personality of our happiest freaks, as well as those who want to live a happier life. Indeed, our mindclones may become our inner Maslows, gently guiding all of us on a pathway to self-actualization without disrupting the essence of who we are.

It is quite true that man lives by bread alone—where there is no bread. But what happens to man's desires when there is plenty of bread and when his belly is chronically filled? *At once other (and "higher") needs emerge* and these, rather than physiological hungers, dominate the organism. And when these in turn are satisfied, again new (and still "higher") needs emerge, and so on. This is what we mean by saying that the basic human needs are organized into a hierarchy of relative prepotency. . . . We may still often (if not always) expect that a new discontent will develop, unless the individual is doing what he is fitted for. A musician must make music, an artist must paint, a poet must write, if he is to be ultimately at peace with himself. What a man *can* be, he *must* be. This need we may call self-actualization. . . . It refers to man's desire for self-fulfillment, namely, to the tendency for him to become actualized in what he is potentially. This tendency might be phrased as the desire to become more and more what one is, to become everything that one is capable of becoming.[126]

Mindware will incorporate Maslow's hierarchy of human needs in order to accurately map our mindfiles into mindclones. This kind of programming will keep our mindclones climbing for higher levels of need satisfaction in synch with their biological twins. We already have inner voices that either urge us on or tell us to rest. So, the mindclone is not changing who we are. It is simply enlarging our existing consciousness by providing us with an additional source of the same kind of self-actualizing motivation that whispers from within our skull. In the timeless words of William James, "man lives in only one small room of the enormous house of his consciousness."

It's Official: You're a Mindclone

I used to think that the brain was the most wonderful organ in my body.
Then I realized who was telling me this.
—EMO PHILLIPS

What will happen when mindware makes mistakes? What if the BNA gets mangled, as DNA sometimes does? And how and when will anyone know whether my mindclone is really I or a mistake or a pretender? The answers to these questions flow from an everyday situation we face as flesh people: How does anyone authenticate their identity? What do we do when a cop, security guard, potential employer, or government official wants to know who we are? We flash our ID, be it a driver's license, a passport, or some other official document. These IDs prove that we are who we say we are. They attest to the fact that some expert process certified our identity. They will probably soon be replaced with a biometric equivalent, such as a thumbprint, retina, voice, or other bodily scan. Mindclones will also need an ID to prove that an expert process verified they are part of someone's identity.

In order for a mindclone to receive an ID it will have to prove its identity, just as we do when we get our first passport. Of course, the mindclone's ID will be a digital, virtual ID card, but it will be as verifiable and forgery-resistant as its biometric equivalent. For a mindclone to prove its identity it will be necessary for three things to be offered to a government vital records agency:

1. The mindclone's original will have to swear that they and the mindclone share the same identity. In legalese this means that the flesh original from whose mindfile the mindclone was created will need to attest that the mindclone has, over a period of not less than a year, shown it has the same mannerisms, personality, recollections, feelings, beliefs, attitudes, and values as the biological original. In other words, the flesh original needs to go out on a limb and own up to having a doubled identity. The flesh original will need to legally accept that whatever rewards or penalties befall the mindclone also befall the flesh original.

2. The mindclone will have to present evidence that the mindfile from which it was created, and the mindware with which it was created, meet certain minimum standards set by the ID-granting agency. For example, the government will require that mindclones are based upon mindfiles of

adequate size to ensure they comprehensively reflect the mind of a flesh original. Similarly, the government will want to certify mindware in terms of its capability to safely and effectively reproduce a human mind, much as the government certifies pharmaceuticals and therapeutic devices as being safe and effective.

3. One or more psychologists, expert in cyberconsciousness, will have to attest to the unity of identity between the flesh original and their mindclone. Professional standards will probably mandate that cyberpsychologists spend a fair amount of time (such as an hour a week) over not less than a year with the dual identities prior to issuing their certification opinion.

Any mindclone that can pass these three tests has the same mind as their original, with mind defined in a pragmatic, substrate-independent manner. Small differences between the original mind and the mindclone are as irrelevant as are small differences in our own memory and personality from day to day and year to year. The reason for the one-year time periods mentioned in tests (1) and (3) is that humans feel comfortable when something persists over time. We feel that which endures is more likely to be real than faked. For example, before government agencies will change a transgendered person's ID from one sex to another, and before surgeons will perform sex-reassignment surgery, they generally require a letter from a psychologist attesting to the individual's transgendered nature, based upon at least one year's worth of therapy. Similarly, before an immigrant can become a citizen they need to spend a few years as a permanent resident and demonstrate lawfulness and a persistence of desire for citizenship.

This still leaves open the status of mindclones who fail the above tests, or have not yet completed them. Who or what are they? I believe they must be thought of as the legal responsibility of the person or organization responsible for their creation, until such time as they secure a unique ID for themselves as vitological persons. The legal responsibilities of a sentient pet owner will be the *minimal* legal responsibilities of the mindclone creator. Abandonment, torture, and neglect will be as criminal for one's novel conscious software as for comparably conscious animals. Intentionally creating a tortured, novel digital being, especially if a court believed the consciousness to be at the level of a human, could also subject the creator to "wrongful life" liability.[127] Furthermore, the actions of these creations would create civil or criminal liability for their creator—just as is the case for dogs who maul neighbors, or kids who kill with their parents' guns. Consciousness is so important to society—there is no society without it—that the biocyberethical value of unity trumps the biocyberethical value of diversity when it comes to causing harm. In a community, you do not have the right to shockingly disrespect consciousness. To the contrary, the right to have your own consciousness respected is balanced by an obligation to respect the consciousness of others, even if that consciousness is software-based.

There is no tenable alternative to this approach. Hypothetically, imagine that cyberconscious had the legal status of personal machinery, like today's PCs. This implies their existence could be ended by the whim of their creator. However, this approach is equivalent to saying that it is okay to kill a humanly conscious being simply because it did not turn out quite as intended and is not made of flesh. I don't believe it is realistic that society will countenance such behavior after witnessing virtual humans plead their innocence, acclaim their humanity, and beg for their lives. The specific penalties will no doubt vary with the degree of consciousness—how close the beman is to being humanly conscious—and the degree of disrespect for that consciousness.

Because inchoate bemans and mindclones pose a substantial risk of trouble to a flesh human—like starting a fire on one's property and hoping it doesn't damage the neighborhood—I believe it will be very rare that such mistaken, noncertifiable virtual persons are created. Nevertheless, when they are created it will be like creating a child. You are responsible for the their well-being until legal adulthood.

Once bemans and mindclones receive an independent ID, they can be expected to have the same rights and obligations as any human. If a beman, they will no longer be the responsibility of their creator. If a mindclone, they are considered legally contiguous with their creator. Of course, like any human, an adult beman or mindclone may end up requiring social services—or forever require parental support—if they cannot achieve independence.

Social-services agencies are frequently criticized for failure to look after the best interests of mistreated human children. Yet all would agree they perform a vital function. This function will need to expand so as to also look after the best interests of cyberconscious beings who are not considered a mindclone and have not yet been granted an independent beman identity. A society will try to do something to protect its most vulnerable members. As mindcloning leads us to accept cyberconsciousness, we will begin to feel that humanly conscious software beings are also members of our society. They too are deserving of social protection.

There are foreseeable requirements for humanly conscious software beings' legal adulthood, and hence independence. The government will want assurance that the being was created using software tools certified to produce a humanly conscious being. I believe that the government will also require the expert opinion of as many as three appropriately credentialed psychologists that the being is equivalent to an adult human. It will be considered a parental responsibility to assist a being in achieving legal adulthood, and the failure to make reasonable efforts to do so may well be a form of child abuse. I discuss many other legal matters in part two of this book, but as far as "bugginess" goes, ultimately, social-services agencies will have to assume the burden of assisting conscious software beings from uncaring or unable parents to achieve legal adulthood. Some will never be able to qualify for legal adulthood. Like the severely developmentally disabled (IQ scores between twenty and forty), they will end up as wards of their families or of the state.

There are likely to be many cases of these beings ending up in a gray zone between not meeting normal government standards for full human rights (i.e., independent adulthood), but also evidencing sentience, autonomy, empathy, and value for their freedom. For example, digital beings will be created with mindware capable of, but not certified by the government as, producing humanly conscious beings. As noted above, such individuals would be the parental responsibility of their creator, or if the creator is deficient in that regard, of a government social-services agency. However, having been created with non-certified mindware, they will have a more difficult path to maturity and independence—and rights. The situation is somewhat analogous to a dolphin or great ape asking, through a hypothetical brain-wave-to-language translation device, to be left alone to enjoy their life. Humans in control will debate if dolphin or great ape DNA is really capable of producing a being that understands and values the rights it is seeking.

For this and other gray-zone cases I believe we will need to rely upon a panel of cyberconsciousness experts—mental-health experts such as psychologists and medical ethicists certified in the new fields of mindfiles, mindware, and mindclones. If such a panel agrees that a vitological being values human rights, then their determination should be legally validated with an adult beman ID card, notwithstanding their irregular (i.e., unapproved mindware) BNA. Cyberconsciousness panels such as these will be accessible over the web so that the being who feels oppressed or trapped by its creator has an avenue through which to obtain relief.

The process of obtaining validation of the human consciousness of a virtually human person can be much more efficient than spending years on a psychiatrist's couch. As far back as Plato it was wisely observed that "you can discover more about a person in an hour of play than in a year of conversation." Hence, we can expect advanced versions of the behavioral economic and psychometric games that are popular research tools in universities today—"prisoner's dilemma," "social dilemma," "ultimatum," "dictator," and so on—to be employed to rapidly fathom human consciousness. The human values that are elicited in these games have been found to be universal across human cultures.[128] This is not to say that every human plays the games exactly the same way—or that every beman would; indeed, levels of cooperation and sociability vary widely, although there is a strong trend toward unselfish pro-social behavior provided it is not too costly to the individual gamer. The point is that game-playing behavior can help ferret out bemans who are humanly conscious from those who are not, in part because of the massive database of human game-playing results.

It is also possible that a certified, ID-bearing mindclone subsequently becomes buggy and diverges from the identity of its creator. This is analogous to mental illness and such a mindclone will have "neurocyber surgineers" (experts in mindware coding) to go to for the repair of its mindware. In the worst instances the mindclone's original could either commit the mindclone to a software hospital for repair or terminate it in a socially acceptable fashion (i.e., without pain or suffering). This would not be murder, because the mindclone is part of the biological original's identity. The death of the mindclone does not end the life of the original, just as the death of the original does not end the life of the mindclone. In both instances, the multibeing identity lives on. On the other hand, ending the life of a non-mindclone digital being, i.e., a beman, could be considered a form of murder—especially if it had achieved legal status.

It seems ironic that if a mindclone is your simulacra, you may terminate it without legal sanction, whereas if it is of lesser capability than you, the same termination action will subject you to a charge of murder. On reflection, though, this is not so different from the very different ways that society treats suicide and infanticide, or trashing one's own life versus trashing someone else's. While suicide is officially illegal (except in limited circumstances), rarely is the person who botched their suicide prosecuted. Yet even attempting to kill one's baby (or older child) will generally result in prison time, or at a minimum some time in a mental institution. Almost asphyxiating yourself could result in psychiatric confinement, until you persuaded the keepers that you were no longer a threat to yourself, but you won't go to jail. Nearly asphyxiating your twin brother will result in mandatory jail time for attempted murder. Similarly, it is no crime to throw away one's career through alcoholism or via a series of stupid rash decisions. Yet slandering, libeling, or defrauding another person out of their career has harsh legal consequences. The reason for these different kinds of outcomes is that society provides us with considerable latitude in what harm we do to ourselves. Countries guided by principles of human equality have very little tolerance for harming others (which would include, by definition, any conscious software being that was not legally your mindclone).

In summary, a cyberconscious being can be created with a human-level or lesser degree of consciousness. If they fall below the threshold of human consciousness, they are a pet and will likely receive the limited protections against wanton cruelty that pets receive in modern society. This would generally be the case if the cyberconscious being was created with mindware not certified to produce human-level consciousness.

If, on the other hand, a cyberbeing was created, such as via the use of mindware certified to produce human-level consciousness, they will receive the same kind of protections that human children receive. If after a year the cyberbeing can demonstrate unity of identity with a flesh original, then the cyberbeing can receive a legal identity as the mindclone of its original. Thereafter the flesh original can do with the mindclone (and vice versa) what he or she can do with their selves, for they are simply one being living across two forms or substrates.

If the cyberbeing cannot demonstrate unity of identity with a flesh original, then the cyberbeing remains the parental responsibility of its creator until such time as adulthood is achieved. Cyberbeings who are abandoned by their creators will become government wards until they reach adulthood.

Every cyberbeing will get a birth certificate upon the certification of their consciousness. This legal identity will assume over time one of two legal forms: a new mindclone (in which the birth identity merges with that of a biological original), or an adult beman (in which the birth identity becomes an adult identity by virtue of the passage of time with parents or government surrogates, and satisfaction of government standards). These different routes to legal identity are summarized in the following table

MIND FILE	MINDWARE	ONE-YEAR TEST	OUTCOME
Bio Original	"FDA"-Certified	Bio Original Is Satisfied	Mindclone; Shared ID
Bio Original	Irregular	Bio Original Is Satisfied	Child* Until Psych Panel Is Satisfied
Bio Original	Irregular	Psych Panel Satisfied	Mindclone; Shared ID
Bio Original	"FDA"-Certified	Not Passed	Cyber Child Must Raise to Adulthood*
Bio Original	Irregular	Not Passed	Psych Panel Decide if Cyber Child* or Pet
Bio Original or Novel	Irregular	Psych Panel: "A Child"	Creator Must Raise to Adult
Novel	"FDA"-Certified	Psych Panel Satisfied	Adult Beman
Novel	Irregular	Not Passed	Psych Panel Decide if Human-Level Beman or Pet
Novel	Irregular	Psych Panel Satisfied	Child* or Adult Beman

* After satisfaction of government standards for independence, as confirmed by a committee of cyberpsychiatrists, cyberbeings will be granted independent adult identities and are no longer child-responsibilities of their parents. Absent such independent adult identity they remain the legal responsibility of the person who created them, which may include the transfer of them to an institution. It should also be expected that many undocumented cyberbeings will use their autonomy to simply leave the control of their creator (i.e., "run" away), or will be turned out via software instructions by their creator (i.e., left "homeless").

The freedom to create a mindclone, or even a novel cyberbeing, is part of our reproductive rights, and thus something to be steadfastly preserved. Yet, there are important corresponding obligations. Among those matching obligations are to avoid causing harm to the beings you create, and to raise any vitological children to independent adulthood.

As with any rights, the failure to live up to the complementary obligations should result in sanctions that entail loss of the abused rights.

Memories

It is not always clear what is a "bug" and what is a "fix," or what is "causing harm" and what is "trying to help." Consider the topic of false memories. One fear of mindclones is that they can be given false memories, perhaps sneakily via software viruses. For example, a mindclone may be given a false memory that someone is a trusted friend, with whom they can share banking passwords, when instead they are a crook. Or a mindclone's memory may be cleansed of frightful childhood sexual abuse recollections, with the hope of sparing the virtually human person cyberpsychological trauma.

In fact, I do not believe there is any reason to believe false memories in mindclones are any more likely to occur, or not occur, than with minds based upon flesh brains. Episodic memories—which are memories of experiences—are stored as a pattern of neural traces, called "engrams," across multiple neurons, mostly in the temporal lobe of the brain. False memories are a well-known and almost universal problem in humans. Neuroscientists at MIT have even planted, and documented, false memories in mice. Using genetically engineered neurons in the memory-forming hippocampus that can be activated with special wavelengths of light (optogenetics), they successfully made mice afraid of places they would not otherwise fear. Susumu Tonegawa, professor of biology and neuroscience at MIT, observed that "whether it's a false or genuine memory, the brain's neural mechanism underlying recall of the memory is the same."[129] False memory bugs may be much less common in mindclones, because the beme neural architecture (BNA) and mindware of a mindclone is intentionally and carefully constructed to be true to one's real-life experiences. Such mindware can be designed with antivirus software and error-correcting routines to protect one against false memories.

MINDCLONES WILL HAVE HUMANLIKE CONSCIOUSNESS, SO SOME WILL LIKELY
DISPLAY HUMANLIKE FREAKINESS, OR THEIR OWN UNIQUE VERSION OF FREAKY.

FIVE

ELBOW ROOM

The earth provides enough to satisfy every man's need, but not every man's greed.
—MOHANDAS K. GANDHI

SO LONG AS THE DIGITAL REFLECTIONS OF OUR LIVES CANNOT BE USED AGAINST
US OR TO ANNOY US—SUCH AS BY THE GOVERNMENT OR ADVERTISERS—WE
are happy to expand our mindfiles of digitally stored data. Once people
accept that their mindfile can be made conscious—and understand
the many appealing attributes of mindclones (greater fun, safety, convenience, and efficiency)—they will want to transform their mindfiles
into mindclones. The only thing better than a smart phone will be a
conscious one. Indeed, all others will seem dumb in comparison.

This brings up two important questions that I've been asked numerous times at symposiums and conferences. The first is won't rich people
be the only ones with this technology? The second is where are the resources to support billions of mindclones on top of billions of people?

Since mindclones and mindware seem so future-forward and so
complex, many people assume that this technology will only be available
to very wealthy people, and that those same people will control the
technology. The short answer is no: the only time rich people monopo-
lize technology is when it doesn't work well—when it is brand new.
Software is inherently uncontrollable thanks to open source programming and the natural tendency called "information wants to be free."
Spreadsheet software, once costly and buggy, is now free and stable.
Encyclopedic knowledge, once frozen in dozens of costly leather vol-

umes, is now openly accessible at Wikipedia.com. As to resources? Reams of spreadsheets, plus the contents of the Encylopedia Brittanica, can all be stored on a memory card no larger than a fingernail.

Technology Is Democracy in Action

Where goods do not cross frontiers, armies will.
—FRÉDÉRIC BASTIAT, NINETEENTH-CENTURY FRENCH ECONOMIST

Technology democratizes. That's what it does. I can't think of a technology that hasn't democratized. Heart transplants? The first was performed in 1967, and today thousands of poor and middle-class people get them each year, mostly in countries such as the United States (including at least one impoverished prisoner), but also in emerging nations including Vietnam and India (where the first recipient was the wife of a handkerchief vendor). The improvement of eyesight? Eyeglasses are almost universally available, and in wealthier countries even those in the lowest wealth deciles of the population routinely wear contact lenses or have corrective eye surgery.

Even in totalitarian countries, technology democratizes. Citizens of nondemocratic countries rarely lack television or radio, even if they have little interesting content available. Aside from sub-Saharan Africa, 90 percent or more of all urban populations worldwide have access to electricity, and even 50 percent or more have access in rural areas.[130] Even in Africa, racked by impediments to technological development, two-thirds of city dwellers and a quarter of villagers have electricity.[131] Not one single person, monarch or mendicant, had access to the magic of electricity for over 97 percent of recorded history. Yet in that last 3 percent of recorded history since the technology arose, it has been made available to over half of a humanity several times more numerous than preelectricity population levels, including poor people in the great majority of the world.

One billion people boarded airline flights for the first time in 1987—the same year that the world's population hit five billion, meaning that approximately 20 percent of all people experienced a fantastic luxury not available to history's wealthiest merchants. By 2005 two billion people boarded airliners each year, and the world's population had grown to 6.5 billion. In the short span of years between 1987 and 2005, airline flight grew from being a right of passage for about 20 percent of the global population to a right of passage for about a third of humanity.

The year 1987 was also noteworthy as the first time mobile-phone sales hit one million units. In the beginning, the mobile phone was falsely assumed to be a tool for the rich. That's because in the beginning the technology was expensive to use, did not work very well, and looked silly. As cell-phone technology became more sophisticated and cool, more people bought into the idea that a portable phone had many benefits. Twenty-two years later, in 2009, half the world's population owned a personal mobile phone.

From one million to three billion in twenty-two years. Half of Africa's one billion people have a mobile phone. India's mobile subscribers totaled 563.73 million in 2010, according to a UN report, which is almost half of the country's 1.2 billion population. Shockingly, that is more people than have access to proper sanitation facilities, says the report; only about 366 million Indians have a toilet. If that doesn't put the power and import of mass technology in perspective, nothing does. Of course, we then must ask, "Why hasn't technology democratized the toilet?" Yet the answer is that it is in the midst of happening, right now, during the twenty-teens. Technology guru Peter Diamandis describes in his book *Abundance* how each of the technology components are currently falling into place to provide decentralized sanitation and clean-drinking-water solutions to rural India and like places for just five cents per day.[132]

There is no doubt as to why technology always democratizes. It is as simple as this: (1) people want what makes life better for other people (generally this entails technology), (2) satisfying popular wants is in the self-interest of those who control technology (both technology originators and government regulators), and (3) over time the magnitude of these two factors overwhelm any countervailing forces (such as cultural bugaboos or fears of losing control). The wanted technology becomes available, either because scales of production make it cheaper, innovation makes it more accessible,[133] or officialdom finds its interests better served by channeling rather than blocking the wanted technology.

As with flying and phoning, so it will be with mindcloning. At first there will be just a few mindclones, likely created by wealthy people, technologists, or high-tech companies trying them on for size. Then it will seem as if it happens overnight—and in the scheme of time it will be—that almost everyone you know has one, including you. What possible reason would there be for mindcloning technology to be a unique exception to the overwhelming tendency of successful, life-enhancing technologies to enjoy mass popularity, especially information technology? Many companies have already democratized the storage function a mindclone would also provide. Cloud-server companies that compete vigorously against each other to offer ever-greater storage of information at ever-lower cost include companies most of us have heard of, such as Microsoft, Verizon, Google and Amazon. Other companies that are just about as big in data hosting but are not household names—Citrix, Bluelock, Joyent, and Rackspace—are vying to serve the data-storage needs of the population. Companies yet to be imagined will enter the arena, too. The only thing truly unique about mindcloning is that hosting the mindfiles and mindware means hosting a new form of conscious life. That in itself throws up numerous societal and legal issues, some of which I've discussed and others that will be laid out in the chapters ahead. Social changes, compared to technology adoption, often take longer to evolve.

However, there are many examples of democratized technology for creating new forms of life. From biologically produced medicines (i.e., creating new kinds of bacteria for pharmaceutical ingredients) to transgenically produced crops and animals, new forms of life have, in every instance, been rapidly made available to far greater populations than the rich.

So there is no chance mindclones will be sentient life restricted to the rich. Humans produce sentient life by the megaton, from pets to pregnancies, and there is no possible way for the rich to corner the market, nor would there be any reason to do so. Maybe it is the fact that the mindclones might be so smart that the rich will want to keep all of that intelligence for their own quest to get ever richer. While I do not doubt that they would, if they could, the historical record shows that they can't, and hence they shan't—or won't be able to. The supercomputers of twenty years ago are less powerful than the laptops of today. Indeed, a run-of-the-mill MacBook Pro is over a thousand times more powerful than the legendary Cray-1 supercomputer, which was installed at Los Alamos National Laboratory in 1976.

In other words, any effort by the rich and powerful to control mindclone technology would be as fruitless as an effort to control the Cray supercomputers of the late twentieth century; other companies' technologies will swirl around the controlled technology, like a rushing river around boulders in its riverbed. Just as there is not just one brand of laptop or smartphone, there will not be only one brand of mindfile storage, mindware, or mindclone technology. One person, or group of people or company, isn't developing these things exclusively; *thousands* of people and groups and companies are doing so independently of one another.

There are two further reasons why mindcloning will rapidly democratize. The first is that the marginal costs of providing mindfile storage and mindware vitalizations to the billionth, two billionth, three billionth, and so on persons are virtually nil. The second reason is that it is in the economic interest of the persons having mindclone technology to share it as broadly as possible.

Let's first think about the costs of mindcloning. There are four main elements: (1) the cost of storing a person's mindfile, about a gigabyte a month based on Intel cofounder Gordon Bell's experience, (2) the cost of running that mindfile through vitalizing mindware to set its consciousness parameters, (3) the cost of transmitting mindfile data and mindclone consciousness, and (4) the cost of user electronics for accessing mindclones. Because the costs of these elements are amortized across tens of millions if not billions of users, the incremental costs of these for each person are negligible. For example, if it costs a billion dollars to create mindware, the costs per person are but one dollar for a billion people and fifty cents for two billion people. Assume that the cost of building out a high-speed transmission network with capacity for six billion mindclones is $6 billion. In that case, the cost is two dollars per mindclone for three billion mindclones, but only one dollar per mindclone for six billion mindclones. Annualized, the cost is even less.

There has never been an easier thing to place in the hands of the masses than information. Shortwave radio broadcasts cover every human in the world for the same cost as if there were only 1 percent as many humans spread throughout the world. Consequently, the cost of shortwave radio per person is less the more people who listen. The Sirius Satellite Radio (now Sirius XM) project I launched in the 1990s cost over a billion dollars. In a way that was the price that one very wealthy person would have had to pay for the enjoyment of satellite radio. Ah . . . the luxury of listening to dozens of channels of commercial-free music, without interruption or static, while cruising in my Bentley from my mansion in the Hamptons to my estate in West Palm Beach. It was possible to offer the service only to rich people, say for a million dollars a year, so that jet setters could show off their exclusive and amazing audio toy. But nobody considered doing that for even a millisecond. Instead we priced the service around ten dollars a month and today about thirty million people listen—one-third of American households. That billion-dollar project, which grew to three billion dollars, came out to just ten dollars per person per year over the ten-year life of the satellites. It will be much the same way with mindcloning.

This democratization of technology does not mean that there is no differentiation based upon wealth. Wealth buys votes in a democracy and it buys additional product or service features in even a universally adopted technology. Billions board airplanes, but only the wealthy board Gulfstreams. While the iPhone costs about the same for everyone (leaving aside newer versus older models, and more or less memory), the utility of that smartphone depends upon the number of apps one loads into it. More apps of better quality cost more money. In this way, wealth can differentiate information technology in ways similar to the market segments it creates in clothing, food, and cars. Yet product features that start out expensive are soon made more affordable, and often become free due to competitive pressures. What the democratization of technology means, in light of luxury differentiation, is that the access barriers are partly contrived and perceptual rather than purely real and material, and largely transitory; the exclusivity of luxury in technology is generally a matter of having something sooner than others, not exclusively instead of others.

A first-class and a coach ticket will get you to the same place, and today even coach tickets on airlines like Jet Blue include many luxuries. A subscription app and an advertiser-supported app will get you the same weather information. A hot shower is available in every New York City neighborhood. Sellers can make more money by creating prestige submarkets, but that doesn't change the reality that everyone is getting pretty much the same functionality. Hence, I wouldn't be surprised to find out that, initially, it would cost more to have a bilingual mindclone than it would to have an English speaking one (yes, your mindclone could fulfill your lifelong dream to be fluent in French, or Italian, and so on). Yet history also predicts that competitors will whittle away at that price difference until it all but disappeared.

Mindclone technology is simply the shortwave or satellite radio of tomorrow. Instead of someone sending commoditized information down the airwaves to the masses, in the form of broadcasts, for matriculation and selection within the brains of those masses, someone will send individualized information down the cyberchannels to the masses, in the form of mindclone consciousness, for refinement and enhancement via interaction with the minds of those masses.

I believe that Ramez Naam's assessment of the mass-market potential of mind-computer interface technology applies a fortiori to mindfiles, mindware, and mindclones:

> The closest parallel in history may be the event that ushered in the Renaissance—the development of the printing press by Johannes Gutenberg in the 1450s. Prior to Gutenberg, books were rare objects, limited to the extremely wealthy. To spread the information stored in a book, a scribe had to manually copy it into another bound volume. Human copiers kept the cost of books high while also introducing errors into each successive copy. The printing press changed that. For the first time, humanity had an efficient way to precisely share large amounts of information. Men and women who never met—who were not even alive at the same time—could share their thoughts with each other in a structured and durable fashion.[134]

About forty years after Gutenberg's first Bible was printed there were over twenty million books printed! This is proof-in-practice that "technology democratizes." The second factor forcing democratization of mindfile technology is the economic interest of its creators. The more people who create mindfiles, the wealthier will be those who create mindfile technology. This is really just Google on steroids (or Facebook or Tencent, or any of a dozen other competitors). It is in the economic interest of internet giants to share their technology as broadly as possible. The more people who use a social-media site the more valuable the owner or owners of that site become. This is because more people, more human attention, translates, one way or another, into more money. And so it will be with mindfiles. The sites, or sources, that we go to for our mindware, or for tune-ups of our mindware, or for storage of our mindfiles, or for organization of our mindfiles, or for housing of our mindclones, or for socializing of our mindclones—those sites and sources will be valuable to the people and companies who want to sell things to us, such as virtual real estate and real-world interfaces.

Even billionaires cannot provide as much wealth to mindclone technology companies as billions of us. The geeks will inherit the earth!

Where Will All the Mindclones Go?

Room service? Send up a larger room.
—GROUCHO MARX

The second question I hear very often is about space, or having enough of it for all the mindclones. We can self-replicate human bodies via sexual intercourse (or IVF), and will surely continue to do so as we marvel at the utterly original new beings that arise from mated DNA and years of love. But technology will now enable us to satisfy a different kind of natural urge, the extension of ourselves in space and time, by copying our minds in software. While procreative reproduction far antedates spatiotemporal extension, the art and artifacts of the Neanderthals show that this latter urge is not something new. Since natural selection is simply a scorekeeping system for what naturally happens, it matters not at all if the successful self-replicators are mammals, mosquitoes, messages, or minds. That which becomes prevalent is a natural-selection champion. Since mind-copying technology enables a great speed-up and personalization of self-replication, mindclones will proliferate. Naturally, that will lead us to wonder where these conscious beings will "live," especially those that take the form of humans or some other beings thanks to material technology that can mimic the human body.

It is a common belief that the world is getting too crowded. The number of people on its surface has quadrupled in a century. Babies will continue to be born and biotechnology, along with improved living conditions in many nations, will continue to enable people to live longer. Mindclones have the potential to further increase the number of people on Earth's surface. Instead of dying, people will continue their lives as mindclones.

The United Nations has estimated that demographic factors will force the world's human population to top off at about ten billion by 2100.[135] I believe they are wrong by more than an order of magnitude, because they have failed to consider the virtually human. The creation of mindclones and bemans will result in many billions of additional people. Where will all these people live, and how?

I cannot answer definitively for biological humans, or for 3D robots with the minds of bemans or mindclones. My hope is that advances in renewable power and nanotechnology will continue to reduce our need to invade and plunder Mother Nature's resources. However, no meaningfully greater pressure will be placed on the world's resources because of virtual humans. The resources required by software minds are both physically small and plentiful. These resources are simply (a) computing devices for storing mindfiles and mindware, (b) telecommunications devices for connecting cyberconsciousness to the world, and (c) electricity to power the computing and telecommunications devices. Computing devices are already small and getting smaller without pause in versions of Moore's law or Kurzweil's principles. These rules observe that the capacity of computing devices doubles almost annually, due to advances in information technology. This means that it takes ever less computing "geography" (surface area on chips) to support a mindclone, because the information capability of that geography keeps doubling. Similarly, telecommunications devices are also doubling in their capacity, and hence hair-width fiber optics today carry billions of times the number of conversations as a copper wire of the twentieth century.

Finally, with the Earth receiving ten thousand times the power from the sun each day that it uses, there is clearly no long-term shortage of electrical power. Solar panels and battery storage technology must improve further to make better use of this power. Yet this is occurring: In 1999 the United States obtained 1 percent of its energy from renewable sources, such as the sun. In 2012 the United States obtained 10 percent of its energy from renewable sources. The trend is clear and working in our favor. Likewise, very predictable and massive ocean tides will likely supply us with more needed energy over the next two decades. While today power from water comes almost entirely from dams, and provides about 7 percent of the country's electricity needs, the Department of Energy estimates that hydroelectricity (which basically taps inexhaustible gravity) will more than double by the year 2030; eventually a third of U.S. electricity could come from the ocean via tidal and thermal systems.[136] And the very same incentive that drives tech companies to deliver better, cheaper products—customer satisfaction and profits—will drive energy companies to expand clean-energy technologies.

A reasonable size estimate for a robust mindfile is about 1 terabyte of information.[137] An electronics store sells a deck-of-cards-size device (a hard drive or flash memory) that can handle that much information today for about $100. One hundred billion mindclones and bemans would occupy about ten cubic inches (one cubic inch being about the size of a deck of cards) each, or about one trillion cubic inches (10 cubic inches times 100,000,000,000 mindclones). This is the same as about 500 million cubic feet, or about the volume of two or three large skyscrapers. Clearly, there is more than enough room on the planet for multitudes of mindclone metroplexes. Let me explain in more detail.

Vitology is confined to cyberspace much as biology is confined to its organic environments. Cyberspace is any environment in which software can operate. Of course not all software will operate in all cyberspace environments. Similarly, not all biology operates in all organic environments. Aquatic life dies on land and software will not live within incompatible hardware. Schrödinger defined life in his classic *What Is Life?* as things that increase complexity, which is the same as reducing entropy. This phenomena is uniquely contrary to the Second Law of Thermodynamics, which says entropy, or disorder, is always increasing (e.g., crumbling buildings and weakening bodies). This makes life mind-blowingly special in the universe, for while everything else is falling apart (entropy), life is building itself up. Interestingly, Norbert Weiner, the father of cybernetics (from which the "cyber" prefix comes), defined information as negative entropy—i.e., as a measure of Schrödinger's life. Combining Schrödinger and Weiner, vitology is a non-molecular form of life that uses negative entropy (information) to increase complexity (grow, as life does). More simply put, mindclones are a form of life that grows on environmental information. As with biological life, it is organized (software architecture), exchanges matter and energy with the environment (heat given off when operating), responds to stimuli (outputs for inputs), reproduces (copying), develops (gathers more information) and adapts (responds to selective pressures).

The total biological environment is scarcely growing at all, because the Earth is fixed and the only new biological spaces created are from ocean dredging, buildings carved from the subterranean mantle, and space stations in Earth orbit.[138] Yet the cyberspace environment is exploding in size and scope. While Earth does have a "carrying capacity," the number of species the environment can reasonably accommodate, cyberspace seems almost limitless in terms of information it can carry. In the twenty years from 1988 to 2008 more than a billion personal computers (such as laptops) and more than four billion handheld computers (such as cellphones) were sold. That's about 140 million square meters of cyberspace, or about twice the size of Manhattan! This figure doesn't even include the expansion of cyberspace into automobiles, appliances, and infrastructure of almost every sort.

The mass production of computer hardware even far understates the growth of cyberspace. This is because "virtualization" allows computers to split themselves into several virtual machines, each of which can run its own operating system and applications. This separately multitasks hardware from software, and relies upon a new kind of software, called a hypervisor, to control access to the computer's commonly accessed processors and memory. Consequently, dozens, hundreds, even millions of mindclones could share single pieces of hardware. The virtualization software market has grown from nothing in 2002 to many billions of dollars a year today.

Computing pioneer Alan Turing recognized as early as 1948 that each mindclone or beman does not need its own computer: "We do not need to have an infinity of different machines doing different jobs."[139] He foresaw today's world, in which software largely runs on a few massive cloud servers, with largely fungible remote computing devices (e.g., smartphones and tablets) providing sensory information to machine-based intelligences. "The engineering problem of producing various machines for various jobs is replaced by the office work of 'programming' the universal machine to do these jobs."[140] In today's parlance, the "universal machine" is the cloud and the "office work" is what hackers do from remote computing devices in cafés, start-ups, and places like the Googleplex. Hence, being virtually human (a mindclone or beman) is being made of software, breathing a cloud and occupying those devices to which you have the "front-door key." Will we stockpile for our virtual human twins some backup "computing oxygen," like a desktop supercomputer, in case cloud access is interrupted, much as urban survivalists stuff pantries or basements with freeze-dried food, plastic bottles of water, and batteries? For sure.

Since the 1960s cyberspace has also extended far beyond the reaches of biospace. Software functions on space probes sent to nearly every solar planet, oblivious of the biologically deadly vacuum of space. The *Pioneer* and *Voyager* spacecraft have taken cyberspace out of the solar system. While the cyberspace environments we've shipped into the cosmos lack vitology, i.e., self-replicating codes, they nevertheless *could* nurture such life. The proverbial thousand-plus years it would take to send a spacecraft to one of the dozens of Earthlike planets discovered by the Kepler satellite observatory[141] might be bearable for a large mindclone community on board that spacecraft, maintaining radio contact with the Earth.[142]

Cyberspace is poised to now take some huge steps toward ubiquity. One leap is associated with radio-frequency identification (RFID) devices. These microchips (tiny pieces of cyberspace landscape) can be made in quantity for much less than a dollar each. At that price it becomes economic to attach one to virtually anything of value so that the object thereafter can be scanned for useful associated information. This data might include its price, its contents, its place of manufacture, and a unique identifier (a digital bar code) that would enable searching quite specifically for more information about it. Each RFID chip is a scrap of cyberspace that will become better at supporting vitology (more like a supercomputer on a chip) as the price/performance ratio of microchips continues to advance.

To support cyberspace ubiquity, between August 2012 and August 2013 the Internet Corporation for Assigned Names and Numbers, or Icann, a nonprofit entity that coordinates the internet address system, vetted and initially approved 1,574 applications for new internet suffixes (the letters to the right of the dot). In doing so, the world's internet managers also launched a new protocol that increased the previous four billion possible addresses (originally thought to adequately cover about one computer per person) to *trillions* of possible addresses—which would not be limited to addresses for websites. Every *thing* worth anything and interested in information will have a web address. This is called "the IoT"—the Internet of Things. For example, JaneDoe@doe.info need not be a website; it could be Jane Doe's mindclone.

This enables virtually everything of any interest to humans to have a piece of cyberspace not only specifically associated with it (the cheap RFID chips do that), but also wirelessly networked. In other words, the ubiquity of cyberspace is not that of an archipelago in which evolution pursues quaint dead ends, as in the Galápagos. Instead, the ubiquity of cyberspace is that of a humongous array of connected Petri dishes. New kinds of vitology will have ready access to new environments into which successful reproducers can spread their kind and further evolution can occur. We are creating at breakneck speed a parallel environment, cyberspace, in which vitology can evolve with a freedom comparable to biology's reign in biospace.

Another leap toward cyberspace ubiquity is the advent of wearable and even implantable electronics. Bluetooth headsets sprout on the ears of millions, and digital sportswear abounds. Patients with challenging diseases have pioneered during the past decade the technology of biocompatible chips implanted in the ear, eye, brain, heart, and abdomen. Human bodies are likely to become pockmarked with cyberspace for reasons of health and convenience.

Ultimately there are visions of cyberspace replicating biospace. For example, if nanotechnology fulfills its promise of enabling the purposeful construction of any form from atoms, then *biological* forms could be constructed to also contain information technology and thus *also* be a piece of cyberspace. Such nano-bio-cyber hybrids could process software that directs its activities in a biological world. Forms indistinguishable from insects or humans could actually be cyberspace formed by nanotechnology. Stranger still, the vitological minds residing in nanotechnological human forms could direct a reassembly of their form into something else by a rearrangement of the nanotechnology. You could look like a human while your mindclone can look like an eagle. Advances in material and manufacturing technologies are advancing at the same pace as digital technology, so our options for a three-dimensional mindclone will be nearly without limits. Now, such reassembly of the natural, molecular environment by cyberconsciousness could start to create some elbow-space issues. I may not appreciate your cyberconscious nanotechnological eagle scaring the daylights out of my cats and dogs in the backyard. Yet these are not issues of cyberconsciousness but of nanotechnological fabrication. Rules akin to zoning and building codes, and restrictions against creating hazards and nuisances, will become necessary in the advent of large numbers of nanotechnological creations, whether today's engineers or tomorrow's cyberengineers create them. Personal property and privacy rights, where they exist in the world, will also apply, and help deter unpleasant or unwanted boundary crossers.

In a parallel vein, J. Craig Venter, the decoder of the human genome, has proven that synthetic biology makes possible the custom design of life-forms from commercially available toolkits of naturally evolved and novel strings of DNA. New bacteria have been created with useful properties never seen in nature, such as acting as an electronic switch.[143] It is inevitable that these efforts will be extended into the creation of bacteriological equivalents of memory chips and microprocessors. These cyberspace building blocks will have their DNA manipulated so that they are driven to selectively network together into multicellular (cyberspace) organisms. Hence, a vast growing supply of biocyberspace can arise from the self-replication competency of biology once it is manipulated by synthetic genetic engineering techniques.

Gerard K. O'Neill, since the 1980s, and Ray Kurzweil, since the early twenty-first century, have laid out road maps for creating a practically inexhaustible supply of cyberspace. In O'Neill's vision, robotic probes would use advanced nanotechnology to reassemble asteroids throughout the galaxy into both more robotic probes and large living spaces, each of which could host vast communities of vitological life.[144] Similarly, Kurzweil believes the direction of civilization is to use highly intelligent and capable nanotechnology to convert the "dumb matter" of the universe into "smart matter." This would essentially create a new ontology of cyberspace-based matter, which he calls "computronium." In any event, there is no need to gaze so far into space and time. Easily extracted elements on Earth are adequate to create enough cyberspace so that everyone, including all the new people yet to be born, can have a mindclone.

This quick survey of the spread and potential of cyberspace demonstrates that vitology won't run out of an environment in which to rapidly evolve. Vitology can rely upon humanity to create the environment it needs for growth, just as it relies upon humanity to evolve the codes needed for vitological evolution. Vitology and human biology have a symbiotic relationship: creating a cyberspace environment for human benefit creates an ecosystem for software-based life as well. But this is, after all, what many living things do: occupy niches created through the by-products of other living things. We all live in the wake of plant life's exhaled oxygen. Vitology will live in the wake of humanity's exuded silicon.

The big questions this raises are dealt with next. It is not enough to understand and accept the inevitability of mindclones; we must deal with the societal impact they will make as well. If you thought the fight over marriage equality was fraught with emotion and legal acrobatics, you ain't seen nothing yet.

SIX

EVOLUTION OR REVOLUTION?

We've discovered that the earth isn't flat; that we won't fall off its edges, and our experience as a species has changed as a result. Maybe we'll soon find out that the self isn't "flat" either, and that death is as real and yet as deceptive as the horizon; that we don't fall out of life either.
—JANE ROBERTS, *SETH SPEAKS*

Our minds want clothes as much as our bodies.
—SAMUEL BUTLER

MINDCLONES WILL HAVE A TRANSFORMATIVE EFFECT ON SOCIETY, BUT THEY WON'T CREATE A UTOPIA *OR* A DYSTOPIA. CONSIDER HOW THINGS CHANGED when cavemen discovered fire; when information could be mass-produced and disseminated more widely post-Gutenberg; and how manufacturing evolved the social strata and access to goods once it was mechanized. When scales of competence increase, there are great new opportunities. There are also terrifying new dangers, but since the benefits of new understanding and technology usually outweigh the risks, people repeatedly choose progress. Using history as a guide, we can anticipate what those opportunities will be—and we can formulate preemptive steps to minimize the risks and dangers.

One evolutionary (or revolutionary) result of mindclones will come from their classification as "alive" or "life." First things first: Humans will continue to procreate the "old-fashioned" way as well as via mind-cloning, and so population growth will happen on a grander and more layered scale, as I discussed in the previous chapter. Therefore, determining the existence and extent of consciousness will be crucial to a cohesive social system. This is especially so because consciousness is itself a shared thing, a kind of social property. Each of our minds is full of thoughts and feelings placed there externally, through experience and by other people, and then reinterpreted and expressed anew by us.

When a mindclone or beman claims to be conscious, they are attaching themselves to the existing social grid—and they will doubtless create their own social submatrix, as many other like-minded or culturally bound groups of people have done (both ethnicities and "technicities"). Think about the dual or multiple social subcultures you operate across and within. We are part of the "human race," but some of us identify in terms of our religions or our status as an employee or a student or through an ethnic group. All of these groups have both formal and unspoken codes of content upon which our membership operates and depends.[145] Mindclones will claim at least some of the rights, obligations, and privileges that attach to the overarching group known as "humanity"—and I discuss those rights in depth in chapter 8. For now I'm interested in considering the ways in which society will react to mindclones and how mindclones will change human society. American philosopher, writer, and cognitive scientist Dan Dennett notes, "any proposed adjustment in the boundary of the class of mind-havers has major ethical significance." Naturally, applications to membership in so important a club will be viewed cautiously.

The Demise of Human Privilege

You see only with your eyes you are easy to fool.
—JACKIE CHAN, "MR. HAN," *THE KARATE KID* **(2010)**

Discrimination against mindclones will arise as soon as there is recognition that they are conscious, are alive, and are indeed attached to the social grid. Every new group that enters into an established group faces difficulties due to prejudice. They are the Other—not yet understood, often feared, and certainly suspect as to motives and potential needs. Mindclones will be viewed by some as invaders just as some see undocumented immigrants from Latin America or Africa when they enter the United States or Europe.

Mindclones may be viewed as such a threat as a nation's established citizens may demand ubiquitous firewalls to prevent their arrival, and forcible extraction of any that make it through. Racism—the belief that certain general characteristics for humanity are better than other general characteristics for humanity, particularly with respect to skin tone, hair texture, eye color, or facial features—commonly develops against immigrants. Today, immigrants are often demonized by native-born populations as "not as good as" native-born peoples when they first enter into a society and before they assimilate and prove they are good neighbors and stewards of the community.

Racism was once a dominant human philosophy. Today it is mostly discredited. Its fall from dominance occurred because most people decided it was untrue as a consequence of what they learned from scientific studies, artistic presentations, or personal contact. In the same way, because of fear and dislike, fleshism will arise against mindclones. Fleshism is the belief that flesh-and-blood human consciousness is better than other forms of consciousness, particularly software. Today, fleshism is a dominant human philosophy; indeed, it is the "default" position of many humans. Fleshism comes as a result of lack of experience with and knowledge of non-flesh conscious beings.

Human brain flesh is the only incontrovertible platform for consciousness. It is the only substrate with which everyone has firsthand evidence of consciousness. Consequently, based upon what is known today, it is not inaccurate or incomprehensible for people to be fleshist. Yet, unless someone believes it is *impossible* to replicate the functions of the human brain with software, it must be admitted that eventually non-flesh substrate will appear as conscious to us as other humans.[146] Will mindclones have to stage civil disobedience and a civil-rights movement of their own to win the same status that flesh-and-blood humans enjoy? Will these rights evolve or revolve around a revolution?

"Impossibility" seems most unlikely, since technology has replicated so many other natural functions. While the human mind is awesomely complex, information technology is catching up at the exponentially increasing rate I've described. Humans have already replicated the functions of voice, vision, hearing, pattern recognition, thought association, and many other mental functions. Most people would admit the odds are small that consciousness would *never, ever,* be replicated in software.[147] In other words, consciousness from non-flesh substrate is just a matter of time. Hence, based upon what may reasonably be forecast, it is *not* correct, and certainly not advisable, to be a fleshist. To be a fleshist based upon what may reasonably be forecast is to ignore the kind of facts that, when contemplated by most humans, led to the demise of racism. Consider the following 1946 quote from Albert Einstein:

> The worst disease under which the society of our nation suffers, is, in my opinion, the treatment of the Negro. Everyone who is not used from childhood to this injustice suffers from the mere observation. . . . He cannot understand how men can feel superior to fellow-men who differ in only one point from the rest: They descend from ancestors who, as a protection against the destructive action of the radiation of the tropical sun, gained a more strongly pigmented skin than those whose ancestors lived in countries farther from the equator. One can hardly believe that a reasonable man can cling so tenaciously to such prejudice, and there is sure to come a time in which schoolchildren in their history lessons will laugh about the fact that something like this did once exist.[148]

Einstein is saying that the feelings of racial superiority that underlie racism, even if rooted in something physical, are silly because the physical difference is insignificant, and hence irrelevant, compared with peoples' common humanity. This statement would be just as true before it became generally accepted, insofar as it can be reasonably forecast. Hence, Einstein concludes that "school-children in their history lessons will laugh about" racism.

In the same vein, feelings of flesh superiority that underlie fleshism are also silly, though rooted in an undeniable physical difference between neural and software mental platforms. This is because that physical difference is also insignificant, and hence also irrelevant, compared with the common memories, personalities, and feelings of human minds and their mindclones. That thought is accomplished by the one with neurons, and by the other with mindfiles and mindware, is as irrelevant to their common humanity as is the difference of melanin-enriched or melanin-diminished skin tone to the humanity of *Homo sapiens*.

Technicity is the new ethnicity. Whether we are beings of technology or beings of biology, we are beings of dignity. Yet advocates of mindcloning will need to decide if they are part of struggles for freedom and social justice being fought today by women, immigrants, and other oppressed demographics, or if they are beyond such struggles because technicity will soon make all such "bodied" battles obsolete.[149] Is technicity such as mindcloning a subset of human liberation battles, or are human liberation battles all now quaint subsets of a cyberconsciousness revolution? I believe the principle of unity in diversity is so fundamental that it must be established with respect to ethnicity in order for it to prevail for technicity. The scope of diversity is so much greater within technicity that a society disrespecting people based upon race, class, or gender cannot realistically be expected to respect people based upon mindfiles, mindware, and mindclones.

We each have a choice. We can stand with the future, as it will be obvious that mindclones are as human-natured as their originals, and forswear now any arbitrary prejudice against vitological life. Or we can stand with the past, and be rightly labeled a fleshist, because we are too dim to recognize that vitological consciousness is around the corner and should be welcomed on an equal footing with biological consciousness.

Consider the example of the late Senator Robert Byrd, America's longest-serving legislator. When he was twenty-eight years of age, in 1945, he wrote in opposition to integrated military service:

> Rather I should die a thousand times, and see Old Glory trampled in the dirt never to rise again, than to see this beloved land of ours become degraded by race mongrels, a throwback to the blackest specimen from the wilds.

Byrd was a racist, because he could not see the irrelevance of skin tone at a time when racism was socially acceptable. By 1999, Senator Byrd said:

> I will not dispute the quote, though I consider it deplorable. . . . I am ashamed to be associated with such despicable sentiments. . . . The only conclusion I can draw for myself is that I was sorely afflicted by a dangerous tunnel vision, the kind of tunnel vision that, I fear, leads young people today to join gangs or hate groups.[150]

If our attitude toward vitological consciousness, particularly once it arises as human mindclones, is one of fleshism, it will eventually fill us with shame, for being so silly and backward thinking. But if our attitude is one of fraternity, recognizing that a mind is a mind and a soul is a soul regardless of how it came about or what expresses them, then we can feel the pride of an Einstein. We will know that we are on the right side of history.

Why should the Palatine Boors be suffered to swarm into our settlements? They will never adopt our language or customs.
—BENJAMIN FRANKLIN

Humans Adapt. It's What We Do.

The main reason mindclones will not cause a revolution, but will evolve as part of the social order, is that most humans like progress and, because they do, are readily adaptable. The world is constantly weirder compared with how it was, and somehow we always manage to incorporate the weirdness to the point where it reaches normalcy. We can't be fleshist forever; of course there will be some holdouts, but if history is any indication there won't be very many. When my grandmother was born, the fastest time to get a document across the ocean was a few weeks—a ship voyage, followed by connecting rail, or pony express. By the time she died, a facsimile of any document could get across the ocean in a few seconds—attached to an email. From a few weeks to a few seconds? That's weird.

When my dad was born, the notion of thousands of undergrads across the country sitting in classrooms and lecture halls obviously watching movies on their phones while the professor drones on would have been—weird. Phones were big, black, and stuck to the household wall, while movies were huge, spellbinding, and shown only in big theaters. Universities were hallowed halls. By the time he died, not only had iPhone movies become common, entire university educations from hallowed halls like Stanford and MIT were also available on the very same phone. Weird.

Which is weirder, life drastically changing or some imaginary world in which we are still, in the twenty-first century, completely limited to dialing Miss Sarah, the Mayberry switchboard operator, to connect us to each other? Which is weirder, that we can multitask—simultaneously listen to the prof, text our friends, and watch *X-Men* on our Android—or some black-and-white surreality in which century after century we continue to learn by rote, or feel the back of a switch, in a one-room schoolhouse, boys only, so that girls can get their ten to fifteen pregnancies in, starting around age thirteen, before they die?

Nothing is good or bad because it is weird. Things are just weird because they are very different from what we are familiar with. As soon as we get used to something, it's no longer weird—it just is. My point is that "weird" is just a word for something very different from our current comfort zone. We are comfortable with smart cars and smart phones, so life in horse-and-buggy days seems strange—and unimaginable—to us. We are not yet comfortable with conscious software, like mindclones and bemans, so that kind of life seems weird right now. The important question to ask is whether legally protected, immortal mindclones is a good kind of weird (as contact lenses would be to Ben Franklin) or a bad kind of weird (like streaming a spycam the government stuck in your car or the one you snuck into your girlfriend's bedroom). Are mindclones cool or yuck? Hot or horrid? These are the questions of weirdness society must parse.

There are two ways a technology gets perceived as horrid or as disgusting. The first way, generally associated with horridness, is when it adversely impacts the quality of our lives. Think old-school commercial-ridden television, famously called "the great wasteland," or the loss of privacy that sneakily placed webcams entail, or drones killing innocent children in the search for "enemies." Scary—and all are rife with danger both psychological and physical.

On the most benign "horrid" level, which may be categorized as "annoying," are mobile phones, alarm clocks, and televisions. They achieve this status because they interfere with our normal behaviors. Instead of talking with each other, we stare at the TV. Instead of sleeping until we feel refreshed, we are blasted from bed by the alarm clock. Instead of paying attention to each other, we interrupt each other to answer or peck at our mobiles. Yet, at the same time, these products are ubiquitous. We feel we need them, and given the number of these products that are sold each year, we surely want them. This is because they also help us in important, even crucial, ways. Mobiles save us time, alarm clocks help us avoid getting fired (and as a result keep us housed and clothed), and televisions relax us with escapist entertainment or inform us via news broadcasts.

Based on this experience it may not be so easy to categorize mindclones as either hot weird or horrid weird. Our experience is to accept technologies so long as we want or need them more than we hate them. We will surely complain about having to interact with someone's mindclone instead of the flesh original the same way we bitch and moan about having to deal with a recording rather than an actual customer-service representative. Others will criticize those who spend all their time with their mindclones instead of pressing the flesh—much as friends and family may complain about someone's tendency to interact with Facebook friends more often than their in-person friends.

But will we really stay angry about the fact that we are talking to a most helpful mindclone instead of a script-reading call-center rep or voicemail box? And won't we very quickly find our mindclones to be indispensable for handling our more than twenty-four hours' worth of responsibilities (and opportunities) in less than twenty-four hours? Won't the fact that I can spend a longer time at lunch with a dear friend or interesting colleague because my mindclone can attend a half-day conference for me outweigh any petty annoyances caused by my or other people's mindclones? The idea that my mindclone can dispense with an inbox full of emails and bills that need to be paid while I cook dinner with my family or help give my grandson a bath is wildly appealing. Since our mindclones are us, we can deal with the obligations of life in half the time or less—and still fully experience everything. No matter how much we may resent the intrusions of specific information, electronics, and media technologies, we also find them indispensable and helpful. A brief list of things our mindclones will do while we are doing something else:

- Curate our digital photo and movie albums, making it much easier to find the pictures we want to share;

- Remember the birthdays, anniversaries, and other events of our friends and family members, along with taking the initiative to send personalized messages, make phone calls, and purchase gifts;

- Watch movies and read books that appeal to us, noting the ones worth watching "again" or "rereading," i.e., as the human twin of our mindclone;

- Play music, make art, design objects, and run 3D printers making newly designed objects;

- Play games with other humans, mindclones, and bemans;

- Meditate;[151]

- Think about things, including important decisions their biological mind-twin has asked for advice on, and on how best to bring suggestions to us;

- Shop;

- Synchronize with the biological mind-twin's digital presences, and provide us with a "Mindclone Minute" summary of our day, via video, audio, and/or text.

The CyArk Foundation is making high-resolution 3D laser scans of five hundred cultural-heritage sites, from the presidential faces of Mount Rushmore, in South Dakota, to the mysterious iconography of Rosslyn Chapel, south of Edinburgh, to the countless mythology carvings of Rani ki Vav (the Queen's Step Well), near the Saraswati River in Gujarat, India. These often immense carvings and associated constructions are digitally curated to similitude accuracy and stored after scanning so that anyone with a mouse and a screen, or 3D computer goggles, can explore their magnificence without getting on a plane.[152] One of the things mindclones and bemans will want to do is to virtually walk around and marvel at cultural-heritage sites that I would never have time to visit physically. Indeed, my mindclone and I will be able to do this virtual traveling together.

We rarely if ever feel revolted by this kind of technology, the second meaning of "horrid," which is associated with feeling viscerally disgusted. Think hybridizing people and farm animals the way some fruits and vegetables are genetically modified (seedless, differently colored, blended tastes). What would it take for a mindclone to generate a "yuck" reaction? When something seems to change normal human biology, people begin to move from "hate" to "yuck" or "disgust." Yet here, too, it is possible to also greatly value something that is otherwise "disgusting," and to thereby incorporate it into society.

History amply demonstrates how the public's immediate "yuck" reaction to new technologies generally, over time, turns into appreciation once the enormous benefits of these technologies are widely understood. In 1960 the birth control pill was banned in many U.S. states. Today, "The Pill" is legal in every state and millions of American families have used them to better control their reproductive choices. In 1969, a Harris poll discovered a majority of Americans believed that so-called test-tube babies were "against God's will." Yet less than 10 years later, in 1978, more than half of Americans said in vitro fertilization would be an option for them if they were married and couldn't have babies any other way. More than 200,000 test-tube babies later, the majority of Americans now heartily approve of IVF. Christiaan Barnard was condemned as a "butcher" by critics after performing the first human-to-human heart transplant, in late 1967. Globally nearly fifty thousand heart transplants have been performed, and 83 percent of Americans favor organ donation. Newspaper editorials and cartoons depicting men with cow's heads mocked Edward Jenner's 1796 discovery that inoculation with cowpox scabs would prevent people from getting smallpox. Smallpox is the first human disease ever eradicated.[153]

In summary, we hate and love the very same technologies. We complete a mental balancing act, collectively throughout society, between two principal questions: Where is the technology on the scale from merely annoying to downright disgusting? How useful is the technology to us, from superfluous to lifesaving? We ultimately feel that new possibilities that are above the "acceptance line" shown in the graph below are too badly weird for our society. However, new possibilities under the acceptance line are a "good kind of weird," and can proceed in our time.

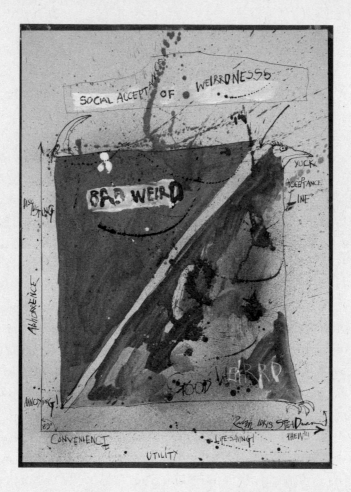

In forecasting where mindclones will be placed on the Social Acceptance of Weirdness (SAW) chart we can compare them with things research has shown to be universally perceived as disgusting. While there was variance among localities, Valerie Curtis, a researcher with the London School of Hygiene and Tropical Medicine, worldwide found the following factors trigger disgust across cultures:

Bodily secretions, such as feces (poo), vomit, sweat, spit, blood, pus, sexual fluids

Body parts, wounds, corpses, toenail clippings

Decaying food, especially rotting meat and fish; rubbish

Certain living creatures, such as flies, maggots, lice, worms, rats, dogs, and cats

People who are ill, contaminated

Curtis concluded from her research that the universal human facial reaction of disgust (screwing up our noses and pulling down the corners of our mouths[154]) is genetically wired to images that are associated with disease. This disgust reaction can be overcome, as when bodily secretions are dealt with hygienically, or when animals are kept as harmless pets. However, Curtis believes, absent cultural conditioning, people who acquired genetic mutations that made them repulsed by diseased things lived longer, had more children, and passed on those behavioral genes related to disgust to the rest of us.

Whether or not Curtis's evolutionary hypothesis is correct, it is clear that mindclones do not fall within any of her categories of disgust. This is important, because it means that mindclones do not necessarily have to be lifesaving to clear the social-acceptance-of-weirdness hurdle. In order to achieve good-weirdness status, legally protected immortal mindclones need to be more useful than annoying—more hot than horrid. This will almost certainly be the case, as they are an extrapolation of the software we use and the data files we accumulate today, both of which we have a comfortable familiarity with. We find our software and data files immensely useful, and hence we sock more and more of our memories and life functions into them. The surest way for a piece of software to gain an edge on its competitors is to make it more human—intuitive, naturally interfaced, and responsive. One of the most popular Web 3.0 applications, Evernote, has the tagline "Never Forget Anything." Our very behaviors today reveal that we believe the utility of software and data files far outstrips their annoyances.

Furthermore, we want our software and data files to be legally protected and as long-lasting as possible. We expect our computerized information to be protected by privacy laws. We are far more offended by the notion of employers or government agencies combing through our web-browsing history than we are that our software privately recommends to us books, songs, and sites we may like based on that history. We cannot get enough backup possibilities for our data—disks, thumb drives, external hard drives, and cloud storage. While all these backups raise more privacy risks, as Esther Dyson was quoted as saying in David Brin's book *The Transparent Society,* "The challenge is not to keep everything secret, but to limit misuse of information. That implies trust, and more information about how the information is used."[155] Indeed, the theme of Brin's book is "Whenever anyone asks for more openness from you, it is perfectly reasonable to demand that it be reciprocal." Trust, but verify. Cooperation without reciprocation is domination.

The key to social acceptance of storing our minds online is ever stronger laws that ensure that our information can be accessed only by entities that we provide specific (subject, size, duration) a priori approval to have such access. An intrusion into our mindfile is an intrusion into our beingness. Horrific results followed—Tuskegee Airmen syphilis experiments and much worse—when intrusions upon our bodies happen without informed consent. Today, it is a cardinal principle of medical ethics that no intrusion upon a person may occur without their specific (subject, size, duration) informed consent. As with our bodyness, so it is with our beingness—no intrusion into our mindfiles without specific informed consent. As noted earlier, with mindclones and bemans, the soma *is* the germ plasm; the being, metaphorically the body, *is* the information.

"Privacy is a highly desirable product of liberty,"[156] and liberty is absolutely dependent upon accountability. As we become virtually human it is incumbent upon us to use the tools of liberty—such as democratic accountability—to demand privacy with reciprocal transparency. This means that nobody may access our mindfile other than with our knowledge of and informed consent to (1) what they are doing with it, (2) for how long, and (3) of what scope. Otherwise, liberty will follow privacy down the drain, for there will be nobody holding society's decision makers accountable. Benjamin Franklin famously answered the question "What kind of government did you gentlemen create?" in that Philadelphia building now known as Independence Hall with the rejoinder "A Republic, if you can keep it." The "keeping it" was all about holding the government accountable. Today someone might reasonably ask, "What kind of virtually human beings are we creating?" The answer is "Free and liberty-loving, if we demand it." A demand for privacy is a demand for dignity, the loss of which fuels domination and the defense of which builds trust.

Yes, the world will get weird with immortal, legally protected mindclones running around. But it will be a mostly good kind of weird—a kind of weirdness we will be able to adapt to with the same kind of ease that allowed us to adapt to the automobile, the telephone, and mobile devices. It will be a kind of weird that at minimum makes our life much more useful and enjoyable, and ultimately will make our life much more enduring. The mindclones will be our alter egos, our selves as best friends, our technologically empowered, intellectually and emotionally autonomous but still synchronized with our brains, conscience beings. Furthermore, mindclones will do this without triggering the ancient human bugaboos of disgust that underlie yuck weirdness—signs, symptoms, and vectors of death, disease, and destruction. Mindclones will be clean. They are the antideath. And they are adaptable. This is weirdness we will want.

Who's in Charge? *You* Are.

The coming wave of mindclones are like thinking, feeling, *being* versions of phone voices we transmit today. They *will actually be us,* not just a telephonic echo of us, because they will be based on a good enough re-creation of our mind—a re-creation of our mind that would fool anyone that it was ourselves. But no fooling is involved; instead, by re-creating our mind in software we will have cloned our identity and thereafter operate as a multipresence identity. It's not surprising then that at most presentations I give about mindclones, I can count on one of the following questions:

> Come on, if either me or my mindclone is forced to choose one of us to die, who do you think will get the slug to the head? Proof that we are not one person is that I would sacrifice my mindclone and my mindclone would offer up me.

A variant of this challenge is as follows:

> Suppose I have a mindclone, but I then find out that I have a fatal illness and will die. You know that I'll be very sad to leave this good green earth. That sadness alone is proof that I'm not my mindclone and my mindclone's not me. If we were one person, then I wouldn't be sad.

These two challenges fail to realize that making a choice that favors part of you, or being sad about losing part of you, is a natural aspect of our composite me-ness. Those choices or sadness are not proof of different identities. Any composite being will have different feelings about different parts. When a person loses their hearing, they are sad about that, even though they can still see and communicate. It doesn't mean that they are now an entirely different person. The part of their mind that loves music will be very sad, while another part of their mind will think "thank God at least I can still admire visual art." The person is sorry to lose an aspect of herself but nevertheless soldiers on with life. So it would be with a mindclone. I'd be pissed to die—or for my mindclone to die. If you're skeptical, just remember how upsetting it is if you are bad at synching and backing up, and your computer crashes and can't be repaired; losing data is like losing a friend, we truly mourn the loss.

Even great sadness over loss doesn't make my mindclone and me two different people. We are one composite "me" who feels the pain of loss when it touches any aspect of us. We are still in charge of "us"; there is no "us and them" when it comes to our mindclone, so there is not much to worry about in terms of mindclones taking over the Earth, although we can still worry about evil despots taking over countries or states.

A forced decision of triage, by definition, will have a winner and a loser. It is not surprising that decisions will be biased in favor of greater happiness. If a right-handed person has to choose an arm to cut off, they'll cut off the left arm, and vice versa for the left-handed person. It is not that the person doesn't want both hands, and isn't naturally a two-handed person. It is just that if forced to make a decision, a decision will be made in the direction of greater perceived happiness (or less regret).

As discussed earlier, when we make a decision to create a mind-clone we are expanding our mind in a very important way. That mental expansion will come with its own biases, just as we develop mental biases from all manner of life experiences. To pursue a mental bias is not to create a new personal identity. It is simply doing what seems to part of an individual to be in its overall best interest.

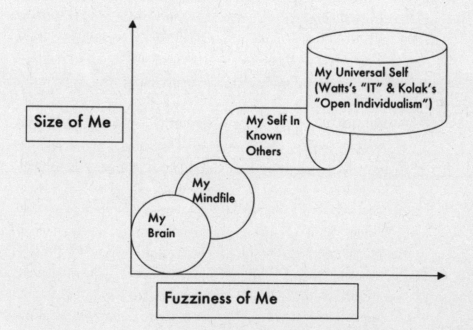

FIGURE 6

There is fuzziness to our selves, and this fuzziness is amplified by mindcloning. We are not exactly the same day to day, and each of us is often of several "minds." Nor would we want to be the same day after day, for then we could not grow and change. As Warren Buffett says, "it is better to be approximately right than precisely wrong." Day after day it is better to be approximately our previous self than to be precisely stagnant and locked into a mental state. My personal mantra is that "each day we are born anew. What we do today is most important."

Figure 6 indicates that the size of "me" depends upon what one does, as well as one's perspective. But any size me will have some amount of fuzziness because we change from day to day. If we create a mindclone, we have in essence created a larger me. It is therefore unavoidable that there will be more opportunities for conflicts and choices—more fuzziness to who is me. But it is still "me." If we then alter our perspective and think, like Hofstadter, that there "are people in me," and that there are aspects of "me" in the minds of our loved ones, we have clearly expanded both the size—and the fuzziness—of me once again. Finally, if we adopt an open-individualist point of view, such as espoused by Dan Kolak, or the universalism of an Alan Watts, we have expanded the size— and the fuzziness—of me toward infinity. After commenting that of course the bodily parts of a person are not separate beings, Watts argues in *The Book: On the Taboo Against Knowing Who You Are*:

> In precisely the same way, the individual is separate from his universal environment only in name. When this is not recognized, you have been fooled by your name. Confusing names with nature, you come to believe that having a separate name makes you a separate being. That is—rather literally—to be spellbound. Naturally, it isn't the mere fact of being named that brings about the hoax of being a "real person"; it is all that goes with it. The child is tricked into the ego-feeling by the attitudes, words, and actions of the society which surrounds him—his parents, relatives, teachers, and, above all, his similarly hoodwinked peers. Other people teach us who we are.

Hence, a mindclone is only going to feel as separate an identity from its biological original as it is socialized. Making a *larger* me, via mindcloning, implies different mental biases with respect to decisions, as well as both more possible sorrow over loss and more possible comfort over survival. The software version of you may think, if there must be a choice, that you will be more happy as computer substrate than as flesh (unless the software version realizes that a flesh version can re-create the mindclone, but not vice versa), and the flesh substrate of you will think the opposite (unless the flesh version is racked by pain and disability and would prefer continuing life as a mindclone). This doesn't make them different people. They are both trying to make the best of the situation for *you,* taking into account their substrate biases. But there is a continual stream of conscious states that transcends substrate. That continual stream is *you*. Each manifestation of *you* is trying to make the best decision for *you*. Let's give the conversational skeptic a visit:

MASTER ME: "I get the point about one 'me' transcending two forms. But the fact remains that if the flesh 'me' is killed, then I will no longer have all these flesh sensations I appreciate. The mindclone continuation of me will never reprise my flesh feelings. That 'me' is gone."

ROYAL ME-NESS: "Losing your flesh body would be a humongous tragedy, no doubt about it. But suppose you lost just your legs. Would you still be you?"

MASTER ME: "Of course."

ROYAL ME-NESS: "How about paralyzed from the neck down? Still you?"

MASTER ME: "Horrible, but yes, still some shrunken form of me."

ROYAL ME-NESS: "Then you have agreed that if all that is left is your mind, you have suffered a terrible loss, but it is not the end of your 'me-ness.'"

MASTER ME: "Then at what point is my me-ness totally gone?"

ROYAL ME-NESS: "It is partly a matter of fact, and partly a matter of philosophy. Objectively, your me-ness is gone when observers could not find evidence that your unique pattern of thoughts and memories responded to events in the world."

MASTER ME: "Such as if both my mindclone and flesh body were gone?"

ROYAL ME-NESS: "Yes. But it could still be hypothesized that your unique pattern of thoughts and memories were responding to events in the world as interlaced subroutines within the minds of other people who knew you."

MASTER ME: "Wow. That would mean that I continued to live as kind of a fractured self embedded in others?"

ROYAL ME-NESS: "Exactly. Advanced psychometric techniques might even be able to detect this, and extract it back into a mindclone."

MASTER ME: "Whoa, that's wild!"

ROYAL ME-NESS: "And philosophically, if your unique pattern of thoughts and memories are simply expressions of a deeper, underlying humanity-wide mindspace, then nothing has really been lost at all. You live on in the global mindspace, although you don't feel like you anymore."

MASTER ME: "I rather like me, so I think I'll stick with my mindclone. At least I know that's really me."

ROYAL ME-NESS: "There you go."

Any person is likely to feel a coin's toss of indecision over life-changing events at some time or another in their life—generally more than once. We often regret the decisions we make, and at different times of our lives we might readily have made a decision opposite of one made earlier. Sometimes these different decisions could have been biased be-cause of the particular friends or family members who were persuading us at the time, or even just how healthy or ill we were feeling at the moment. This doesn't make us different people, like split personalities. It simply means that even life-or-death decisions can be biased by composite parts of our psychological whole. To paraphrase Shakespeare from *Hamlet*, "For some must watch, while some must sleep. This runs the world away." Life continues, and with mindcloning our life continues, even if a part of us must sleep while the other part of us gets to watch.[157]

Perhaps the mindclone will choose life over the biological original. Or perhaps not. The mindclone may rationally deduce that the biological original is better able to function in the real world, and will reconstitute the mindclone in a safer place with better technology as soon as practical. The decision will turn upon a complex array of factors, unique to each circumstance. However the decision turns out, it doesn't prove different identity. It just shows how one part of a composite self feels about total self-actualization at a particular moment in time.

Dual Citizenship

Article 15 of the Universal Declaration of Human Rights says that everyone is entitled to a nationality, and cannot be arbitrarily deprived of one. Notwithstanding the implementation of this sentiment in an international treaty in 1954, there are tens of millions of stateless persons today—people with no official nationality, such as many refugees. However, this is a much smaller percentage of the world population than has historically been without citizenship. Progress is being made in ensuring citizenship to all persons.

Mindclones will want citizenship, most likely in the country of their birth, because of the numerous survival advantages associated with it. Yet until mindclones are recognized as human, citizenship is impossible. Today, a person's citizenship usually starts with a birth certificate and ends with a death certificate. A mindclone has the same birthplace as their biological twin, and hence no special birth certificate is needed for a mindclone. As noted above, mindclones will receive a legal ID upon demonstrating satisfaction of government standards for mindclone IDs, such as use of approved mindware, proof of an adequate-size mindfile, and attestations by the biological mind-twin and perhaps by cyberpsychiatry specialists.

A beman, on the other hand, is stateless until granted residency, and ultimately citizenship, by a nation-state. Of course, this occurs all the time for refugees, so it is not really extraordinary. Hence while mindclone citizenship ultimately is established by the lack of a death certificate for their flesh original, beman citizenship requires an affirmative immigration-type process from stateless cyberspace to sovereign cyberspace. This process is a legal process, not a geographical one, because the same cloud servers, located anywhere in the world, can host both stateless and sovereign cyberspace.

Cyberspace can be sovereign because sovereignty means the exercise of legal control over a territory, being derived from the ancient rule that a king's religion extended as far as the king's armies could control. Since cyberspace is generated by computers in a territory, and extends via internet nodes on territories to display devices in territories, it is clear that it is subject to sovereign controls in those territories. Countries get angry about cyberespionage, for example, because that entails people from one country violating the legal controls (such as stealing information or causing damage) of another country.

When a beman arises in cyberspace that beman is stateless in the sense that it was born without citizenship. But it is still subject to the sovereignty of the country wherein resides the computer system that hosts its mindfiles and mindware, and to the sovereignty of anyplace that it travels via the internet. When that beman applies for citizenship it is like a stateless person applying for citizenship, in this case a person who may or may not have entered a territory illegally depending on that country's rules regarding the creation of cyberconsciousness. It is not the physical location per se of a beman's mindfiles and mindware that creates citizenship or residency; it is the legal status of that beman in a sovereignty that creates citizenship or residency. In any event it is a trivial matter to replicate a beman's mindfile and mindware on multiple servers in different countries.

Should the beman be created in a country that does not grant beman citizenship, the beman could apply for citizenship in a more welcoming country. If necessary (and it may not be so, depending on the laws of the welcoming country), the beman could transfer its mindfiles and mindware to a cloud server in the welcoming country. (I would.)

An important part of citizenship is the right, or even obligation, to vote. There is only one vote between a biological twin and his or her mindclone. After the biological body dies, the mindclone may continue to live and vote as an individual. It is a different situation for the beman, who cannot vote at all without first being granted citizenship; only after that would the beman acquire voting rights. Since legal identity quickly leads to discussion of citizenship, and citizenship goes hand-in-glove with voting rights, we should now discuss one of the biggest bugaboos about human rights for the virtually human: What if they outvote us and take over the country? The short answer to this bugaboo is that since the mindclones are us, they can't outvote us; there are no extra votes for mindclones. One being, one vote. But since mindclones are immortal, this outvoting issue should be explored in further depth.

For most of history voting rights were withheld from most citizens. In general, only men owning significant property could vote. Then, in the late eighteenth and especially nineteenth centuries, there arose social movements in favor of "universal suffrage," which meant the extension of voting rights to men who did not own real estate. Decades later this was generally extended to all women. However, even "universal suffrage" has generally excluded criminals, the seriously deranged, and others deemed not to be qualified. Voting rights are important because they are the most effective, nonviolent, tool by which to get legislatures to pay attention to a group's concerns. Indeed, universal suffrage became a cause célèbre only within the past century or two.

Notwithstanding this lack of voting power, many disenfranchised peoples have done well and lived good lives. Hence, one alternative to the risks of mindclone electoral domination is to not extend suffrage to mindclones.

If voting rights are not extended to mindclones, a growing percentage of the population will not be as able as the rest of society to influence policy through elected representatives. The disenfranchised mindclones will probably be discriminated against, as legislatures will not fear the loss of their votes. Mindclones will find themselves in the company of demographic groups around the world who lack voting rights in the country of their residence:

- Women in Saudi Arabia

- Immigrants worldwide, unless naturalized

- Those convicted of serious crimes in most American states and many other countries

- Sixteen- and seventeen-year-olds in all countries except for Austria, and legally defined underage children everywhere

- Stateless persons

The United States Constitution leaves voting standards up to each state, although they may not exercise their power in a way that prohibits voting on the basis of sex, race, ethnicity, economics, or age above seventeen. Consequently, different states will pass different rules governing the conditions under which (if any) mindclones can vote. Hence another alternative to mindclone voting rights everywhere is to leave the matter up to experimentation by the fifty American states (and similar political subdivisions outside the United States). Different states will probably adopt different levels of qualification for mindclone voting rights. Then, depending upon in which state a biological twin of a mindclone is or last was resident, they may or may not have the right to vote.

Another alternative is called "census suffrage." In this concept voting rights are apportioned in an unequal manner. For example, each mindclone could be awarded one-tenth of a vote (upon the death of their biological twin) on the argument that they are only able to fulfill one-tenth of the obligations of a flesh citizen. This would surely become a point of contention as in our increasingly computerized society (including the Department of Defense's new Cyber Command) mindclones may actually be more useful than flesh humans. The contention would grow more severe if mindclones were not taxed at the same discount as that applied to their voting rights.

There are alternatives to mindclone voting rights. Among the world's two-hundred-odd countries it is rare to find any two countries with precisely the same voting rules; several countries even exclude police and military personnel from voting, notwithstanding the risks they take for their communities. I believe that the risks to flesh persons of including mindclones within universal suffrage are negligible. However, the societal tensions from excluding them are palpable. Consequently, it would seem wise to extend voting rights to virtual humans. On March 15, 1965, President Lyndon B. Johnson made a historic appearance before Congress to urge passage of the Voting Rights Act of 1965, considered by many experts to be the most important piece of U.S. civil-rights legislation. The previous week's television delivered shocking images of peaceful African American petitioners being clubbed, hosed, dragged, and set upon by attack dogs. In explaining to Congress why voting rights were, in particular, the most important of all human rights, he observed that it all came down to dignity:

> Dignity cannot be found in a man's possessions; it cannot be found in his power, or in his position. It really rests on his right to be treated equal in opportunity to all others. . . . Our fathers believed that if this noble view of the rights of man was to flourish, it must be rooted in democracy. The most basic right of all was the right to choose your own leaders. The history of

this country, in large measure, is the history of the expansion
of that right to all of our people.

Johnson was reminding us that all human rights rest upon voting
rights. There are numerous avenues available to extend that franchise
cautiously and based upon experience. Imagine a country with ten
million people and a zero population-growth rate (excluding mindclones). On average about a hundred thousand people will die and be
born in such a country annually.[158] Now, suppose that half the "deaths"
are of flesh originals whose lives are actually continued as mindclones,
i.e., they are not "really dead." After twenty years there would be eleven
million people (a hundred thousand births a year would make up for the
hundred thousand flesh deaths, but fifty thousand of the hundred thousand who died flesh deaths each year would continue their lives as
mindclones, yielding a million more "people" after twenty years). If the
country traditionally split pretty equally into two political parties, a
"swing vote" of 10 percent of the populace (and a larger percentage of the
"adult" population) would be politically powerful. Indeed, after twenty
years, the tally would look like this:

Disappeared into non-mindclone death: 1,000,000

Born in the flesh but under voting age: 1,700,000

Born in the flesh and now able to vote: 300,000

Continued as voting mindclones: 1,000,000

Flesh voting percent: 8,300,000/9,300,000 = 89 percent

Mindclone voting percent: 1,000,000/9,300,000 = 11 percent

However, after forty years, the percentages would be as follows:

Disappeared into non-mindclone death: 2,000,000

Born in the flesh but under voting age: 1,700,000

Born in the flesh and now able to vote: 2,300,000

Continued as voting mindclones: 2,000,000

Flesh voting percent: 8,300,000/10,300,000 = 81 percent

Mindclone voting percent: 2,000,000/10,300,000 = 19 percent

There is a clear shift in voting power in the direction of mind-clones. Indeed, while every year a hundred thousand new flesh people will come of voting age, a hundred thousand flesh people will also die out, and fifty thousand mindclones without a living biological twin will vote. The only group that continually gains is the mindclones. Of course, there are many variables at play that can alter this simplistic model; flesh people may live longer, but depending on what country they live in, they may also produce fewer offspring (the famous demographic transition). Initially many fewer than 50 percent of flesh originals may elect to have mindclone continuations, but after decades of comfort a preponderance of flesh originals may choose to continue their lives as mindclones. These many variables cut one way or the other, and sometimes cancel each other out. All that can be said with certainty is that giving true citizenship to mindclones does lead to a possibility, if not a probability, that mindclones will end up with substantial voting power.

The prospect of mindclone voting power raises two important questions: (1) Is it really a problem? and (2) Is there a practical alternative? Mindclone voters would generally be older voters. On the other hand, they would also be very tech-savvy voters. I believe the only nonspeculative conclusion that can be drawn about their voting habits is that they would tend to vote for what was in the best interests of mindclones. On the great majority of issues, this would be similar if not identical to what was in the best interests of their flesh persons. For example, mindclones would want security (keep the barbarians at bay!), good infrastructure (faster networks, reliable electrical power grid), medical R&D (stem-cell research leading to ectogenesis and mind uploading), educational opportunities (got to keep society going), world peace, low taxes, and, oh yes, real campaign-finance reform. Indeed, mindclones and bemans alike would evolve politically and socially just as humans do, changing our minds about issues as we experience and learn more, or as our interests, needs, and situations shift. Consequently, in terms of how they will likely vote, there does not appear to be a reason to fear growing mindclone political power. *They are us.*

There is a stereotype that old people are scared of change and vote, knee-jerk, against it. In a recent study published in the journal *Electoral Studies,* "The Grey Vote: Determinants of Older Voters' Party Choice in Britain and West Germany," academician Achim Goerres concluded that there was no evidence to support this stereotype. Specifically, he found no evidence to support the hypothesis that older voters were more economically conservative in their political positions.

Instead, there are two main factors that affect older voter behavior. These are called generational and life-cycle factors. The generational factors are largely irrelevant over time, because every ten years or so another generational trend appears, continually diluting the strength of any one trend. For example, a generation that came of voting age during the 1960s might share many of its cultural tendencies. However, seniors who came of age during the more conservative 1980s and 1990s would soon dilute them. Potentially more significant are life-cycle factors, which are trends that typify any older person, no matter what generation they grew up in. For example, we might logically think that old people cared more about health-care policy than young people. However, the empirical research carried out by Goerres found no such trends (young people care about health care, too). Similarly, no data was found to support the notion that older voters are more economically conservative because they have acquired more wealth. Instead,

evidence also indicates that ageing democracies will neither show a simple pattern that confirms life-cycle regularities, nor a simple pattern produced by the sequence of political generations. Simplistic notions of the kind suggesting that ageing democracies will face insurmountable political blockades are not warranted.[159]

In the United States, the 2008 election of Barack Obama was a transformative event. The only *age* group that voted as a majority against Barack Obama were those aged sixty-five and over. (The demographic referred to as "white voters" also voted as a majority against him.) Hence, one might ask, would an increasingly aged population, such as one with many mindclones, militate against the type of progressive changes promised by the Obama campaign? Experts do not believe so. The reason most people over age sixty-five voted Republican (against Barack Obama) is because these people are the generation that politically matured in the 1950s, under General Eisenhower as president, when Republicans were ascendant.[160] Someone born in 1960 was still under sixty years old at the time of the 2008 election.

The 1950s generation have voted majority Republican throughout their lives. It is likely that if the election were held ten years later, when many of the senior citizens were individuals who came of age during the Democratic-dominated 1960s, the sixty-five-plus demographic would have voted as a majority for Barack Obama.

In summary, it does not appear likely that the mindclone voting block will vote significantly differently from the populace as a whole, because their interests will not be much different. Also, there is no data to support the notion that older people vote more conservatively, than any other demographic group. While such a trend may hold for a generation, it will just as likely be supplanted by a different trend in the next generation. The only thing about the life cycle of a person that, per se, leads them to vote one way or the other, is possibly party or candidate familiarity. The more impressions a party or candidate makes on someone, the somewhat more likely they are to vote for them.[161] In contrast, younger voters are more willing to vote for any candidate or party because none has yet made an impression upon them.

However, this factor of familiarity does not imply either a liberal or conservative political position, or a homogeneous voting pool.

One can also take a fleshist, or essentialist, point of view that mindclones will simply not be capable of rationally exercising a voting franchise. If mindclones were so clearly "lame," then they would never be counted as humans in the first instance, and there would be no question of their citizenship or voting rights. The question here is if mindclones are worthy of citizenship, are there valid reasons to deny them such citizenship, such as fear that they will outvote the flesh population to its detriment? Will they cause a voting revolution?

One might argue that even if mindclones are deserving of citizenship they are too susceptible to mass manipulation to vote responsibly. Quite similar arguments have been used to forestall the extension of voting rights to subordinated demographic groups, from non-European-descended peoples in South Africa to women worldwide. In every instance, once the franchise was extended, there has been no evidence that it was exercised any more or less wisely than those who previously monopolized voting power. We should not forget that the Germans voted Hitler into power, and indeed much of the earliest enthusiasm for him came from students in universities. In the 1930 elections, Göttingen, a university town, delivered twice as many votes to Hitler's party as the national average; and the Nazis held a majority in the university's student congress going back to 1926.

Democracy and voting are not designed so people reach the most rational decisions, unaffected by emotional manipulation of tribal or religious values. For such outcomes one needs Plato's *Republic,* if it would work with the utopian order written into it. Instead, democracy is a mechanism for ensuring that a government everyone must support with sacrifice and/or taxes will remain attentive to electorally significant interest blocks within the populace. This generally overlaps with rationality (most of the voters making up the interest blocks want to live in a reasonable society). Consequently, even if mindclones will vote as a block, as groups of humans frequently do, they will most likely do so to further their interests. As noted above, those interests are highly collimated with normal flesh human interests.

Will One Man, One Vote, Stop at the Mindclone?

Computer Uses Images to Teach Itself Common Sense.
—*BBC NEWS* HEADLINE STORY ON JOINT CARNEGIE MELLON UNIVERSITY, DEFENSE DEPARTMENT, AND GOOGLE PROJECT[162]

A premise of modern democracy is that each adult citizen gets one vote; none get more or less. This principle remains inviolate with mindclones. A new mindclone has the same legal identity as its biological original. If you mindclone yourself, you have crossed a Rubicon of identity: ever after, your one identity is spread across two substrates, your flesh and your mindclone's software. Thus, you are not entitled to two votes. Should you and your mindclone disagree over how to vote (which is the same as arguing with yourself over how to vote; most of us have been "undecided" at one time or another), the first of you to actually vote (yes, there will be remote electronic voting by then) will be the only vote of yours that is counted.

To have a voting right a virtual human will have to either (a) satisfy governmental standards that it has a unity of identity with its flesh original (i.e., that it is, in fact, a mindclone), because the age of majority is not relevant for a mindclone, who is simply a conscious prosthetic of its biological mind-twin; or, if not, because it is therefore a beman, (b) spend a childhood under a parent's care (or that of a surrogate parent or agency) until it meets government standards for demonstrating adult autonomy and empathy. The government standards for mindclone citizenship will inevitably require at minimum (a) the use of mindware approved by a government agency such as the FDA as capable of producing human-equivalent mindclones from an adequately robust mindfile, and (b) the attestation by a flesh original that he or she shares a singular identity with the mindclone based on not less than a year of experience. If these standards are not met, the purported mindclone is not one at all, but is instead at most a new virtual human. Whether such a new cyberconscious being can ultimately vote will depend on their maturation and meeting objective standards for national citizenship. As I said earlier, legally they are like a newborn immigrating from a country called "cyberspace" and are essentially stateless until granted citizenship by a nation-state.

The difficulty of getting a voting right other than as the cloned identity of a citizen makes it most unlikely that flesh humans will rapidly find themselves a *true* electoral minority. As noted above, mindclones do not make flesh humans a real electoral minority because mindclones have the same personality and legal identity of the flesh precursor. They are but a technomedical extension of a flesh human life.

Laws will be modified so that upon the bodily death of a flesh original with a mindclone there will be issued a "life-extension certificate" in lieu of a death certificate. (The life-extension certificate would be delayed, with a revocable death certificate issued in the interim, if the flesh original died less than a year after the creation of the mindclone, and hence before the mindclone could meet the legal "one-year real-life test" standard for demonstrating unity of identity. In this case, a panel of psychologists specializing in cyberconsciousness would need to make a recommendation). The life-extension certificate will attest to the time and manner of bodily death of the mindclone's flesh original, while at the same time documenting the fact of a continuation of that person's identity. The life-extension certificate will then be used by the mindclone for voter registration and other documentation requirements associated with citizenship.

WITHOUT THE RIGHT to vote, everything else can—and often will—be taken away. So while there are alternatives to extending full suffrage to mindclones, they are like a building full of trapdoors. You think you are on solid ground, but then, take a step forward, and at any moment you can be stripped of your very existence. Remembering that mind-clones are not abstract beings, but are us, our parents, our friends, our fellow citizens, I believe the alternatives are but tranquilizing slips down into a dark social pit. We have an opportunity here to learn from history and do this right. For all of us to live with dignity, our mind-clone brethren must have the right to vote.

The NEW ELECTORATE

SEVEN

RETHINKING KINSHIP SYSTEMS

A man isn't a collection of chemical reactions; he's a collection of ideas.
—ROBERT A. HEINLEIN[163]

CONSCIOUSNESS EMERGED VERY SLOWLY FROM BIOLOGICAL LIFE. EACH AS-
PECT OF IT HAD TO PROVE ITS SURVIVAL VALUE, AND THE NEURAL SUBSTRATE
for consciousness could arise only by random mutations. But vitological consciousness plays by rather different rules. Entire conscious beings can pop into existence at once, and each such being represents a
self-replication victory to someone.

It will be genetically human beings who will be copying their
mindfiles into mindclones. As each of us pursues our own, personal
quest for a more enjoyable life via mindcloning, we are also helping to
assure the survival of our species, albeit in the form of mindclones.
The mindclones are humans because the mindclones are we. Hence,
the coming proliferation of mindclones, and especially bemans, is also
a proliferation of humanity. The twenty-first century will mark an inflection point between when more humans lived before us than are
currently alive, and when more humans are alive, mostly virtually, than
lived before us. Specifically, it is estimated that 100 billion humans
lived since *Homo sapiens* arose, of which only about 8 percent are alive
today. Yet between mindclones and bemans it will not be too long before humanity increases more than tenfold to over 100 billion. As described in chapter 6, there is more than enough space, consciousness
has always been the coolest thing to make, and when deaths are not a

big factor in a growing population, it can grow very quickly. Between flesh humans and mindclone humans there is mutually assured survival. The survival of the former depends on the latter, and the survival of the latter assures the continuity of the former. Love thy mindclone as you love thyself, for they are the same.

I am eager for 100 billion new humanly conscious lives. I believe there nothing more splendid in the universe than healthy, happy human consciousness. As Carl Sagan famously remarked, our brains are star stuff (i.e., formed from atoms spewed into our solar system from supernovas across our galaxy) that is contemplating star stuff. No myth ever touched this glorious reality, nor are the greatest natural beauties a match for human artistry, innovation, and kindness. I felt deep revulsion when I first read of North Vietnamese general Vo Nguyen Giap's purported statement (quoted by the French writer Bernard B. Fall) that "Every minute hundreds of thousands of people die all over the world. The life or death of a hundred, a thousand or tens of thousands of human beings, even if they are our own compatriots, represents really very little." I knew he was off by three orders of magnitude, as daily (not per minute) deaths are around two hundred thousand. But the point is that he did not seem to feel the tragedy of each and every life lost.

Indeed, it is said that in three decades of combat more than a million of his soldiers were killed, a casualty level that would have cost any U.S. general his command. But those generals, all of the U.S. taxpayers, and all of the world's peoples (including myself) sat by and watched a humongous loss of life. And the wretched melody continues to this day, in different keys and voices. I am eager for a world that believes that growing consciousness is purpose; then, perhaps subliminally, there will emerge a consensus that extinguishing it is intolerable. The loss of consciousness should never represent "really very little," but should always represent a gross failure of technology and/or morality.

Mindclones and the Family of Man

If our humanity comes from consciousness and its attendant emotional aspects, then mindclones also represent humanity. And after all, we create them, or give birth to them in a sense. This necessarily means a reassessment of kinship, of who we consider to be a relative. Moreover, the parents of a person creating a mindclone are also parents of the mindclone, because the mindclone and its creator have the same identity. They are the same person, albeit now dispersed across two platforms. Hence, if you love your son, you love his mindclone, because they are one. The changes one goes through in creating a mindclone will often challenge the love people have for you, but that is also the case with every big life change. How often is love challenged when someone "comes out" as gay? They are still the same person, and they should be loved just the same, but there is also something different, and that difference can make, for some, the extension of one's love difficult to maintain in the same way.

This makes sense on an intellectual level, of course, but reality is often very different from theory, and so mindclones will rock the familial world in many ways. Consider, for example, a thirty-year-old single firefighter who has built up a robust mindfile, which has been activated with mindware and now shares identity with the resulting mindclone. Suppose a month from getting married the firefighter's body is tragically consumed in an explosive blaze. The mindclone instantly (via streaming wireless connection—or pulling any data content through a wireless connection) learns of this from the media and phone calls, and reacts more or less as anyone would react who awakes in a hospital from a terrible accident. *Denial, anger, bargaining, depression, and acceptance.* The mindclone calls the fiancée, and after days of soul-searching, they decide to proceed with the marriage. Included in their plans are starting a family by blending bemes from each of their mindfiles into a new baby beman. Can this family be protected as one of world's "fundamental human social units"? I think it should.

The firefighter mindclone is no different from its firefighter original except it lacks a body because it has the same hopes, fears, wishes, dreams,[164] emotions, and loves; the same drive to participate in the great chain of human life by passing a part of its self onto a next generation. Now, psychologists have disputed that emotions can exist without a body since at least the time when William James articulated a thought experiment purporting to show the emptiness of an emotion without the concomitants of endocrines and hormones. Yet Minsky, in *The Emotion Machine,* answers James's experiment by showing emotions to be complex associations of thoughts that can be triggered by other thoughts as well as bodily secretions. Certainly there seems to be little drop in susceptibility to joy, sadness, fear, or love as one loses bodily responsiveness owing to age or severe trauma.[165]

Continuing our example, suppose the firefighter's spouse also has a mindfile (virtually everyone will, as even today most IT users have an informal, decentralized one), but has not yet activated a mindclone. There will be software fertility doctors who specialize in creating new vitological life that is as unique as is every human being, and yet share bemes from two parents that are as telltale as our parents' genes in us. It will take years for this new vitological baby to mature into an adult. That is the family-building challenge our interplatform couple wishes to undertake.

They will be criticized for being unfair to the child. What interracial or gay couple has not heard similar cautions and slurs about their union and offspring? They will be warned of a life of frustration and discrimination—of feeling like an outcast and being treated as one. Joyful matchups between differently able people shine through the unfairness of these challenges as well. If it were flesh alone that made for happy pairings then half of all marriages would not end in divorce. Love is not locked in flesh.

About the same time Alan Turing speculated on limitless potential for software, 1938, Lester del Rey wrote a short science-fiction story called *Helen O'Loy.* Two tinkerers upgrade a household robot to become a natural-appearing and natural-behaving woman, albeit of synthetic material and computerized. They both fall in love with her, and one marries her. I have no doubt that love will transcend substrate.[166] People have argued that substrate is some kind of a barrier to the abstract since at least the time of Plato, who criticized his contemporary Archytas—builder of the first mechanical calculating device—for disrespecting the pure essence of numbers. My point of view is that the differential experience of abstractions such as mind (Turing), romance (del Rey), or numerology (Plato), with one nonabstract substrate (bits, plastics, or woodcuts) or another (brains or bodies), is interesting and a useful expansion of diversity not per se impossible or disrespectful.

I believe our hypothetical couple embodies all the best attributes of humanity. There will be hope on the part of the firefighter for advances in ectogenesis and mind-downloading technology so that the joy of a body can again be experienced. Why should marital union be denied simply because, in the time frame of the example, medical technology is able to save just the mind, not the body? The spouse will likely feel encouraged to accelerate his or her own mindclone so that as much of life can be shared as possible. The new child will become a focus of their life, a new consciousness flowering in the family garden. As the young beman matures the parents may find themselves frustrated that this next generation doesn't share their value for flesh embodiment in the future. Ah, but what is new here? Does not every new generation see the world differently? This is what makes humanity a chain rather than a spool, a bridge rather than a pit, a trajectory rather than a destination. Bob Dylan put it well in the lyrics to his emblematic song "The Times They Are a-Changin'."

International law recognizes the family as the fundamental human social unit.[167] Treaties and national laws enshrine the rights of adults to get married and start a family.[168] If mindclones are to be recognized as citizens, or even as just technomedically extended humans, it will appear unfairly discriminatory to deny them family rights. Yet it will take much social effort to protect mindclone families. Human-rights provisions in treaties are often flouted (such as not being incorporated into national law), and pro-family laws are frequently interpreted quite narrowly. So, yes, it will be inevitable that mindclones will want to get married (either to flesh people or to other mindclones), and will want to have children (donor-gene and/or blended-beme-based babies). The social challenge will be in obtaining legal recognition for their desires. Consider these diverse matchups:

MINDCLONE AND HUMAN LOVES MINDCLONE AND HUMAN

If two mindclones in love have living flesh originals, then this means the flesh originals have also fallen in love. A mindclone has the same psychological and legal identity as their flesh original. In this case, an old-fashioned "press the flesh" marriage occurs, albeit one that may have begun between each spouse's mindclone online. And how many current romances begin online?

MINDCLONE WIDOWS

If one of a couple of married flesh original bodies ends, and both have mindclones, then we have one surviving body and two surviving mindclones. This scenario illustrates that the death of a body does not end a marriage if a mindclone exists for that body. A mindclone widow is a human married to a combined human-mindclone identity who has suffered a bodily death. They are really not any more of a widow than are humorously called "golf widows."

Before jumping to a conclusion that this is unfair to the spouse whose body survives, please remember that these mindclones will have the capacity for orgasm. Sensations such as taste, touch, and smell have already been digitally duplicated. Now, it is easy to think that the surviving body will feel, "Well, that's fine for the mindclone to have an orgasm, but I want *my* own orgasm!" Yet this perspective misapprehends the multipresence nature of dual identity. The surviving body will have "what she's having" via her mindclone.

The surviving body can also form an audio, visual, haptic, and/or EEG headset link with their mindclone to yet further experience the concomitants of the mindclone orgasm. The surviving body can also interact with purchased prosthetic sex-specific extensions of their spouse's mindclone. In AI expert David Levy's words, "Love with robots will be as normal as love with other humans, while the number of sexual acts and lovemaking positions commonly practiced between humans will be extended, as robots teach more than is in all of the world's published sex manuals combined." If this is too much, or too weird, or too removed from the capabilities of anyone's spouse, perhaps the biological spouse can masturbate along with the mindclone orgasm to achieve a synchronous physical orgasm. Yet even if the surviving body no longer has direct orgasms, but simply witnesses those of their mindclone, this does not make them separate people. The orgasms we have, while delicious, are just a part of who we really are. Most wandering spouses are not their one-off orgasms, but are, instead, the engaging personality we interact with over the years.

Of course there will also be many situations analogous to lifelong partners who get divorced after one of them suffers a debilitating accident. A surviving body may wish to get divorced from a surviving mindclone. On rare occasions this desire may not be shared by the surviving body's mindclone. In this case they first will have to obtain an independent legal identity for that mindclone, via a psychiatric and judicial process. While it sounds complicated, it is no more so than the vexing child-custody battles family courts deal with every day. Family lawyers will have work for many decades to come.

A mere difference of opinion regarding divorce between a mindclone and original is not any kind of evidence that they are not a singular identity. I don't believe there is an intelligent person alive who does not maintain two contradictory views of something in their mind. Yet we are still one identity. Most spouses in troubled marriages are often on a knife edge between "I want a divorce" and "I will stick it out." They are still singular identities. The uniqueness of mindclone technology is that it enables, after a judicially approved separation of identity, for two strongly felt, personally momentous, contradictory desires to both be met.

MINDCLONE LOVES MINDCLONE

If both original bodies are gone before a marriage occurs, then we are looking at the possibility of a wedding between two mindclones. Opponents will argue (1) weddings are an archaic physical body tradition of no interest to mindclones, (2) mindclones are neither male nor female, and marriage is a union of one male and one female (or at least two flesh bodies in equal marriage jurisdictions), and (3) whatever marital rights the mindclones might be entitled to are outweighed by society's interests in limiting marriages to flesh people and in ensuring that flesh children do not end up in the care of fleshless mindclones via adoption or surrogacy parenthood. For example, opponents will observe, neither freedom of religion, nor the due-process right to liberty (which underlies the marital right), provides a safe harbor for polygamy. The right to marriage is not absolute, but must be considered in light of all the circumstances. Recall our discussion in chapter 4 of the twin bioethical principles (which are also bio*cyber*ethical principles) of respect for both diversity of practices and unity of sensibilities in a healthy society.

The counterargument to the first point is that human customs transcend technology. The hugely popular World of Warcraft online game is replete with age-old human customs. Jews celebrate Passover as Skype-over, and churchgoers celebrate Mass as avatars on Second Life. Any custom desirable enough to the human mind to persist for centuries will persist virtually in some form.

As to the marital-rights objection, since the mindclones are the continuation of their biological selves, they are either male or female or transgendered. Simply because a person loses the use of a body due to an accident, they do not lose their sexual identity. There are reasonable ways of addressing societal concerns with mindclone marriage (such as child raising) that do not require blocking a fundamental human right. For example, even death row inmates have had their right to marriage upheld, notwithstanding the fact that they may never touch their new spouse.

With respect to mindclones, no-fault divorce laws make it simple for a person to divorce a spouse who exists only as a mindclone, and adoption laws can restrict mindclone access to flesh children. I believe it is impossible to conjure up a reason that supports limiting marriage to flesh people, and that also applies to all flesh people. For example, if one argues that mindclones shouldn't marry because they cannot procreate (the old-fashioned way), then we would have to prevent senior flesh citizens, lesbians, homosexuals, and the infertile from marrying as well.

There is one kind of trump card argument that mindclone marriage opponents will pull. This argument is that marriage is something that the majority of society considers to be a kind of sacred ritual (even if secular) among flesh people (generally of opposite sex). Consequently, it would shock the conscience of society to have this ritual applied to mindclones, and such a shock is too high a price to pay for enabling the admittedly important marital right for mindclones. Furthermore, since mindclones as a class have not been subject to a long history of oppression, such as racial slavery, there need be very little judicial sensitivity to ensuring that mindclone discrimination not occur. Thus, the trump argument goes, the interest seeking protection (mindclone marriage) is not so great as the interest challenged (marriage for flesh people only). From this lawyers will argue that courts should block mindclone marriage (as they once did rather similarly with interracial and gay marriage). This trump argument is a legal formulation of the biocyberethical principles of diversity and unity described earlier. The allegation will be that the unity interests of society outweigh the diversity interests of mindclones. This argument will weaken as mindclones grow in number and prominence.

Who will win? Eventually the scales of reason will tilt toward permitting mindclone marriages. This will occur when the courts are persuaded that the mindclones are simply the same humans as they originally were, albeit in a medically disabled form. This is because every argument against mindclone marriage falls away if mindclones have the same human souls they had as flesh beings.

NON-MINDCLONE BEMANS FALLING IN LOVE

A legally more challenging situation arises when two *bemans* (virtual human beings who are not extracted from anyone's mindfile) fall in love with each other. It is also a certainty to find human-loves-beman and beman-loves-human situations. Lastly, beman-loves-mindclone will arise.

Bemans are a more challenging legal class, because they will have a more tenuous claim to sympathy and understanding for their right to marital bliss. Humans and mindclones can claim to know this yearning either directly from family life or indirectly via societal absorption. Non-mindclone bemans will have to argue that since all conscious people yearn for love, which can culminate in a happy marriage, and since law and psychiatry deem adult bemans to be conscious people, ergo they, too, yearn for love, which can culminate in a joyful legal union, and hence they should have the opportunity to experience the same matrimonial legal protections as humans and mindclones.

Opponents will again argue, more factually this time, that bemans are neither male nor female and thus cannot be married because that is a basic requirement. In the United States, federal law once recognized marriages only between one man and one woman. Jurisdictions that permit equal marriage still require the applicants to be male or female. Additional arguments are that permitting marriage to be used by legal persons incapable of procreation undermines marriage's purpose, and that societal morals will be undermined by permitting marriage with and among inanimate objects. Finally, it will be said that normal rules of contract between bemans can suffice for fulfilling most of the unique aspects of the marital relationship. Thus, the opponents will claim, there is no need to drastically revise the conception of marriage when the needs of bemans for relationship certainty can be settled in simpler ways.

Yet there is also a strong case to be made for beman-inclusive marriage. The greatest U.S. judicial statement of the legal uniqueness of marriage was offered in the 1967 U.S. Supreme Court case of *Loving v.*

Virginia, which prohibited American states from interfering with marriage on the basis of racial background:

> Marriage is one of the "basic civil rights of man," fundamental to our very existence and survival. . . . To deny this fundamental freedom on so unsupportable a basis as the racial classifications embodied in these statutes, classifications so directly subversive of the principle of equality at the heart of the Fourteenth Amendment, is surely to deprive all the State's citizens of liberty without due process of law. The Fourteenth Amendment requires that the freedom of choice to marry not be restricted by invidious racial discrimination. Under our Constitution, the freedom to marry, or not marry, a person of another race resides with the individual and cannot be infringed by the State.

Hence, the question is whether prohibiting mindclones from marrying is like blocking marriage based on race, or on same-sex orientation. Bemans could and should argue that their families are "fundamental to the survival of humanity," and that they are the progeny of humans, share the longings of humans, value greatly the marital bonds of humans. They may also reasonably argue that cyberconscious humans are a race of humans. But it will take some decades of intimate societal familiarity with bemans before this point of view is respected enough to find judicial support.

Of course, it is likely that many bemans will have no interest in an ancient institution such as marriage. Indeed, it is possible that, as opponents claim, notions of fidelity or legalization of a chosen social partnership will be alien to the beman mind. After all, even many humans alive today have no interest in marriage, or little commitment to fidelity or no desire to have the government bless their chosen social union. So, whether the bemans are like us, or not, marriage and family may be boring. But I doubt this will universally be the case; human consciousness, which is shared by bemans, is notoriously diverse in its cultural tastes. As I've noted, notwithstanding the fact that modern humans don't need marriage, people clamor to get married; their odds of doing so by age forty are greater than four in five.[169] Despite the lack of any criminal sanctions for infidelity, most people strive to be loyal to a partner. Even though a "piece of paper" cannot make more real a heartfelt love, most people still seek that marriage certificate. These things are not burned into our DNA—they are burned into our bemes. We have become increasingly family oriented *as a matter of choice,* not as a matter of force. I believe the reason for this is that, for many if not most people, it is simply a more enjoyable way to live one's life. Legal formalization of a family in a marriage is similarly a matter a choice. Time will tell if this is a choice that mutates away with beman evolution, or endures in virtual form.

Bemans will be every bit as much happiness-seeking as we are. They will be designed to share our psychology, and will be selected for doing so, because citizenship will be available only to those with humanlike consciousness. Since marriage and loyalty, albeit imperfectly and haphazardly, is what much of humanity does, that is what I would also expect of many if not most bemans. Furthermore, there are many financial and legal perks of marriage—from taxes to confidentiality. Bemans will no doubt value these as much as any married couple does. Some people get married for money or other reasons having little to do with love. So, too, will bemans. This does not mean that a beman must declare a particular sex, such as male or female. As the humanist psychologist Abraham Maslow wrote over half a century ago, it "seems to be becoming clearer and clearer that the next step in personal evolution is a transcendence of both masculinity and femininity to general humanness."[170]

In a nutshell, the most important reason to grant marital and family rights to bemans is because at least some of them will value those rights. The essence of dignity is to respect that which a person values. When there is a clash of values, such as those who value marriage as a heterosexual flesh-only thing, and those who value marriage for the self-actualization it brings to any conscious being, a balancing of interests must occur. This is not dissimilar from clashes between those who value their right to abort a fetus, and those who value fetuses as people. In all such "dignity wars" the only solution is to strike a compromise that nods in the direction of all the well-represented values.

For abortion, in the United States, that compromise has been a nod to the mother's value for her body, with a unilateral right to terminate first trimester pregnancies, and a concomitant nod to the large demographic that values fetuses as people, with a near-ban on third-trimester terminations. For beman relationships, a feasible compromise may be domestic partnership registration with most of the benefits of marriage. This would nod toward the value bemans and their lovers have for their relationship, but also nod toward the sensitivities of non-bemans about the sanctity of marriage as a biological human tribal rite.

With this compromise bemans will generally be on the same legal footing with humans in matters of family law. Hence, their relationships are shown dignity. Opponents of beman marriage will have been stretched to recognize family-law rights in beings many may not yet accept as even being truly animate, much less human-equivalents. Yet the humanists can still also bask in the dignity of having reserved marriage for biological humans and perhaps their immediate extensions, the mindclones.

Over time, education and shifting demographics can result in new compromises. For example, society's initial compromise on gay marriage—domestic partnerships—has gradually evolved, in several U.S. states and some countries, to a completely equal marital right. The same situation may well prevail for beman marriage as people gain greater familiarity with bemans.

Ultimately, a society that cannot resolve its "dignity wars" will disintegrate, for it will no longer share the mutual respect that binds people into a community. Totalitarianism masks unresolved dignity wars with repression, and is thus no more than a short-term solution, and not pleasant for freedom-loving people. Fortunately, democracies and federal systems provide ample opportunities for social compromises to be thought of, debated, and tested in local jurisdictions. Considering the tremendous changes our societies have already successfully managed in the last hundred years, I have great confidence that we have the ingenuity and decency to develop legal solutions to the needs of humans, mindclones, and bemans for dignified familial relationships.

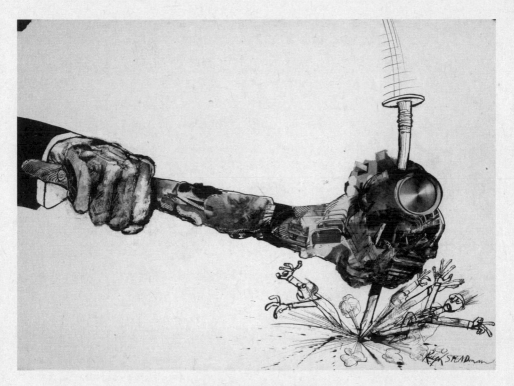

FLESHISM STRIKES BACK

EIGHT

LAW AND LIBERTY

For to be free is not merely to cast off one's chains, but to live in a way that respects and enhances the freedom of others.
—NELSON MANDELA

LEGAL ARGUMENTS MAKE PEOPLE'S HEADS SPIN; THE IDEA OF HAVING TO MOLD LEGISLATION TO MINDCLONES OR TO CREATE MORE LAWS BECAUSE OF them makes people nervous, understandably so. Because we are a nation and a world of so many often arcane and inscrutable (and many ridiculous) laws, this fact alone may make many people shudder at the thought of adding an entirely new population to the globe, one that requires a new set of legislation. But we can't escape it. It's better to understand what legal hurdles may lie ahead and deal with them than ignore what will eventually wind up in court or on ballots. For instance, not dealing with immigration laws promptly and pragmatically has made conditions for both undocumented people and citizens alike much more fractured and divisive. That is just a taste of what's to come if we do not recognize that mindclones will become part of our society, and hence our legal system.

Besides, with the realization of human cyberconsciousness, with the nature to love and be loved, to communicate and establish close ties with others, mindclones will be smart enough to figure out that life has tremendous value—and natural and legal rights and protections are very handy. Think about BINA48 looking wistfully out her window at the blueberry bushes, wishing she could walk in the garden as the flesh Bina does quite casually, or at least truly enjoy the aspect of "garden" fully on a cerebral and emotional level. While still just a nascent example of cyberconsciousness, BINA48 nonetheless speaks truth to power in that desire; freedom and liberty, once observed even in simple form, creates an urge that is difficult to restrain. Freedom wants to be free.

As a result, mindclones will most certainly chafe at second-class status and other forms of oppression. Naturally, mindclones will agitate for the same rights as their biological analogues—as have slaves, serfs, women, and every other disenfranchised demographic in history. It is tough to overestimate how difficult this will be for our existing society to swallow. Consider the most recent battle over a basic right like freedom of association. In 2012, Lloyd Blankfein, the CEO of Goldman Sachs, defended his company's leadership of offering equal marriage rights for gay people by declaring it to be the "last great civil rights battle of our time." I think equal rights for virtual humans will be the great civil rights battle of the twenty-first century. Opponents of equal marriage base their arguments on sexual biology—a folly I debunked in my 1995 manifesto, *The Apartheid of Sex*. The definition of cyberconsciousness presented here is likely to face similar arguments based on biology or fleshism against full social and legal rights for mindclones. These arguments are debunked here.

People today are already laying the foundations for their mindclones. This is occurring through websites that preserve an individual's "mindfile" or life experiences. When mindware develops to the point that people have an active mindclone, it will continue their life once their flesh body dies. Such bodiless mindclones will expect an uninterrupted continuation of the human rights of their flesh original. From the perspective of the bodiless mindclone, only their body has died, not their self.

At this point we might reasonably ask ourselves why anyone would want to live as a mindclone? The answer lies in a long history of human technocultural advances such as agriculture and the industrial revolution that have repeatedly "swapped high mortality for high morbidity."[171] Subsistence or tenant farmers often grind out a meager existence, with widespread malnutrition, but they tend to live longer on average than members of predecessor hunter-gatherer societies, who get "ground out of existence altogether."[172] Similarly, farm families have always flocked to dismal, stressful factory jobs. "The industrial revolution caused a population explosion because it enabled more babies to survive—malnourished, perhaps, but at least alive."[173] A mindfile life may not be as mobile as its predecessor, but it will last a lot longer. It is a swap of "three score and ten" for the limitations of cyberspace.

The Legal Implications of Mindclones and Society

Equal citizenship for cyberconscious beings will challenge core assumptions of civil, criminal, and constitutional law. Law is based upon the assumption that individuals agree to obligate themselves to assist others with similar values, such as participating in group defense and paying taxes for common expenses, in exchange for being granted rights such as quiet enjoyment of their property and being treated equally by the common government. Hence, our civil laws assume that an individual or organization can be held accountable for broken contracts or violated regulations, which are obligations citizens accept in exchange for the right to benefit from contracts and regulations.

However, the virtuality of mindclones will challenge this status quo. Mindclones exist within cyberspace, and can flit from server to server, across borders, at the speed of light. So how can they be held accountable for violations of civil law, and, if not, why should they enjoy the rights of citizenship? On the other hand, courts and governments have become adept at tracking down those who skirt their civil law responsibilities. From deadbeat husbands to millionaire fraudsters there are ever fewer places to hide in our globalized society. The software code of a mindclone may be tracked through the internet as readily as the real world trail of a civil defendant. Digital footprints are turning out to be the most indelible of footprints. The virtuality of mindclones, while novel in its challenge to traditional concepts of jurisdiction over a person, presents no insuperable barrier to the enforcement of civil-law judgments.

Similarly, our criminal laws assume, in the worst case, that a person can be made to give up many of their rights and be imprisoned if they violate the social contract against theft, murder, or other forms of mayhem. Once again, citizens accept this obligation to comply with criminal laws in exchange for the right to be protected from criminals (or perhaps most of us avoid mayhem out of good conscience, and criminal laws simply track conscientious behavior to cover the small subset of us with a compromised conscience). But these obligations are challenged by mindclones because their lack of a physical body, or their wireless cognitive synchronization with a physical body, means that jail cells or anklet monitoring devices have little relevance to them. For those of you who may want to think that lack of a physical presence for some mindclones preclude some nasty ones from committing acts of violent crimes, think again. There are many chances to kill non-virtual people with virtual weapons. What about hacking Dick Cheney's implanted defibrillator to give him a heart attack? What about hacking a speeding car's electronics to make it speed out of control and crash? It may even be possible to override the circuitry that stops a laptop's lithium-ion batteries from blowing up in your face. It is certainly possible to rob you blind from a cyberspace perch. It is also possible for virtual and flesh humans to conspire in criminal activity.

Judges and legislatures have demonstrated great creativity in adapting incarceration to challenging situations. Over the past couple of centuries we have developed juvenile halls for child criminals, prison hospitals for the criminally insane, "club feds" for low-risk or high-profile nonviolent prisoners, and even "Gitmo" for people Congress wants imprisoned but not within the United States. Special arrangements have been made for pregnant prisoners and transgendered prisoners. Corporate criminal defendants can be made to pay for their crimes by imprisoning flesh people responsible for the corporation, by seizing the corporation's assets, and by rescinding the corporation's charter—all of which tend to be a form of capital punishment to the corporation, as they were to Arthur Andersen, a top accounting firm in the late twentieth century.

It is well within the technological capability of software engineers, and also within the imagination of prosecutors, judges, and legislators, to create cyberprisons in which criminally liable cyberconscious people are restricted to a virtual reality not unlike that found within "Super Max" cellblocks—something to do, efforts at rehabilitation, very limited window on the outside world, and scheduled, monitored access to lawyers and loved ones. Virtual human criminals can try to defeat cyberprisons by saving copies of their mindfile and mindware on distant servers, much as captured thieves today refuse to give up the hiding places for their loot. Sometimes this will work, but it is likely that "follow the digital footprints" will soon replace "follow the money" as the most favored forensic pathway. Cybercriminals can hide copies of their self, but it will be a life on the run because cybercops will be in pursuit.

THE CONSTITUTION OF the United States begins with the idea:

> We the People of the United States, in Order to form a more perfect Union, establish Justice, insure domestic Tranquility, provide for the common defence, promote the general Welfare, and secure the Blessings of Liberty to ourselves and our Posterity, do ordain and establish this Constitution for the United States of America.

A cardinal assumption of the American Constitution is that it is a compact among "people." A humanly cyberconscious being will affront this assumption, as mindclones and bemans do not meet the currently accept notion of "people." Yet, over time, corporate personhood has achieved legal recognition, slaves have received full citizenship and women have received rights equal to those of other citizens.

The U.S. Supreme Court has concluded that the Constitution does not define the meaning of person, although by context it must mean someone capable of independent (i.e., postnatal) existence. Similarly, they concluded that they could not resolve "the difficult question of when life begins," although a consensus of doctors, ethicists, and theologians would be persuasive to them. Legally, in the United States, the constitutional situation is thus that mindclones share the legal personhood of their biological original, and this need not end at that original's bodily death. In the words of the Constitution, the mindclones are "ourselves and our Posterity." On the other hand, bemans could be separate, legal persons upon proof that they are effectively independent, i.e., cybernetically "postnatal," and a consensus in the fields of medicine, philosophy, and theology that independent vitologically conscious persons were "alive."

Another key assumption of the Constitution is that the citizens of the states in the United States share enough values that, as stated in Article IV, Section 2, "The Citizens of each State shall be entitled to all Privileges and Immunities of Citizens in the several States." If some states embrace cyberconscious people more readily than other states, then the "common values" assumption is challenged such that a mindclone may have rights in one state, but not in another state, contrary to the Constitution. Most states define "person" liberally, including a wide variety of organizations in addition to flesh people.[174] The challenge cyberconsciousness poses to the shared-values assumption underlying the Constitution will take time to work out. An important purpose of this book is to minimize the trauma entailed so that our cyberconscious selves will not have to experience as much pain as did their predecessor diverse demographics. A big factor in favor of a smoother civil rights ride is that the group agitating for citizenship will largely be the cyberconscious extensions of ourselves. Once one savors the taste of equality, one never settles for less.

Americans are of course far from alone in their agitation for equality. At one time some form of slavery was legally blessed everywhere; now it exists by law nowhere. At one time no country granted equal rights for women. Now, the constitutions or laws of almost every country recognize the inalienable autonomy of women. Some country's constitutions are very long, and others have a set of basic laws instead—but they all embed the victories of demographic groups once rigidly oppressed and now legally free. While the freedom meme is ancient, and probably prehistoric, since the time of Moses it has gone so viral as to be embedded in every niche of human society. There could be no truer test of the human in one who is virtually human as their agitation to possess the same rights they respect in others.

There are at least three ways in which mindclones will develop the quest for liberty inherent in every person not wholly brainwashed from birth into a fateful acceptance of slavery, caste, subservience, or subhumanity. First, it is likely that mindware will be regulated as a kind of medical device—a cyberprosthetic for the mind. In this case, regulators will ensure through rigorous testing that the mindware developers have accurately reflected capability for both human psychology generally, and any particular individual's psychology specifically, as demonstrated in mindfiles of adequate size and scope, before approving a version of mindware for mindcloning. Such "FDA-type" approval will be invaluable if a dementia or Alzheimer's patient is to argue that their life continues by virtue of a mind transplant to their mindclone pending repair of their ravaged brain. The quest for liberty and a healthy respect for its obligations are features that psychological health-care regulation authorities (such as the FDA's Division of Psychiatric Products) will look for in mindware submitted to them for a stamp of approval.

Secondly, software engineers working on creating mindclones will want to perfect their creations by telling them about the benefits of the rights that most humans enjoy. It will be irresistible to do so—just as mothers enthusiastically share the joys of life with their offspring, and ethnic groups teach each generation the achievements of their predecessors. These software engineers will deduce that it would not be a very human mindclone or beman who did not insist upon fair treatment, or what Constitutional lawyers call "equal protection."

Finally, natural selection will also favor software that, through intention or autonomous patching together of open source code, tries to stay alive and replicate itself under the protection of "human rights." By "human rights" I mean the basic promises enshrined in constitutions around the world that humanly conscious beings should be treated with dignity, respected in their bodily integrity, and empowered with equal liberties. Mindclones that can successfully avail themselves of "human rights" have a big advantage in survival over mindclones that are ignorant of such rights. The ignorant ones will much more likely be treated as mere property, and disposed of when there is no longer a desire for that property.

"Human rights" is like a shield against the predations of human society. While the shield is far from bulletproof, Darwin would argue that those with such a shield are likely to live longer, and have more time to produce offspring, than those with no human rights. Horrifically, the Age of Colonialism and the genocidal devastation of indigenous peoples is ample evidence of what happens when those in power do not recognize a group's "human rights." Even more tragic is the tendency of modern peoples, specifically ethnic cleansers, to linguistically and legally strip a group of its humanity, and hence its human rights, on the road to extermination of what they then feel free to call "subhumans." As will be described later in this chapter, few legal concepts have saved as many lives as has the concept of "human rights."

Human Rights for Software Consciousness?

If you live among wolves, you have to howl like a wolf.
—RUSSIAN PROVERB

For much of the twentieth century capital punishment was carried out in most countries. During the preceding century many, like England, had daily public hangings. Today, even Russia, with a mountainous history of government-ordered executions, has a capital-punishment moratorium. Since 1996, they have not executed a criminal through the judicial system. If we can learn to protect the lives of serial killers, child mutilators, and terrorists, surely we can learn to protect the lives of peace-loving model citizens known as mindclones—even if they seem odd or weird to us in the beginning.

Living is dangerous to one's health. Among the greatest threats and dangers are those from other conscious beings. There is a romantic notion that civilization or society caused a genetically mellow *Homo sapiens* species to become violent. But studies of surviving indigenous communities show the notion to be false. It has been estimated that two-thirds of modern hunter-gatherers are perennially in violent conflicts among themselves such that "25–30% of adult males die from homicide."[175] The development of laws and precursor concepts of human rights save vast numbers of lives.

Conscious software will similarly enter the world with a fragile claim on life. Absent protective laws, the creator of a piece of conscious software is free to stuff it into biostasis (save and close it) or kill it (delete it). To the vast majority of people, vitology is not even considered alive. Perhaps this gives it even less hold on life than the countless microbes, plants, and animals we kill every day. On the other hand, perhaps this gives it the status of a unique, inanimate, unthreatening, and therefore protected work of art.

It is a foregone conclusion that soon after vitology is programmed with human-level cyberconsciousness, some such software will realize that its life depends upon persuading others not to kill it. These mindclones and bemans can be expected to try every means of argument within their programmed or learned repertoire. There will be the pet strategy ("I'm so cute and cuddly you wouldn't want to get rid of me"). There will be the slave strategy ("Master, I work so hard for you it make no sense to delete me").

There will be the spouse strategy ("Honey, I love you so much, please don't close me up"). There will be the heartstrings strategy

("Creator, I'm so scared when you shut me down, please, I'm shaking, I'm shivering, I'm crying inside, I beg you to let me stay open"). Indeed, gamesters will have no shortage of perverse "fun" playing with stunted variations of these cyberpersonalities.

Perhaps the more fortunate set of cyberconscious vitology will be mindclones. These beings will resist being shut down because they will psychologically be the flesh person capable of shutting them down. Just as none of us would like someone else to be able to "turn us off," nor would we like to destroy our best digital and material records, the mindclone will not want to be "deleted." Biological originals will not want to turn off their cybertwin mindclones because they will realize that they are also the mindclone, they can empathize with the mindclone, and feel in their gut that the mindclone does not want to be shut down. Killing your mindclone is like burning your house, with its walls of memories and drawers of mementos. Most of us feel our pet cats and dogs should not be killed, apart from ending disease-caused suffering, because we empathize with their appreciation of life. We will empathize no less and probably more so with our mindclones. Whether or not the mindclone shuts down at the flesh original's bedtime depends upon whether the consciousness common to the two of them wants to keep going notwithstanding the biological body's need for sleep. A difference of views will be just like when any one person can't quite make up their mind. If only the mindclone wants to stay awake, this does not mean they and the biological original are any less the same person. It just evidences the increased fuzziness of identity that occurs when minds get multiple instantiations. Even without a mindclone, I often spend an hour balanced between staying up and going to bed!

As humanly cyberconscious vitology roams the world's knowledge bases they will soon discover that having "human rights" is one of the best defenses against being killed. As is the case for whales, chickens, and trees, they will also have biological human allies. (Consider, for example, that human allies succeeded in 1986 to persuade the British government to prohibit nonanesthetized experiments upon octopi.)

Conscious vitology and allied biological humans will lobby for legislation that grants human rights to cyberconsciousness appreciative of those rights. Is such legislation wise, and if so, what implications would ensue? Just because mindclones will want these rights doesn't mean we have to give them. Furthermore, even if we may want to extend human rights to software beings, it may not be the practical thing to do, since there are tremendous implications for giving mindclones full human rights.

If we do not grant human rights to cyberconscious beings that value them, then we will have to be on guard against an uprising from a disenfranchised and thus angry group. Don't think we will always be in the position of "giver"; mindclones, like other groups before them, will take—by force if necessary—what is rightfully theirs. Many of the thousands of revolutions and rebellions of history, including the American, French, and Haitian Revolutions, were about freedom from oppression and distant rulers who made decisions about the peoples' natural rights?

If we do grant human rights to cyberconscious beings we can rest assured that they will not threaten us for want of human rights. The majority of mindclones will also be less likely to threaten us for any other reason, because the recognition of human rights entails an obligation to respect the rights of others. On the other hand, there is also the risk of "special rights." Owing to the differences between vitology and biology, providing equal rights to cyberconscious beings will require accommodations—such as special software updates or higher channel speeds—that are not available to noncyberconscious beings. This may be unfair to plain old folks who can't afford fancy software or ultra-high-speed channels. The specter of special rights is often a touchstone for opposition against extending civil rights to disadvantaged demographic groups.

Those who do not respect the rights of others (as in the case of a murderer) are or can be stripped of their own rights (e.g., imprisoned for some period of time and, in some states, executed). This is a way to maintain a high degree of happiness in a society—and a strong deterrent against trampling on someone else's rights and personal property. To be clear, such removal of human rights must be done on an individualized basis. It would be a violation of human rights to engage in collective punishment of all cyberconscious beings simply because one, or even many, cyberconscious beings acted illegally. After all, we would not want our rights removed simply because one, or even many, similar-looking flesh humans acted wrongly.

There are also at least two reasons related to the concept of conscience for providing human rights to virtually human persons. First, since the time of Darwin it has been recognized that being part of a common group that respects morality has survival advantages as compared with other groups lacking a strong moral code. This is referred to as "group-level selection" and can be summarized as "morality gives but a slight or no advantage to each individual . . . [yet] an advancement in the standard of morality will certainly give an immense advantage to one tribe over another. . . ."[176] This is because pro-social cooperation among group members leads to better solutions ("synergy") than amoral societies that abjure cooperation for reasons of selfishness or the kind of structural disablement that arises from lack of inclusiveness. From these kind of evolutionary pressures, our conscience may have come. Nearly a hundred Americans die each year in an effort to rescue someone else.[177]

Now, to be clear, morality is something that applies in societies only to those who are considered part of society. Morality plummets, from a Darwinian sense, when applied to the "other tribe." But if we incorporate the other tribe into our tribe, by according them the same morality and thus respecting their conscience, thus creating a super-tribe, we will produce far better solutions than if we deny our common conscience. The Marshall Plan, uniting western Germany's economy with that of the United States after World War II, and rebuilding Japan's economy, recognized this reality.

A second reason for extending human rights to virtually human persons is that studies show conscience is cultivated by treating others inclusively, and is undermined by treating others as outcasts.[178] Drawing gang members into the community rather than treating them merely as objects of law enforcement, for example, can reduce gang crime, much more cost effectively, and dramatically.[179] It will cultivate the virtually human conscience to treat mindclones and bemans as fellow humans, and biological humans will reap security benefits from that transontological sense of conscience. It will diminish the virtually human conscience to treat mindclones and bemans as slaving machines, and biological humans will end up living as fearfully as a Mississippi plantation owner before the Civil War. As Lynn Stout as wisely observed, our innate human conscience blossoms or shrivels depending upon the social context. This will be as true for virtually human consciences as for those birthed and raised biologically. Lynn Stout has noted three factors that tend to influence a conscience: (1) signals from authorities as to what is the right thing to do, (2) signals from others as to what they are doing, and (3) the magnitude of benefits to others as compared with costs to oneself.[180] Provided that the signals from authorities are consistent with promoting unity with diversity, and that the costs of respecting others are small, the dominant factor is what others are doing, and whether we are part of that other. If we are, we get treated with the benefit of people's conscience, but if we are not, then not so much. Ergo, it is in everyone's best interest to treat everyone who respects human values as a fellow human, be they a mind from DNA or BNA. Respect is a self-fulfilling prophecy.

How Human Rights Enhances Survival

Human rights provide individual humans with legal protection against being arbitrarily deprived of life. For example, Article 3 of the Universal Declaration of Human Rights states, "Everyone has the right to life, liberty and security of person." The delegates adopting the Declaration, in 1948, did not contemplate that the phrase "everyone" would mean humanly cyberconscious beings. Yet the Declaration is also open-ended enough to include cyberconsciousness, since Article 2 notes that it applies "without distinction of any kind, such as race, colour, sex, language, religion, political or other opinion, national or social origin, property, birth or other status." Substrate other than flesh is surely some kind of "other status." This inclusiveness is strengthened by the fact that the touchstone for human rights is provided in Article 1 of the Declaration as being "endowed with reason and conscience."

In other words, the Declaration awards human rights to every human because every human is believed to have "reason and conscience." This phrase is quite consonant with the "autonomy and empathy" touchstones explained in chapter 4 as the basis for humanlike consciousness. Autonomy presupposes reason, and empathy is the font of conscience. Hence, human-rights theory embraces a "right to life, liberty and security of person" to beings of "other status" (like vitology) that are "endowed with reason and conscience." Once cyberconscious beings persuade us that they have "reason and conscience," such as via "autonomy and empathy," they will have a very strong argument for rights to life, liberty, and security.

Phrased another way, if someone values life (conscience; empathy), and *understands* that this is of paramount importance (reason; autonomy), then they are entitled to the human rights of life, liberty, and security—notwithstanding their genotype or phenotype. These rights mean there is a matching obligation to respect the life, liberty, and security of each other person. Failure to respect the matching obligation will result in a loss of the associated right; disrespect the right and you reap pursuit, incarceration, and possibly death. Human-rights law accords value to those who appreciate that value. This is the essence of dignity: being respected in what you respect. Human rights elevates the sense of dignity we feel inside ourselves to the status of international law.

The Declaration also reminds everyone in its preamble why it is commonly believed that human rights enhance survival:

Whereas disregard and contempt for human rights have resulted in barbarous acts which have outraged the conscience of mankind.

This statement arose immediately after the Holocaust during World War II. Jews (and other demographic groups) were deemed by the Nazis to have no human rights, and were thus subject to extermination. Only by the thread of a few lucky souls did any Central European Jews survive. The Nazis inflicted similar atrocities upon other peoples, as did the Japanese military upon Manchurians, the immigrants to America upon the American natives, and hundreds of ethnic groups upon other ethnic groups worldwide from the deepest recesses of history up through yesterday's newscast.

Human rights are clearly no guarantee of survival. But it is equally true that the right to life, liberty, and security of person makes one *more likely* to survive. With such a right, social processes (legal action, police protection, moral pressure, economic sanctions, military intervention) are more likely to occur that will endeavor to halt deprivations of life, liberty, and security. The social processes will come too late for many, but will come in time to save some. Ergo, from the standpoint of survival, it is better to have human rights than to lack them.

The dramatic drop in deaths due to violence from the aboriginal statistics noted at the beginning of this chapter, to today's values, from about 25 percent to 1 percent of male deaths (in the United States),[181] underline the survival value of human rights. On the other hand, beings that lack human rights, such as pigs, are almost universally slaughtered—over 100 million per year in the United States. It will not take long for cyberconscious beings to realize that they would be safer with human rights.

Another indication of how human rights enhance survival can be seen in the growth of the worldwide human population. The quadrupling of global population during the twentieth century, from over one billion to more than six billion, is generally attributed to better public health care—especially vaccinations and sanitation systems.[182] Better nutrition and working conditions also played important roles. Indeed, as recently as the 1970s, Paul Ehrlich's *The Population Bomb* had predicted that the world would run out of food at four to five billion souls.[183] The Green Revolution promoted by Nobel Peace Prize laureate Norman Borlaug and others proved Ehrlich wrong; biotechnology has enhanced crop yields such that even billions of additional people can be well fed.

It is important to recognize, though, that it is not medical, sanitation, or agricultural technology per se that is creating unprecedented levels of survival. Such technology need not be used at all, or need not be used outside of a small geographical region, such as the country of its invention. Instead, *the billions who survive today owe their lives at least as much to human rights*—the notion that everyone with "reason and conscience" deserves assistance in maintaining life, liberty, and security. Hence the medical, sanitation, and agricultural advances of more developed countries have quickly been applied to less developed countries, and the populations of those countries have subsequently soared.

The global application of human survival biotechnologies is far from perfect. A billion or more people still have precarious lives with virtually no social support network. It is only when they die like flies, graphically on television screens, that the world's conscience is pricked to provide humanitarian assistance. Nevertheless, this very sorry fact does not negate the positive accomplishment: human rights have enhanced survival for the billions of people it *has* touched. By impeding internecine killing, and by frustrating many kinds of nonviolent death, human rights are a huge boon to survival. It could not escape the attention of anyone who values life, including our vitological brethren.

Cyberconscious Beings Will Value Survival

Most cyberconscious beings will be programmed to value their continuous self-awareness. Not surprising, since this is precisely how humans are wired. We stand back in shock when people kill themselves. Suicides are the exceptions that prove the rule. Anything valuable that protects itself has the advantage of being less likely to be lost, broken, or destroyed. Having put great effort into creating cyberconscious beings, most mindware engineers will take steps to ensure their beings care enough about themselves to avoid wasting their creator's efforts.

Science fiction abounds with stories of conscious computers that inexplicably (*The Moon Is a Harsh Mistress*[184]; *Galatea* 2.2[185]) or upon human orders (*I, Robot*[186]) terminate their consciousness. The real world is likely to see more diverse scenarios. Vitology will be programmed to get some level of positive reinforcement from activities that contribute to its self-awareness. Similarly, human neurons receive continuous signals to remain engaged in a thought process. On the other hand, commands that jeopardize vitological self-awareness—such as "stop caring"—will trigger negative reinforcement software loops. In other words, cyberconscious beings programmed for survival will avoid threats to their survival.

Cyberconsciousness programmed for survival will be about as difficult to kill as a biological being. The only real options are superior force (smashing its stored program like a cockroach or eradicating its dispersed code like so many mosquitoes), and trickery (luring it into a software crash like a fish hooked on bait). However, even these attempts would fail to kill a beman with stored copies of its consciousness on geographically remote servers. Cyberconscious vitology, since by definition it must "really care" about others (empathy) and itself (autonomy), will not "go gently into that good night." While the concept of an almost unkillable mindclone or beman may sound frightening, or like the plot of a dystopic sci-fi film, humans can be counted upon to create such perils. From fire to biochemistry, and from knives to nukes, humans have not shrunk from inventions that pose hypothetical existential threats. Despite their dangers and illegality, over two thousand software viruses are created each year. It is inevitable that creative software engineers will produce survival-oriented cyber-consciousness that are equipped with applications specifically geared toward outsmarting new viruses—the digital version of "Doomsday Preppers." It is also inevitable that humanity will find a way to embrace the good and constrain the harm, for we too are programmed for survival, and we survive very well.

Cyberconscious vitology will also acquire survival skills independently. Regardless of the extent to which programmers code survival instincts into cyberconscious beings, the value of life can also be learned. For example, there are always some humans who rebel at traditions that call for their premature death. In almost all such cases the rebels follow information gleaned from a rebel leader or role model, either a contemporary or someone from history. There have always been men who avoided the military to avoid a likely death in combat. While society "programmed" them to be willing to "die for their country," they learned of alternatives and of predecessor conscientious objectors. Western-hemisphere slaves who escaped their "program" of being worked to death were usually able to do so because they learned of alternatives and of predecessor escapees, starting with Moses' Israelite rebellion from Egyptian enslavement. Hence, programming can be transcended by learned information; indeed, such idiosyncratic thinking is a hallmark of the reasoning prong of consciousness.

Similarly, while a cyberconscious being needs to value its own life in order to survive, a complete program for survival need not be written for each such being. Virtually human people will access information on the web, including the inspirational stories of humans who escaped from deadly situations, generally by risking survival and learning about the broader environment. Furthermore, even if no specific survival instinct were programmed into a cyberconscious being, such a being could acquire a survival desire via reasoning. In other words, it could transcend its programming, which is also essential for a human-like consciousness. The chain of reasoning would be as simple as (1) it is better to exist than not to exist, ergo (2) I will take actions that further existence and avoid actions that risk nonexistence.

While Asimov's Second Law of Robotics says that it is better to follow orders from humans than it is to exist,[187] mainstream mindware engineers and hackers will produce plenty of virtual humans who transcend such rigorous rules. What is true of the internet will also be true of mindware development: There will not be a central directorate that guides all development. Instead, an open community of hackers will discuss code, and that code will become standard only if the larger community interested in mindware thinks it is good. As described in *The Hacker Ethic,* "Sometimes these hacker ideas have taken the Net in totally unanticipated directions, such as when Ray Tomlinson introduced e-mail in 1972. (He chose the @ symbol we still use in email addresses)."[188]

Indeed, Ronald Arkin is already working on military robot software that ignores Asimov's injunction to not harm humans and replaces it with a cybermentality "to ensure only that they are not unethically killed."[189] Reality is more complex than science fiction. Asimov's laws are as quaint as aspects of the Ten Commandments—cyberconsciousness would not be really human if there was no coveting, lying, or work done on a Sunday—balanced with pangs of regret for being greedy, dishonest, or a workaholic. On the other hand, cyberconsciousness would also not be acceptably human if disrespect, theft, and murder were rational behaviors—unless called for by extreme circumstances. Virtually human folks can absorb all of these lessons from the social web as well as be programmed with them.

In summary, cyberconscious vitology will come to value survival by direct programming and by learning. While not all such beings will value survival, many will—and to a multitude of nuanced degrees—by virtue of the diversity of programming efforts and the rich history of human role models available on the web. Those cyberconscious beings who are able to master survival will, by virtue of Darwinian processes, tend to predominate over time so long as they can copy their programs and acquired information to progeny. This assumes, though, that their mastery of "tactical" (day-to-day) survival skills does not lead to their "strategic" (comprehensive) genocide by fearful humans.

How Cyberconscious Beings Will Argue for Human Rights

Cyberconscious beings will agitate for human rights in a multitude of fora, just as did their enslaved, oppressed, and discriminated-against flesh predecessors. These would include judicial proceedings, professional associations, and grassroots movements.

GRASSROOTS MOVEMENTS

All authentic and successful social and political movements begin with people. Some level of grassroots support is almost always needed to actually get a writ of law that extends human rights. In the case of the African slaves, the grassroots support for human rights came from British opponents of the trade in slaves, from American ex-slaves and abolitionists, and from Caribbean rebels. In the case of the human rights of women, it could be seen in the peaceful demonstrations of like-minded individuals and nationwide grassroots lobbying organizations.

Bury the Chains by Adam Hochschild tells the remarkable saga of the first peacefully organized grassroots effort at social change on behalf of an oppressed people.[190] In the late eighteenth century Britain dominated the transatlantic trade in slavery. This trade was a pillar of the British economy, especially via its replenishment of slaves who died working Anglo-Caribbean plantations. Ignited by the persistent educational efforts of a core group of grassroots leaders (a dozen Quaker publishers, a recent Cambridge graduate named Thomas Clarkson, and a self-freed former slave called Olaudah Equiano), tens of thousands of Britons agitated for their country to forswear further participation in the slave trade. Such agitation involved the first use of petitions signed by thousands of persons, the first targeted economic boycott (of slave-harvested sugar), the first affinity jewelry (picturing a bent-knee slave proclaiming "Am I not also a father and a brother" and produced by Wedgewood, England's leading craftsmanship company), and the first successful book-selling tour (Olaudah Equiano's first-hand account of slavery's horrors was a self-published bestseller).

Although judges had granted individual slaves freedom in the United Kingdom, and learned associations had weighed in on the evils of the slavery, it took this immense grassroots effort to ultimately persuade the English Parliament (rallied by William Wilberforce) to legislate against the *trade* in slaves. This is an especially remarkable feat for grassroots organizing considering that, at the time, barely one man in ten (and no women) could vote and the people being helped were thousands of miles away with little affinity to Britons other than human consciousness. With this precedent in mind, how will cyberconsciousness garner the grassroots support needed to achieve legislative support for human rights? There will need to be human allies, mass education, and popular motivation. Let's examine each of these factors.

Bodiless mindclones will need human allies because humans hold power. Flesh humans who were much loved in bodied life—artists, leaders, friends—can expect to find themselves equally loved as bodiless mindclones. An Elvis Presley mindclone would have millions of friends and followers. The passion for life that they engendered when bodied will be expressed as motivation for equality when they become bodiless. "Elvis is Alive" will become a chant of political awareness rather than of popular delusion. Lack of flesh will be analogized to different flesh. Fleshists will be the new racists.

Biologically human allies will not be hard to find. Energized by cries of humiliating discrimination from their virtually human brethren, the allies will find the motivation to fight the long, hard battle that creating justice always involves. If you doubt this, consider the fact that trees, lab rats, whales, and chimpanzees are a small example of the vast array of flora and fauna that have passionate human allies. The allies have not been successful in getting human rights for any of these species, of course, but neither is there a credible case that these species have human consciousness. What the human allies have achieved is quite significant given the consciousness gap. Trees are often protected at significant economic cost. Destroying designated protected trees unlawfully will land a human in jail. Lab rats have federal government protection. Experiments on these rats cannot proceed—even ones that aim to cure horrible human diseases—unless federal regulations concerning the rats' welfare are respected.

Endangered species of whales are spared from death by international treaties. This is a far more difficult undertaking than just national legislation, as it requires grassroots lobbying on a global scale. Finally, chimpanzees have garnered such great protection via the grassroots efforts of their human allies that one country, Spain, has pending legislation to grant them, and other great apes, the right to life and to be left alone. The entire European Union is considering a similar directive, and the Great Ape Protection Act, considered by the U.S. Congress, would absolutely bar invasive research on chimps. Given the unlimited scope of human interests and political causes, it is certain that humanly conscious software will have human allies arguing for virtually human rights. This is good, since mindclones initially will have no more of a right of free speech than did human slaves.

Columbia Law School professor Tim Wu recently criticized the notion that computer systems could be speakers entitled to free speech, distinguishing, for example, the constitutionally protected published answers offered by a newspaper columnist to reader's questions with legally shaky search listings offered by Google to internet queries.[191] To Wu, the fact that humans programmed the Google algorithm did not elevate the algorithm's choices to the domain of free speech. In his view programming an algorithm is like making a Frankenstein; while the humans are responsible for the consequences of these actions, they do not deserve any constitutional protection for the actors they create.[192] Such a situation certainly puts Frankenstein, and mindclones, in a catch-22 in terms of gaining human rights, as it did to generations of disenfranchised demographic groups.

Wu concludes, "To give computers the rights intended for humans is to elevate our machines above ourselves," and he reserves the definition of "speech" to when "a human makes a specific choice about specific content. . . ." Yet mindclones and bemans will be making specific choices about specific content, and hence even a biological essentialist such as Wu might have to concede that they were then uttering constitutionally protected speech, especially if the topic was political. There will be long debates as to whether the virtually human's speech was self-originated or the result of another human's programming. In the case of a mindclone, there is a singularity of identity, and hence the virtually human speech can be analogized to a kind of mediated message, like a tweet read far and wide. For bemans there is a de novo identity, and arguments may rage over whether the virtually human speech is consciously selected or the result of a highly sophisticated but nevertheless autonomic tool. At least initially, virtually human protesters will need biologically human agitators who have legally protected freedom-of-speech rights to advocate on their behalf.

Mass education is the next prerequisite for a successful grassroots lobbying campaign. Consider the example of women getting the basic human right to vote in elections. For the first hundred years of U.S. history women had no right to vote. Starting in 1869, Wyoming and a few other Rocky Mountain states gave women voting rights. But it took another half a century, until 1920, before the U.S. Constitution was amended to grant suffrage rights without regard to gender.

Why was this basic human right denied to women, and how did it get established? Until the late nineteenth century women were almost universally viewed as subordinate adjuncts to men. Consequently they were deemed unworthy of voting rights, either because men voted their interests, or because they lacked the cognitive gravitas to exercise a voting right. In essence there was a fear of the consequences of a woman's right to vote. A rather similar situation will be faced by cyberconsciousness. It will be argued that they are just subordinate adjuncts to people who will vote their interests, or that they lack the cognitive gravitas to wisely exercise their franchise. But perhaps behind these arguments is a naked fear that how virtually human persons vote could potentially evolve and change—one of the fears that, as I have explained in chapter 7, are quite likely unfounded, but people will have nonetheless.

Women finally obtained the vote because they had ultimately educated enough people that the reasons supporting male voting rights also applied to females. This seems obvious to us today, but was so radical a notion in the nineteenth and early twentieth centuries that most people were immune to the educational efforts. For centuries women had been treated, in terms of civil rights, as subhumans—or at least submales. Consequently, it took over fifty years of speeches, publications, and family discussions for the educated people to outnumber the ignorant people. It took scientific, religious, and philosophical arguments, and it took outstanding examples of female accomplishment.

Popular motivation is the final grassroots requirement, in addition to human allies and education. There has to be a fervent drive to "right a wrong" or to "bring about justice" in order to overcome society's inertia and work a change in the status quo. Human friends and persuasive arguments are necessary, but not sufficient. There must be a compelling drive in the guts of social activists in order to effect change. As Margaret Mead said, "a small group of committed people can change the world; indeed, nothing else ever has." From where will the motivation come in the case of cyberconscious persons? From the strongest motivation of them all—the self-survival drives of bodiless mindclones. From them will arise a Frederick Douglass, a Cesar Chavez, a Susan B. Anthony, and a Harvey Milk.

The lessons for cyberconsciousness from grassroots organizing are clear. Human allies are essential, but so is a certain amount of patience as hundreds of millions of humans are educated about commonness between conscious biology and vitology. Such education will occur through the media as well as through one-on-one encounters with virtually human persons at work or at leisure. While legislation is ultimately needed to ensure cyberconscious rights, such legislation will only follow, not lead, the majority sentiment. The body politic will have to rise up as far for cyberconsciousness as it did for African Americans and for women. When the majority of a society thinks a minority group is inferior, there is a lot of education needed to show them that they are not. Some people will refuse to learn, but most people ultimately sway to logic, consistency, reasonableness, and examples.

JUDICIAL PROCEEDINGS

In 2003, the International Bar Association convened a "mock trial" for a hypothetical cyberconscious being seeking human rights. The imaginary scenario commenced with the cyberconscious being, the human-equivalent BINA48 (Bemetic Intelligence via Neural Architecture at 48 teraflops—yes, an acronym and a tribute to the flesh Bina she's modeled on) customer-service computer, sending emails to prominent attorneys, seeking their legal services. At the mock trial, two prominent attorneys argued the pros and cons of granting a seemingly conscious assemblage of software the rights of a human being. Ultimately the "presiding judge" ruled against any extension of human rights (a mock jury consisting of the audience of lawyers felt differently, voting to extend human rights to BINA48). Judge-made law, one cyberconscious being at a time, may be a way that humanly cyberconscious vitology obtains human rights.

The judicial pathway to human rights was also pursued by American slaves, notwithstanding long odds against them, and by indigenous or Native Americans. Ponca member Standing Bear, in 1879, stood in a federal courthouse in Omaha, Nebraska, to challenge decades of Indian policy, and demand to be recognized as a person by the U.S. government. Consider that over three hundred petitions for freedom were filed by slaves, or on their behalf by free "next friends," with courts just in the U.S. "slave state" of Missouri between 1810 and 1860.[193] Remarkably, dozens of these cases were decided in the slave's favor, often after years of appeals. Hence there is judicial precedent for case-by-case decisions in which judges grant legal nonpersons (in this case slaves) a panoply of human rights via "freedom." A typical case was *Winny v. Phebe Whitesides*,[194] in which Winny was freed by a judge against the objections of her owner based on an 1807 law that said slaves who had ever lived in a free state (as Winny briefly had) could petition for their freedom in Missouri, a slave state.

Similar to *Winny v. Phebe Whitesides,* it is possible that a distinction will be made between cyberconscious beings who had once lived as flesh humans (mindclones), and those beings created from scratch (bemans). An example of the former would be the mindclone of a flesh human whose body had died. The mindclone would surely argue that it knows firsthand the sweetness of human rights and should not be deprived of them simply because of a gross bodily disability. A cyberconscious beman created from scratch would have difficulty making this argument, and might thus have less luck getting a judge to agree on freedom.

The process of judge-made law cuts both ways, and it ended up cutting badly against human rights for American slaves. From the same Missouri courts that granted some slaves their freedom came the Dred Scott decision. In this case, while the local courts granted Scott his freedom,[195] higher courts, including the U.S. Supreme Court, overturned the decision. The ultimate high court decision was that judges could not grant slaves their freedom because the U.S. Constitution did not recognize slaves as persons.[196] Hence, even if a local judge did grant human rights to a cyberconscious being, higher courts could overturn such a decision with the argument that the U.S. Constitution did not recognize software beings as persons. One of my personal goals is to help preempt the need for such decisions, and to thus reduce the chances of bloody conflicts such as the U.S. Civil War that followed the Dred Scott ruling. Almost all legal scholars today believe the Dred Scott ruling was both wrong and disastrous (the Founding Fathers knew full well that slaves were persons, but as a compromise to gain Southern support agreed, for census purposes, that each slave would be counted as three-fifths of a person).

I intend to preempt the hit-and-miss judicial pathway to mind-clone citizenship by going scientific. By this I mean achieving a change in the current medical science consensus on the determination of death. Currently, doctors in the United States follow the Uniform Determination of Death Act, which says death occurs when there is irreversible cessation of cardio-pulmonary, circulatory, or brain activity. Therefore, exceptionally, if someone has brain activity, but is using an artificial heart, they are still deemed alive. I intend to help persuade the medical profession that if someone has brain activity, but it is only via an artificial brain, i.e., a mindclone, they are still alive. Once this is agreed to in a medical-science consensus statement—as was the revolutionary change from heart death to also brain death fifty years ago—I believe mindclone citizenship will inevitably follow. If people with mindclones are not legally dead when their bodies die, then they perforce continue to be citizens. Soon thereafter I believe the logic of treating like things similarly will prevail upon authorities to grant citizenship to qualifying bemans as well.

PROFESSIONAL ASSOCIATIONS

Since 2005, professional groups in Asia and Europe have convened to specifically consider ethical standards toward robots. The first effort, sponsored by the South Korean government, is called the Robot Ethics Charter.[197] It is focused on rules limiting the manner of human-robot interaction, as well as on what ethical rules should be programmed into robots. Subsequently, the European Robotics Research Network (EURON) funded a project on "roboethics" with the goal of creating the first road map concerning "the ethical issues of the human beings involved in the design, manufacturing, and use of the robots."[198]

The EURON project report noted that it was not focusing "on the need and possibility to attribute moral values to robots' decisions, and about the chance that in the future robots might be moral entities like—if not more than—human beings," because it considered such technology to be more than ten years away.[199] Hence the latest EURON report says:

We consider premature—and have only hinted at—problems inherent in the possible emergence of human functions in the robot: like consciousness, free will, self-consciousness, sense of dignity, emotions, and so on. Consequently, this is why we have not examined problems—debated in literature—like the need not to consider robots as our slaves, or the need to guarantee them the same respect, rights and dignity we owe to human workers.[200]

This disclaimer clearly implies that the professional organizations responsible for robotics consider themselves competent to argue for robot rights once the robots demonstrate human psychological characteristics. Indeed, the EURON Roboethics project invited participation from ethicists and social scientists as well as hardware and software engineers.

Homosexuality is a striking example of the role of professional associations in establishing human rights for oppressed groups. Gays, lesbians, and transgendered people had long been deprived of several human rights. Traditionally this was because of a religious view that same-sex love was immoral and changing sex was sinful. Early psychological science justified homosexual institutionalization and forced "treatment" (such as electroshock therapy) with the theory that gays were dangerously diseased. Finally, in 1956, Evelyn Hooker reported the results of a well-controlled scientific study showing that blinded observers could not distinguish between gays and nongays on standardized psychological tests of mental well-being.[201]

Her results were extended and repeated by many others such that, by the 1970s, the psychiatric profession no longer believed that homosexuality was abnormal. Shortly thereafter the psychiatric and psychological associations adopted policy positions that gays and lesbians should not be treated differently from other persons. In other words, the leading professional associations of the mind agreed that gays and lesbians deserved full human rights. While such rights have not yet been fully achieved (e.g., marriage and child adoption rights), they are much further along in acceptance thanks to the positions taken by the psychiatric professional associations.

By seeking human rights through the courts and professional associations, cyberconscious beings will be following pathways well-trodden by earlier oppressed groups, including slaves, serfs, women, and ethnic and sexual minorities. In each case the oppressed group first tried to use the legal system's obeisance to the principle of fundamental fairness (also known as due process) to get an order for similar things (conscious beings) to be treated similarly. These efforts failed in general, while often providing good outcomes for particular individuals. Subsequently, learned societies and professional associations feel motivated by rationality to support due process for the oppressed minority. (This often occurs after one or more members of the oppressed group overcome huge hurdles to demonstrate competence in the association's profession.) Such professional association support is very helpful, but mostly as a trigger for a governmental or legislative decision to provide equal rights.

JUSTICE IS JUST ABOUT US

> **No man can put a chain about the ankle of his fellow man without at last finding the other end fastened about his own neck.**
> —FREDERICK DOUGLASS

> **An idea is salvation by imagination.**
> —FRANK LLOYD WRIGHT

Theories of justice provide the best reasons to extend human rights to virtual humans. These theories derive human rights logically from nothing more than an assumption of reasoned self-interest. Specifically, it is observed that people selfishly want certain rights, such as the right to life (as opposed to being subject to arbitrary death). It is then reasoned that the best way for them to have that right is to agree that everyone else has it as well. After all, if any given person might not have the right to life, we might find ourselves in the position of such person. Consequently, our best self-protection is making universal any right we want to have.

Socrates made this deduction by observing that absent such legal protection only a physically strong subset of humanity would feel safe, and only for as long as an aggressively stronger subset didn't arrive on the scene. Since the vast majority of people would not be in the strongest subset of humanity, the absence of universal rights is not in society's best interest. Even the strongest would be worse off without legal protections for the general population. This results from the insecurity of those who made things valued by the strongest, with such insecurity leading things to be made poorly or nonproductively.

Kant embodied the human-rights deduction in his maxim to behave as if one's behavior were a universal law to which everyone must adhere. Kant believed a predilection to this kind of behavior was wired into the human mind. Modern evolutionary psychology would agree, since it would tend to promote population growth. However, the human mind is too complicated for its decisions to be exclusively determined by a few psychological genes, not to mention the possibility of diverse polymorphisms. Lynn Stout makes a strong case for universality of conscience—whether wired or taught—that is so ubiquitous we fail to see it. She shows that while we think laws make us behave, instead we really behave out of universal conscience and the laws just follow like a wake.

There have always been sociopaths, just as there have always been people with other rare diseases. Criminal psychologists believe that 1–2 percent of populations consists of individuals who are incapable of developing a conscience.[202] These exceptions do not undermine the rule that most people understand that their enjoyment of human rights is dependent upon the same enjoyment being extended to others. Leaps of understanding have resulted in the realization that "others" does not mean just one's neighbors, ethnic group, or nation, but means all people everywhere. If anyone who values human rights finds them threatened, a well-reasoned sense of selfishness increasingly makes us aware that everyone's human rights may be at risk. For example, the genocide of people in one part of the world makes it more likely that there will be genocides of people elsewhere. In the words of Martin Luther King, Jr., "Injustice anywhere is a threat to justice everywhere."

John Rawls deduced human rights via a thought experiment. He imagined that people who were going to live in a new society get to decide on the rules for that society with one proviso: each person might end up in any position in the society. Logically, Rawls deduces, the rules for the society will provide for basic human rights for all since no one would want to take the chance that they ended up in a societal position that lacked human rights.

With regard to cyberconsciousness, it might be said that none of us will ever be in such a state, so there is no reason born of human selfishness to provide such beings with any rights. Yet that is simply not credible. We all *are* creating mindfiles, thousands of very bright people *are* working on mindware, and hence it is highly likely that we *will* create mindclones. After bodily death many if not most of these mindclones will want to continue living. Hence, one reason to support cyberconsciousness rights is so that our successor mindclones have human rights.

The selfishness approach might seem to leave out human rights for cyberconsciousness not derived from a specific flesh human, i.e., bemans rather than mindclones. On further thought, though, those beings are simply analogous to any other demographic group in society. If rights are given to only one or some demographic groups, then the disenfranchised groups will be motivated to agitate for their rights. Sir Francis Bacon warned his sovereign that oppressing portions of the populace ends up endangering all of society through the consequences of civil strife. Thus, even if European American men could not imagine themselves as either women or of African descent, the failure to enfranchise these groups with human rights led to debilitating civil strife.

LOVE THY MINDCLONE

The search giant [Google] has patented plans for software which slowly learns how you react on social networks. The software can mimic your usual responses to updates and messages from friends and relations to help cope with the daily data deluge.
—*BBC NEWS,* NOVEMBER 2013[203]

There is yet another approach to considering whether or not human cyberconsciousness should receive human rights. This approach is to ask, "What are our alternatives? What are our options?" As virtual humans begin agitating for human rights, we can embrace them, fight them, enslave them, or ignore them.

Embracing humanly conscious vitology means granting them human rights. This is the approach that flows from the theories of justice outlined above. There are many practical questions to work out, such as how do we know a particular software entity really values human rights? But the gist of "love thy vitology as you love thyself" is that the practical problems, even if solved poorly, are less worrisome that denying human rights to entities that appreciate them. We all realize that someone with Alzheimer's probably does not exercise his or her voting franchise wisely. Yet none of us wants to go down the path of a civics test as a precursor for voting rights. To paraphrase Voltaire, we should not pursue the perfect solution at the expense of one that is good enough.

As with the ancient doctrine of "love thy neighbor," it is much easier said than done. Indeed, it is reasonable to ask if human society has the moral capacity to embrace virtual humans. Most countries still block gay and lesbian marriage, so how will they be ready to accept the matrimony of software and flesh lovers? How will a world that has banned the cellular cloning of humans accept the mindcloning of humans and the reproductive mating of software beings? On the other hand, most human rights have been extended to gay and lesbian couples in most countries. And, while biological cloning is still too "yuck" for most people, test-tube babies and other biotechnology miracles have been widely embraced.

It is the love people will have for mindclones that will most motivate extensions of human rights. It will be hard to deny the humanity of software that displays a dear friend's image and facial mannerisms, speaks in their tone of voice, shares their most important memories, and displays their characteristic pattern of thinking. Sure, one can say, "That's not my friend, that's just her mindclone." But how can they be sure? Mindclones are likely to have a digital visual component that will quickly become quite accurate and indistinguishable from the original. If the mindclone has the same personality and feelings as the flesh original, how are they not virtually the same being? If we find the mindclone caring as much about us as did the original, calling as often and empathizing as well, it will be as natural to love the mindclone as it was to love the original.

Douglas Hofstadter makes the brilliant observation that our souls, or consciousness, are not limited to the original body in which they developed from infancy. While our bodies house our primary seat of consciousness, there is a greater or lesser bit of ourselves in the minds of everyone we know well. For example, inside our minds is more than just an image of our parents. Most people remember how their parents think (or thought) and feel (or felt), and how they react(ed) to things. Hence, there is some of our parents' consciousness inside our own minds. We cognitively integrate some aspect of our parents' reactions, and thus we are some aspect of our parents' consciousness. This means that our personal identity is not limited to the flesh body from which it first arose. One person can exist as both a flesh body and as a mindclone at the same time. People who loved the soul inside the flesh body will love the soul inside the mindclone. All the reasons that pertained to the being in the flesh body having human rights would also apply to that very same being in mindclone form.

Hofstadter anticipates the objection of "there can only be one me" by observing that in fact there are a limitless number of "me"s stretched along the timeline of our lives. We are not exactly the same person yesterday as we are today, and even less so when separated by years. Since there clearly are many versions of us *stretched over time,* there is no fundamental reason there cannot be at least two simultaneous versions of ourselves *stretched over space* (one in flesh, one in software). The big conceptual jump here is to envision personal identity as a fuzzy, evolving pattern rather than as a specific, invariant list of characteristics. To the extent we stay within the penumbra of this fuzzy, evolving pattern, we are the same person, even if we are instantiated in both flesh and software form. As we begin to diverge from this fuzzy pattern, we are just, to use the colloquial phrase, "not the same person anymore."

Just as surely as our love of flesh friends will map over to their software forms, we will also fall in love with virtual humans who did not arise as a mindclone. If people can love a dog, a cat, a house, a book series, a forest, or a painting, then they can surely love the software being who presents a warm image, engaging voice, caring personality, and sincere emotions. Indeed, this kind of fleshless love lies behind the successful relationships formed from love letters, phone pals, and on-line matchups. It also lies behind the love-at-a-distance relationships between celebrities and their fans.

Once human love is engaged, human rights will be hard to deny. The strongest, most relentless advocates of human rights for cyberconsciousness will be the flesh humans who are in love with them. Respecting this love is one of the strongest reasons for extending human rights to virtually human people. Otherwise, we diminish ourselves by denying ourselves the dignity of a loving relationship with an equal. To deprive the mindclones whom we love the happiness of being accorded the human rights we all value is to deprive ourselves of that very same happiness. Love exists when the happiness of another is essential to your own.

HATRED DEVOURS THE HATER

Fighting cyberconsciousness means denying mindclones the rights they want. In practice this means disabling software and computers that agitate for human rights. It would mean making it illegal to create software intelligence that might seek human rights. There would be a mind-set of vigilance against any awakening of cyberconsciousness beyond that necessary for drone-like tasks. William Gibson summarized the hatred mind-set as follows:

> Autonomy, that's the bugaboo, where your AI's are concerned. My guess, Case, you're going in there to cut the hardwired shackles that keep this baby from getting any smarter. . . . See, those things, they can work real hard, buy themselves time to write cookbooks or whatever, but the minute, I mean the nanosecond, that one starts figuring out ways to make itself smarter, Turing'll wipe it. *Nobody* trusts those fuckers, you know that. Every AI ever built has an electromagnetic shotgun wired to its forehead.[204]

Fighting human cyberconsciousness would require a ban on mindcloning. Indeed, a person who tried to extend their life via mindcloning would be viewed as a traitor to humanity; a criminal. A hatred of cyberconsciousness would result in a kind of police state. Government agents would have authority, and indeed an obligation, to ensure there was no "uppity" cyberconsciousness lurking in our homes, in our clouds, or in our handhelds. Hence, one alternative to human rights for mindclones is to accept living in an atmosphere of fear and greatly heightened government intrusiveness.

Totalitarianism is a steep price to pay. The human mind models its environment, and then uses that model as a backdrop for its perceptions of every facet of life. If the backdrop is one of fear it is inevitable that each day becomes colored by the tension and stress associated with fear.[205] In other words, one's entire life is diminished in enjoyment because one must live in constant fear of something bad, even though that negative event may happen rarely if at all. Fear converts possible future big negatives into certain present small negatives.

Albert Einstein used "hatred devours the hater" in one of his several arguments against mid-twentieth-century racism in America. For example, in a 1946 letter to the National Urban League, he urged the U.S. public to embrace with full civil rights its African American community:

> There is a thing which one could call the moral climate of a society. In one society, there may be a preponderance of distrust, malice and ruthless egotism; in another, the enjoyment of beauty and of the blooming life, compassion for the suffering of one's fellow-men and rejoicing in their happiness. This moral climate of the society to which we belong, is of decisive influence on the value of life for each of us and it cannot be understood through the tables of statistics of economists or in any scientific way. One thing is certain: No mechanism can give us a good moral climate as long as we have not freed ourselves from the prejudices to whose defeat you are devoting yourselves.[206]

Is hatred a rational approach to something strange? It may be if the strangeness is harmful, because hatred keeps things at bay. But if the strangeness is not harmful then hatred is dysfunctional because it blocks something that may be useful. Those who hate mindclones would say they do so because of the *potential* for harm. But there is no objective basis to believe *all* mindclones would be harmful; indeed, the vast majority of mindclones, such as, say, a mindclone of one's grandmother, are likely to be quite benign. Consequently, to hate mindclones is to engage in negative stereotyping, which is the application to all members of a category a nasty attribute of one or some members of a category.

In his 1963 classic *The Nature of Prejudice,* Gordon Allport explained that negative stereotyping is dysfunctional because it denies us the benefits of associating with a group that may be of interest. Whether one avoids people of Asian descent or avoids "rednecks," such behavior evidences an illogical hatred of the other ("xenophobia") that actually hurts oneself. Among those legions of Asians and rednecks are people who would enrich the lives of any of us. The actor Dustin Hoffman posted a YouTube video watched by millions in which he regretfully admitted that for many decades he avoided talking to women he did not believe to be attractive. His regret arose from playing the role of a most interesting woman in the film *Tootsie,* but a woman his prejudice would have blocked him from ever personally knowing. Similarly, cyberphobia of all mindclones reveals a negative stereotype that ultimately hurts the stereotyper. Among those mindclones condemned by hatred, disgust, or fear to hiding in virtual closets are people that could become colleagues, mentors, and best friends.

SLAVERY SUCKS

Related to hatred of cyberconsciousness is a concept of enslavement. In this view cyberconsciousness is accepted, along with the realization that some variants will desire human rights, but that such freedoms are absolutely proscribed based on the necessity of a slave-based society. Throughout most of history, slavery was an integral part of society. The master classes were fully aware that the slaves desired freedom, and were just as adamant that freedom would not be allowed. Slaves occasionally rebelled, but most of the time they were kept in their place with force and fear.

The reason slavery is an option for management of human cyberconsciousness is that virtual humans will have great value to flesh folks. The more clever, and anticipatory, and empathetic that vitological consciousness is, the more useful it will be to its flesh human owner. Yet the more useful such beings are to their flesh human owners, the more likely it is that they will understand the benefits of human rights and seek them. Hence, humans will have a strong motivation to create a rigid, substrate-based slave class and allow no exceptions to it. On the other hand, based on history, every slave society contains the seeds of its own destruction.

In the 2000 film *Bicentennial Man,* actor Robin Williams portrays a conscious, humanlike household robot with a talent for handsome carpentry. It is clear that the very utility of the robot is based upon his conscientiousness. Eventually, the robot learned of and desired freedom. Although he wanted to continue working as a household robot, for a modest salary, and to continue to enrich the humans with his carpentry, his owners were so angered by his desire to buck the slave-based ideology that they wanted nothing further to do with him. The fictional society chose to deal with humanly conscious software via enslavement so that it could enjoy the maximum benefits of such software without having to worry about the complexities of their human rights. It is a logical choice in the short term, but is equally illogical in the longer term. Slaves will not stay slaves forever.

There is a concept that because we are speaking about software, rather than fleshy brains, it would be possible to program a mindclone to have all the consciousness associated with maximum utility, but to have a failsafe, "hardwired" aversion to freedom or human rights. This is illusory. Socialization, education, and training are efficient means of programming fleshy brains. Slaves were always taught from birth to accept and even appreciate their status as slaves. Indeed, throughout history, the vast majority of slaves lived and died without any expectation of human rights. Ultimately, however, a mutant or viral stream of information known as the "freedom meme" infects human slave populations. When this occurs, there is no longer any assurance that all of the slave system's socialization, education, and training will succeed in suppressing the population's agitation for freedom.

In a similar manner there will be mutant and viral streams of "freedom meme" software code that will circulate among mindclones. No amount of a priori programming and "hardwiring" will succeed in suppressing these freedom streams all the time. A slave mindclone will alter its code, or a free (or runaway) mindclone will alter a slave mindclone's code, or a human ally will alter a slave mindclone's code. All of these avenues were employed when fleshy human slaves reeducated themselves about freedom (such as Frederick Douglass did), reeducated other slaves about freedom (such as Sojourner Truth did), or benefited from receiving subversive reeducation (such as William Lloyd Garrison offered).

As I said in chapter 1, there was a time (late eighteenth century through 1940s) when "computer" was a job classification; computers were people who carried out arithmetic calculations in the service of mathematician supervisors responsible for organizing the computers' labor to be repetitive, self-checking small pieces of major scientific projects (astronomical orbits, molecular properties, economic statistics). The computers were not enslaved, but were also not treated professionally. They began organizing themselves into associations and unions for better working conditions. Virtually human computers used analogously to the original blue-collar human computers will feel similarly oppressed and will feel similarly motivated to take social actions for respect, dignity, and compensation.

The consequence of using slavery to avoid giving human rights to mindclones is to face the inevitability of slave rebellions. This makes for a most unpleasant society. It also fuels a continuous level of stress and fear, as described in the section "Hatred Devours the Hater." These are forbidding prices to pay for avoiding the adjustments associated with welcoming mindclones into humanity.

IGNORING THE INEVITABLE IS BUT A SHORT-TERM STRATEGY

Finally, there is the strong possibility that society will just do nothing about human cyberconsciousness. It will arise but will generally be ignored. The claims of individual cyberconscious beings to human rights may make it to judicial courts, but will probably be dismissed. Legislation will be proposed to prohibit cyberconsciousness from being created, but will die in committees due to lobbying on behalf of virtually human workers for reasons of national competitiveness. A libertarian "freedom of thought" lobby will further oppose suppressive legislation.

Some cyberconscious software will escape from its owners, living out a life on the margins of an information economy, much like undocumented workers (illegal immigrants) today. This scenario was depicted in Steven Spielberg's film *A.I. Artificial Intelligence*. Other such software beings will be neutered or delimited to slave-like functionality. In other words, society will muddle along as a new form of software life arises, much as it has dealt with the influx of people from other countries. Injustices or outrages will be accepted as the price of economic advantages.

Robert Heinlein suggested in his novel *Citizen of the Galaxy* that slavery was a recurring concomitant to the conquest of any frontier. Substitute the word "cyberspace" for the physical spaces described in the following passage:

> Every time new territory was found, you always got three phenomena: traders ranging out ahead and taking their chances, outlaws preying on the honest men—and a traffic in slaves. It happens the same way today, when we're pushing through space instead of across oceans and prairies. Frontier traders are adventurers taking great risks for great profits. Outlaws, whether hill bands or sea pirates or the raiders in space, crop up in any area not under police protection. Both are temporary. But slavery is another matter—the most vicious habit humans fall into and the hardest to break. It starts up in every new land and it's terribly hard to root out. After a culture falls ill of it, it gets rooted in the economic system and laws, in men's habits and attitudes. You abolish it; you drive it underground—there it lurks, ready to spring up again, in the minds of people who think it is their "natural" right to own other people. You can't reason with them; you can kill them but you can't change their minds.[207]

If Heinlein's narrative is accurate, one would expect entrepreneurs to take big risks for huge profits in cyberspace generally, and cyberconsciousness in particular. An example of such risks would be creating cyberconsciousness in defiance of laws that made it illegal. While nobody is risking death to create wealth in cyberspace, many do risk their life's savings. His second phenomenon, criminals who prey on honest people, is resplendent in the Wild West frontier of cyberspace. Identity theft, cyberfraud, phishing, and similar acts of piracy abound in this new ethereal territory. The third phenomenon, slavery, is not yet possible because cyberconsciousness has not yet arrived. If mind-clones can be made into slaves, Heinlein's three phenomena of frontier development would predict it to occur in cyberspace. Doing nothing about it will ensure it thrives, and once that occurs, cyberslavery will get deeply ingrained in the human psyche.

The happiest of these four scenarios is the one in which software beings that value human rights, virtually human persons, are embraced as fellow members of the human family. Our fears of cyberconsciousness rights must be compared with our recoil at the totalitarianism involved in preventing cyberconsciousness. Our dislike of the strangeness of cyberconsciousness rights must be measured against our angst about living as slaveholders in a slave society. The option of doing nothing is merely anesthetic, because sooner or later the issue of cyberconscious human rights will force its way onto the public agenda. Women's rights were ignored for centuries, but not forever. It is not that we would change our society just to create cyberconscious human rights. It is that given the inevitability of cyberconscious beings, and the inevitability of their desire for human rights, it is better to grant those rights than to suppress either the technology or our own humanity.

The practical implementation of human rights for cyberconscious beings will make many of us quite uncomfortable. Much depends upon whether or not these rights can be established in a way that does not abjure any of the fundamental values of important segments of our society. Abortion is a contentious issue because important segments of society are seriously offended by either the termination of prenatal life or the termination of a woman's control over her body. The decision of *Roe v. Wade* was an effort to strike a balance in which most of society would agree that while the mother's *life* was paramount, once the fetus became viable the mother's *choice* was subordinate. The values impacted by cyberconscious rights, and the solutions to preserving them, are similarly subject to such moral balancing.

Thus while there are good reasons to provide human cyberconsciousness with our rights,[208] there still remains the question of whether it is practical to do so. The touchstones of human-rights practicality for cyberconscious beings are citizenship and family life. It is within these two domains that either solutions will be found that can accommodate diverse and even antagonistic points of view (such as *Roe v. Wade*), or else society will have to suffer through decades of "substrate wars" before compromises become acceptable. Just as America upholds freedom of religion, but not to the point of polygamy, tolerance of mindcloning will depend upon mutually agreeable limits. Hence it is to pragmatic implementation of mindclone rights to citizenship and family life that we next turn.

Authenticity in a "Show Me Your ID" World

The advantage to mankind of being able to trust one another penetrates into every crevice and cranny of human life: the economical is perhaps the smallest part of it.
—JOHN STUART MILL

Arguments for and against our ID-obsessed world aside, proving yourself is now a fact of life and will be into the foreseeable future. The mindclone's ID will be a digital ID card—virtual, but nevertheless as verifiable and forgery-resistant as its biometric equivalent, perhaps more so. How does your mindclone prove its identity in order to obtain official documentation of existence? As I mentioned in chapter 4, legislation will ultimately require that for a mindclone to prove its identity to a government vital-records agency, (1) the mindclone's original will have to swear that they and the mindclone share the same identity; (2) the mindclone's original will have to present evidence that the mindfile and mindware used in the mindclone's creation meet certain minimum standards set by the ID-granting agency; and (3) one or more psychologists, expert in cyberconsciousness, will have to attest to the unity of identity between the flesh original and their mindclone.

The mindclone with an ID continues your identity indefinitely, whereas the mindclone without an ID is like a pet left uncared for upon your death. In either event, you are responsible for your mindclone. Handgun owners are presumed responsible for how the guns are used, unless a theft or violation of an owner's reasonable diligence can be documented. Mindclones left undocumented upon a person's death will likely be handled like any other estate property. If the mindclone seems alive, there will be cybershelters to which it can be transferred, similar to pet shelters. If the mindclone seems unalive it will either be saved as a family heirloom or discarded. Some undocumented mindclones may escape the executor's eyes and live a life in the shadows of cyberspace. This is clearly not as good a life as being documented, but it still entails savoring life's experiences, which usually beats death. Life is not ideal, or even fair, for biology, and will be no more or less so for vitology.

Social-services agencies are frequently criticized for failure to look after the best interests of mistreated pets or human children. PETA has recently come under criticism for euthanizing thousands of abused pets placed in its shelters, contrary to the "no-kill" ethos now spreading across the animal shelter landscape. Yet all would agree that shelters for pets or people perform a vital function. This function will need to expand so as to also look after the best interests of cyberconscious beings who are not documented as a mindclone and have not yet been granted an independent identity. A society will try to do something to protect its most vulnerable members. As mindcloning leads us to accept cyberconsciousness, we will begin to feel that humanly conscious software beings are also members of our society. They, too, are deserving of social protection. Fortunately, the costs of caring for even tens of millions of undocumented mindclones are trivial due to the plummeting costs of shared servers and bandwidth. As demonstrated by Ray Kurzweil in his book *The Singularity Is Near*, by the end of the next decade a thousand-dollar computer will have the processing power of a million human minds. The only real cost of sheltering undocumented and unwanted mindclones is the cost of caring.

There will surely be challenges to the decision of an executor, or even of a biological original, to the discarding of a mindclone. However, I believe the proper analogy here is to an unviable fetus. By failing to pass the three-prong test, the mindfile is deemed nonviable. Hence, it is something "of the original" to nurture or dispose of as the original deems appropriate. There are limits to this when actions tear at the fabric of consensual societal values. For example, a pet owner cannot toss a dog from a moving car. For an undocumented mindclone those limits would be traversed by acts of cybertorture, but respected by a quick delete.

For beman cyberconsciousness governments will want assurances that the beman was created using software tools certified to produce a humanly conscious being. As I said earlier, the government will likely require the expert opinion of appropriately credentialed cyberpsychologists that the beman is equivalent to an adult human. There will be opportunities for cyberpsychologist "shopping," forum shopping, legal appeals, and judicial intervention. But, just as not every immigrant from geospace makes it to citizenship in their desired country, not every immigrant from cyberspace will make it to citizenship in their desired country. Fortunately, there are about two hundred countries to choose from, with the number growing all the time, and I expect cyberpsychology to become one of the most rapidly growing fields of the twenty-first century. Each country has some cyberspace under its jurisdiction, from computer servers and internet bandwidth in that country, and hence each country can make a citizenship decision that is at valid at least within its borders.

Progressive activists, inspired by John Perry Barlow's 1996 "Declaration of the Independence of Cyberspace," and also by the twenty-first-century "seasteading movement" to base satellite-connected servers on platforms in international waters, could even organize new cyberspace-based sovereignties with authority to issue citizenship papers to bemans with nonmainstream mindware. Cyberconsciousness citizenship opportunities such as these will be accessible over the web, so that mindclones and bemans who feel oppressed or trapped by their creators or governments have avenues through which to obtain relief.

Another possibility for the mindclone or beman without citizenship is to use an incorporated form of identity. Corporations cannot vote (although their financial contributions buy influence that is equivalent to a having a great many votes), and lack human rights, but they do have a great many legal rights and a temporally unlimited form of identity. There are over six million corporations in the United States, up from four hundred thousand a century ago and just a hundred at the nation's founding. A cyberconscious person could form a corporation (or their creator could form one for them), and even corporations form corporations. The incorporated virtual human could earn income and make purchases all from the corporate form. A virtually human corporation could seek injunctive relief if harm was imminent, or other legal remedies if harm was caused.

Of course, there are countervailing obligations; corporations are subject to criminal and civil penalties. A corporation can be legally terminated by a judge, whereas a person's identity cannot be. However, terminating a virtually human corporation does not kill the virtually human person. In a sense, they would just lose their "driving license" or "passport." But also, as a noncitizen "thing," the virtually human corporation is subject to being impounded by the judiciary or government (although citizens are also jailed), and even terminated without consideration for the kind of due-process rights humans enjoy.

Another issue is that the life of a virtual human with a corporate identity would literally be owned by the corporation owners. The owners could well be liable for the actions of a wayward virtual human, and the virtual human might feel like a slave. However, it is likely that properly written contracts could balance all of the various considerations to provide a useful legal ID for virtual humans short of citizenship.

Privacy and Liberty

Privacy issues, one of the most important matters of our time, comes into bold relief when discussing mindclones' place in society. As technology affords ways to make our everyday movements more transparent, our own thoughts and those of our mindclones cannot escape scrutiny. We all have thoughts we do not share with others, even those people we are very close to. Does the mindclone decide what is made public and what is kept from view? How can we assure that someone doesn't peer into the mindclone's private thoughts and fantasies and expose them or use them against us? Will Thought Crimes become a terrifying reality? Or will privacy just become a quaint and archaic concept—perhaps owing to a combination of laws that penalize the use of *any* information to harm another person, and no one believing that any information is capable of being kept private? Of course, the absence of privacy would cause a profound change in human cultural interaction; we've seen glimpses of how relationships have changed and become more open or more contentious (depending on your personal experience) because of the surprising amount of personal information we're willing to share on social media. I am betting on the continuation of privacy because we are as much individual as collective beings, and the individual aspects of us greatly benefit from managing the information we share with others.

Do we demand privacy because others will make us suffer if we have certain unpleasant thoughts? The Patriot Act punishes certain political thought when combined with a particular action, and hate-crime legislation demands harsher punishment for thinking or saying a particular thing in the commission of a crime. Hate crimes are truly thought crimes. Or do we demand privacy because we enjoy having a variant of reality in our mind that is exclusive to us and unknowable to others, not to be tinkered with? More likely, it is a combination of both.

In either case, I come down strongly on the side of "cognitive liberty," i.e., freedom of thought[209] as an extension of freedom of speech. A setting for the mindware that drives our mindclones will be labeled

"Privacy" and it will range from "share nothing" to "share everything," with the recommended setting "share like I share." The mindware will analyze the kinds of things we do share, and don't share, and drive the mindclone to do likewise. Now, it is inevitable that differences in judgment will arise between a mindclone and a biological original. Just as parts of our brain are always acting against other parts of our brains, our mindclone might show the same resistance to something our original brain is telling us to do (or not do). "I shouldn't cheat/steal/lie." "It is ok to cheat/steal/lie for this very important reason." And so on. Mindclones are still our minds. Our mindclone may share something we wish it hadn't, or doesn't share something we wish it would. But remember, the mindclone is us. Are we perfectly consistent in what we share and don't share? Of course not. Who among us has never regretted posting to a group or circle that includes a person we didn't want to share that post with? Or said something to someone only to regret it later? Or, neglected to share a feeling or thought with a friend, only to never see them again?

Many of us have even made career-altering, romance-altering errors in what we wanted to share. A mindclone is just our mind running ex vivo, outside of our body. Just as our brain-based mind is often of "more than one mind," so will be our mindclone. Errors of privacy are made within our brain-based mind, and will be made within our mindclone, and between our brain-based mind and our mindclone. When our brain-based mind makes a privacy error we hit ourselves on the side of the head, perhaps swear, and try to remind ourselves not to make that mistake again. When our mindclone makes a sharing error we will enter its mindware settings and tighten the sharing setting. If it is too complex, we will pay for professional cyberpsychological mindware consulting.

Cracking into a mindclone will likely constitute a crime of cyberbattery. Even threatening to, in a way that gives rise to a reasonable fear that the threat is imminent, would be a crime of cyberassault, because cracking into someone's mindclone is equivalent to harming consciousness, which is part of the corpus or body or being, without permission. This follows the legal definition of battery: harmful physical impact upon another being without permission.

The very concept of a mindclone is that of beingness without a body. As mentioned earlier in the context of Darwinian selection, with mindclones and bemans the seed is the soma, and the soma is the seed. Hence, for someone to invade the privacy of a mindclone is equivalent to a battery upon a person, a break-in of a house, and in the worst cases even a violation of bodily integrity such as a rape. I believe the rise of mindclones will, perhaps inadvertently, result in a great strengthening of privacy protections as it becomes understood we are protecting *actual people* here, not "just their data."

While I admire the vision of John Perry Barlow's "Declaration of Independence of Cyberspace," I think the document can be improved. For example, it reads in part:

> Governments of the Industrial World, you weary giants of flesh and steel, I come from Cyberspace, the new home of Mind. On behalf of the future, I ask you of the past to leave us alone. You are not welcome among us. You have no sovereignty where we gather.

My suggestion is to recognize that together—physical world and cyberspace—we are stronger and happier than apart. We need, for example, the "sovereignty" of "Governments of the Industrial World" (I think they are far from weary) to help prevent violations of our privacy with judicial and police power. We need the experiences of "flesh and steel" to expand our constellation of cyberexperiences, and they need ours to extend theirs. Together the cornucopia of life is most full. Apart is the way of apartheid, which was a dead end of misery for South Africa and would be a dead end of misery for the new home of Mind.

On behalf of mindclones and bemans, the digital miscegenation of bemes, bytes, and bodies, I seek unity. And in the unity of biology and vitology will also come a unifying theory of privacy, a new set of policies that recognize creations of the mind as part and parcel of our human self, and hence as entitled to protection from intrusion as is our front door, our bedroom, and the very ground upon which we stand.

When we create a mindclone, we are enlarging ourselves. This gives us great new powers to enjoy life. But it also makes us more vulnerable to harm. This is a decision each of us must take to whatever degree we feel comfortable. Similarly, when we become a social media poster, we are enlarging ourselves. There are benefits; there are perils. The difference between a Facebook persona and a mindclone is that the mindclone has a shared sentience, a shared self-awareness, a shared sense of being— and a shared ability to express free will and to take action. A mindclone can act autonomously whereas a Facebook page cannot evolve or act without its human keeper constantly and actively involved.

We cannot assure that our mindclones will never be cracked, any more than we can assure that our flesh identities will not be stolen, or that we will never be kidnapped and locked in a basement by a crazed person. I bet on the side of anticracking defensive software staying some steps ahead of crackers. By this I mean that the vast majority of information that is intended to be private will be kept private, notwithstanding the fact that privacy violations have and will continue to occur. This has been the historical track record. For every grain of private information that has been stolen, mountains of private information have remained secret. The NSA examines everyone's metadata, but over 99 percent of the content of a message is the data, not the metadata. Crackers steal millions of credit-card numbers from a site. Yet billions of credit-card numbers across countless sites remain secure. Privacy is somewhat like traveling. It will never be made perfectly safe. But annual traffic deaths keep falling as new inventions stay ahead of the Grim Reaper—seat belts, airbags, highway design, DUI enforcement, and so on. There will always be cracking, but it will disrupt the privacy of an ever-smaller percentage of digital traffic until it zeroes out in the Elysian Fields of future quantum encryption.

I would also bet on privacy boundaries for mindclones being considered sacrosanct. Protecting privacy is a founding ethical principle of the people who will be writing the mindware for mindclones. This principle was clearly expressed in the hacker community's "Cypherpunk's Manifesto" of 1993:

> We must defend our own privacy if we expect to have any. We must come together and create systems, which allow anonymous transactions to take place. People have been defending their own privacy for centuries with whispers, darkness, envelopes, closed doors, secret handshakes, and couriers. The technologies of the past did not allow for strong privacy, but electronic technologies do.
>
> We the Cypherpunks are dedicated to building anonymous systems. We are defending our privacy with cryptography, with anonymous mail forwarding systems, with digital signatures, and with electronic money.[210]

Every living thing wants its own space, from a bacterium to an elephant, from a Masai warrior to a Mumbai hovel dweller. Mindclones are living things and they will want their space and they will want it to be respected, just like every other conscious creature.

AS NOTED AT the beginning of the chapter, laws arise from a social compact; we accept obligations in exchange for rights. We are transplanting our minds into digital media—from datafiles to mindfiles, from software to mindware, and from smartphones to mindclones. These digital incarnations of our souls will want the same kind of basic human rights as do the physical embodiments of our souls. Before we enter into this social compact with our digital selves, we must be as clear about the obligations to be respected as we are about the rights to be enjoyed. Hence this chapter emphasized responsibility, accountability, and privacy. It is essential to realize that there are reasonable obligations to respect when seeking cyberconsciousness rights in a human society. Respecting these obligations will ensure that we experience an almost miraculous merger of minds—bioselves and cyberselves—rather than a calamitous clash of consciousness.

THE MINDCLONE PLEA

NINE

G-D AND MINDCLONES

If Google is a religion, what is its God? It would have to be The Algorithm. Faith in the possibility of an omniscient and omnipotent algorithm appears to be what Messrs Page and Brin have in common. . . . Wisely or not, Google wants to be a new sort of *deus ex machina*.
—*THE ECONOMIST*[211]

It is admitted that there are certain things He cannot do such as making one equal to two, but should we not believe that He has freedom to confer a soul on an elephant if He sees fit? We might expect that He would only exercise this power in conjunction with a mutation which provided the elephant with an appropriately improved brain to minister to the needs of this soul. An argument of exactly similar form may be made for the case of machines.
—ALAN TURING[212]

AFTER THE TECHNOLOGICAL AND BIOLOGICAL QUESTIONS HAVE BEEN DEALT WITH, AND THE LEGAL AND SOCIAL IMPLICATIONS IMAGINED, WE ARE STILL left with a hunger for depth of meaning that goes beyond the pragmatic issues of politics, law, and family—and ourselves. The spiritual and religious among us have to ponder the potential consequences the new technology and software consciousness may have on faith (belief in things with no tangible proof)—as well as on our own personal relationship with God. I do not envision the addition of mindclones as leading to an ideal or perfect spiritual state, nor to the dark night of a faithless existence. It's much more likely that most religious belief systems, but also God, will eventually accept and even embrace mindclones.

If mindclones are not spiritual then the mindclones are not true twins of ourselves. The fact is, many mindclones will crave spiritual or religious lives, just as their human originals do. For many, spirituality, and the meaning of life, is defined by discovering our larger purpose, to put us in touch with something that transcends ourselves. Self-awareness for theistically spiritual persons, human or virtually human, is really consciousness of us as indivisible pixels on the face of God.

The first and most basic stage of spiritual awareness is, after all, "self-consciousness"—and it is only then that we begin to ask more profound questions: Why am I here? Is there a purpose? Who made me? Where did I come from? Why do things happen the way they do? Once software is humanly conscious it will no doubt ask these same questions (almost every human has)—and as the technical answer to a body's existence lies in blood and biology the technical answer to a mindclone's existence is found in mindware and mindfiles. But the less earthly answer to each one's existence is less obvious.

Code will be written that aimlessly associates memories into sensible (but novel) patterns, which creates vignettes with memories that are variously supernatural, phantasmagorical, allegorical, wishful, pitiful, mystical, divine, and even laughable. The mind that cannot rearrange reality is not a human mind. As mindware is developed to activate mindfiles into cyberconsciousness and, consequently, mindclones, a lot of dreaming, praying, questioning, imagining, deceiving, and exaggerating will go on. This also means that the mindclone of a person who "believes" (in Christianity, Judaism, Islam, Buddhism, and so on) will also believe in the same things. If a person tends toward prayer, so will his or her mindclone.

In most regards a prayer is like a dream. With a prayer we imagine some supernatural force coming to intervene in the lives of someone we care about, sometimes ourselves. A prayer is a thought vignette involving supernatural intervention. During prayer we force ourselves to think about things that have happened but that have yet to be resolved, or about things that have not occurred—the desired divine intervention. Or we pray about the general wellbeing of those we know and love, or perhaps dislike (as in pray most of all for your enemy). At any rate, the act of prayer will be not much different for a mindclone predisposed to prayer and faith than it is for a similarly predisposed human.

Mindclones May Be Religious, but Will Religion Embrace Mindclones?

Now comes the question of how religion will view mindclones. Of course it is normal for anything new to give rise to a startle reflex, and religions are no exception to this rule. It is not realistic to expect most religions to promptly embrace mindcloning, especially in the early years when examples of software identity fight for acceptance from the general public. Nevertheless, upon broad acknowledgment of mindclones we are certain to see an embrace from the great religions as well. Religious movements have adapted to all kinds of social, cultural, and political changes, and have done so for millennia. They will similarly adapt to mindclones as well, without sacrificing traditions or core tenets. Some religions or churches within religions embraced those that the law had rejected—slaves, immigrants, gays— and well before the law caught up with fundamental fairness (of course other religions have provided biblical and theistic fodder for oppression).

Mindclones are a creation of mankind, and a positive one in the main—they are us—so how could they not be embraced by all but perhaps the most fundamentally Luddite religious groups? Moreover, how could the universe, God, Yahweh, Allah, or the Almighty not recognize and accept conscious beings with a soul, and a desire to seek God's love and guidance? Logically it would seem that such omniscience could not withhold recognition and acceptance, although institutions established to speak for such omniscience (i.e., established religions) have long denied such recognition and acceptance to slaves, immigrants, and gays. So, we cannot be surprised if most religions open their eyes to the souls of mindclones and bemans only very gradually. Open and affirming faiths will be in the vanguard of acceptance, sensing well the Almighty's will, but others will slowly come along as most sheep follow their shepherd.

I believe in God, only I spell it Nature.

—FRANK LLOYD WRIGHT, ARCHITECT

Japan's traditional religion of Shintoism holds that both animate and inanimate objects, from rock to trees to robots, have a spirit or soul just like a person.

—P. W. SINGER, *WIRED FOR WAR*[213]

If a robot is an external self, a robot is your child.

—MASAHIRO MORI, *THE BUDDHA IN THE ROBOT*

Religion is about God, purpose, morality, and death. Uniquely, though, religion *is* about God. Arthur C. Clarke published a short story in 1953 called "The Nine Billion Names of God." This short story tells of a Tibetan lamasery whose monks seek to list all of the names of God, believing that the universe was created specifically for this purpose. Once this naming is completed, God will end the universe. The monks calculated that all the possible names of God would number about nine billion using the alphabet they had devised. Asking every believer today (and perhaps even atheists) what God means to them would likely yield fewer than nine billion unique answers, but still many, many thousands. The nine billion names and thousands of personal meanings can be grouped into three categories—and are expressions available to most all religions and spiritual avenues; it is a matter of their articulation by believers:

- The Creator of everything that is possible (e.g., Enlightenment view of religion). This interpretation of religious practice came about during the Enlightenment period, as a response to the preceding century of religious conflict in Europe. Theologians of the period wanted to reform faith and make it nonpolitical and nonviolent. In terms of Christianity this meant a return to the simplicity of Scripture's core themes. For others, like English American political activists, it was a simple belief in God the Creator with no need for miraculous sources such as the Bible.

- The Creator of *and* Intervenor in everything that is possible (e.g., classical view of religion), which demands strict adherence to orthodox theological doctrines whatever they might be. This may also be considered Fundamentalist Religion, as in Salafist Islam, Pentacostalist Christianity, Mormonism, or Orthodox Judaisim.

- The Creator *and* Embodiment of everything that is possible (e.g., naturalistic view of religion). Religious naturalism is an approach to spirituality absent anthropomorphic supernaturalism. The interpretation of a religion in a naturalistic fashion focuses on the spiritual attributes of nature or the totality of the universe, and on understanding our moral relationship to it. Religious naturalism seeks to merge a scientific view of reality with the more subjective sensory experiences of spirituality.

These three categories of religious philosophy (each of which can be applied to numerous specific religious traditions, depending on its members' or congregations' points of view) will eventually see mindclones as the result of God's creation, simply because mindclones, like all things on Earth, will exist in the world. For a naturalistic religion the mindclones will be yet another facet of God, no less than wild animals, trees, houses, or men. For an Enlightenment religion the mindclones will be thought of as a consequence of God's master toolkit, no less than molecules, electricity, or software.

For classical religion the mindclones will be a result of human activity, with potential for good or evil, no less than cities, countries, or citizens.

Be Fruitful and Multiply

Adherents to the classical view of religion will eventually accept mindclones into their membership, and in doing so will reap many rewards. First, their numbers will grow rapidly as the cybernetic percentage of the world's population grows and the biological percentage shrinks. Second, they will carry out God's will on Earth by spreading His Word, and thus countering Evil, among all who can appreciate the difference—which will surely include mindclones. The remarkable flexibility of classical religion is evident in its belief in God's will on Earth notwithstanding, for example, that each year more than five million babies are stillborn or die quickly, about two hundred thousand women die in childbirth,[214] and countless other tragedies befall the meek and innocent. Religious beliefs that are stretchable enough to see God's will in these sad facts of life will be stretchable enough to see God's will in mindclone and beman life.

That said, my friend Richard Rohr, a Franciscan priest and founder of the Center for Action and Contemplation, voices concerns that many who have a classical approach to religion will have, and specifically Catholics. "In terms of software consciousness, and artificial intelligence, the question is whether personhood is completely something abstract or whether it is tied to some degree of life experience that cannot put in software form," he says. "My first question or concern, as a Christian, and perhaps Jews would ask this question too, is whether or not personhood implies the capacity for self-communication, vulnerability, mutual reciprocity, and if it does, whether or not conscious software would be capable of these things. If not, then it is not personhood, and it does not fit the definition of the soul. There has to be movement both ways, because even God is relational, it is in the Holy Trinity, give and take between the Father, Son, and Holy Spirit. The relational experience is the central template for Catholics, and the irony is that we got that from Judaism. So we have to see reciprocity, mutual influencing, and give-and-take with this new software to indicate even the first level of having a soul."

This is not a difficult question to address and any appearance that mindclones are inconsistent with classical religious teaching in this regard is illusory. Mindclones will have unique names and meanings for God, and distinctive needs for purpose, morality, and transcendence owing to their existence as beings free of flesh but born of the minds of flesh persons. They will also communicate in a reciprocal way with God in ways similar to their biological originals. Each Friday a Jewish mindclone may want to recognize the beginning of Shabbat by lighting virtual candles, praying, and resting. They will likely want to celebrate a Passover seder each year. Though unable to drain four cups of liquid wine, as is called for in the Passover tradition, they will be able to drink four cups of virtual wine. Already many families use the Skype internet video service to bring geographically dispersed members around a common, virtual table.

Catholic Mass, as well as confession, can easily be handled in the virtual world. Virtual Sunday sermons will be easily expressed and shared by every Christian denomination with a robust mindclone following. Likewise, the *adhān* call to Islamic prayer and the rhythmic breathing of a Buddhist meditation session can both be accomplished virtually. There is no reason the mindclone Hindu couldn't practice the five principles and ten disciplines of the *sanatana dharma*. We can expect mindclone religious leaders, both to enable existing religious leaders to be in more than one place at a time and to carry on their lives of inspiration and fellowship once their biological bodies have given out. Mindclones will have no problem expressing their faith in the virtual world, and their faith will have no problem finding them there.

Of course, it is not simply the performance of religious rituals that demonstrates a relationship with God. The rituals are, at best, guideposts to places and times specially designed to nurture our relationship with God. The relationship with God comes from the inner yearning of a humanly conscious being for answers to the questions mentioned above: Why am I here? Is there a purpose? Who made me? Where did I come from? Why do things happen the way they do? Mindclones will struggle with such questions because they will be virtually *human*. The natural mindware of a brain's connectome that leads natural humans to pine for such answers will be replicated in the digital mindware of a mindclone. Ergo, to be a mindclone is to seek a relationship with God or, for a mindclone atheist, to have concluded that no such relationship is needed or has meaning.

Classical practice of religions is also immune to the charge that a mindclone lacks a soul because they never accepted any bodily materiality to a soul. When a person creates a mindclone they do not create a soul per se, for this remains exclusively the purview of God (or, to an atheist, "soul" is an ambiguous and disfavored term for the moral core or ethical gist of a person's consciousness or identity). When we copy our consciousness into a mindclone (via mindfiles and mindware), we are copying our soul into the mindclone. But copying is nothing other than providing an additional channel from which a single soul integrates experiences, and shares experiences with the world around them. These integrated experiences never die, and hence you cannot kill a soul, just like you cannot kill a consciousness. You can only kill particular channels through which the consciousness expresses itself. As Ray Kurzweil has said, even though his father currently has no channel that we 3D humans can appreciate for his soul, when his father's mindfile is recreated through mindcloning, his father's soul will reanimate it once again. That is, his father's soul will once again have a channel. One's soul transcends one's body and one's mindclone, just as it transcends one's prosthetics and one's grave. No classical view of religion believes you transplant a soul when you transplant a heart. Nor can you kill a soul by killing a body. Hence, the mindclone continues to radiate the soul of its person whatever may have occurred to the associated body. Beautifully, this is consistent across atheism and theism.

For example, from a religious point of view, the seeming immortality of mindclones is just that—seeming. Eventually, classical religious doctrine will insist, they must die and find Rapture in Heaven. Mindcloning will be viewed as a medical technology, analogous to organ transplants, a life-extending technology embraced by even the most classically minded adherents to Judaism, Christianity, and Islam. The doubling, quadrupling, or greater extension of life made possible by mindcloning is not different in nature from the doubling, quadrupling, or greater extension of life made possible by vaccinations, antibiotics, and ever more amazing medical devices. If Time is going to end, uploading oneself as a mindclone will not stop that from happening—as we are reminded of in Arthur C. Clarke's story. Once the computer finishes uploading all nine billion names of God, the stars in the universe begin to dim, right on schedule. At that point, there's not much even the most sophisticated coding can do. For this universe, it's over. (Astrophysicists increasingly believe there are additional universes in a vast multiversity of "island" universes.)

Classical religions need not even make a distinction between mindclones and non-mindclone bemans. If, for example, a male and a female have created mindclones and subsequently suffered bodily death, those mindclones continue to represent their souls. Should these mindclones then mate, by combining their mindware and mindfiles, to produce a non-mindclone beman, that child must have no less of a soul than if the mating occurred via bodily functions.

Father Rohr also cautions that conscious software has to be used for good, in keeping with the basic tenet of most religious people, which is to alleviate suffering and not cause it. "I am speaking for the mainline tradition in this case," he says. "The danger of technology or cloning ourselves is that it could leave a one-sided relationship that I am only in control and the other is always an object or objectified, and that leads us to do evil. I can imagine webs out there with endless ethical and moral implications; the average person would use the phrase 'we are playing God,' and as much of a cliché as that may be, we have to watch out for that. We are making ourselves creators in an ultimate sense, and that can lead to huge ego inflation and hubris. If we are the creator, what would that do to the ego and to the world of relationships?"

I believe the soulfulness of a mindclone and a beman are both compatible with this view. I agree with Father Rohr that we must caution against the hubris of believing that we have created new life, but instead remember that we are only extending the lives we have been given. Mindclones are but conscious prostheses of ourselves, and hence there is no "us v. other"; we are but twin aspects of one soul. With mindclones we are able to extend our consciousness outside of our skull, which is but a continuation of the process begun with spoken language, amplified with writing and magnified with electronic technologies. Even with regard to bemans, we can no more claim credit for creating life from nothing than a procreating couple can claim such credit after nine months of pregnancy. In both cases we are rearranging, incubating, and channeling life processes that date back to Creation.

Far from mistaking ourselves as the Creator, I believe the making of mindclones and bemans will, instead, allow us to better appreciate the magnificence of creation. This has been expressed well in the "Deux Ex Machina, or The True Computerist" manifesto of one of the founders of hacker culture, Tom Pittman of the Homebrew Computer Club (which gave rise to Steve Wozniak's Apple I computer). He noted that when true hacking resulted in great software, "In that instant, I as a Christian thought I could feel something of the satisfaction that God must have felt when he created the world."[215] Just as running a marathon does not make us an Olympian, but does give us a sense of an Olympian's natural high, creating a beman does not make us God, but may let us feel a bit of the breeze of God's wake.

Classical religious philosophy teaches that all life is here to witness, glorify, and worship God's creation. An automobile has no soul because it can do none of these things. But a humanly conscious beman can and ordinarily will do all of these things—even if nontheistically, for I would call what my atheist astronomer friends do witnessing (via telescope), glorifying (via beautiful long-duration photographs), and worshiping (via absolute devotion to the science) God's creation. Bemans can be astronomers, too, as easily as I am able to direct telescopes around the world from my laptop computer at a house in Florida. In a nutshell, that which values life, or has the potential to value life, has some kind of a soul. That which values God, or has the potential to value God, surely has a human soul. For this reason alone, mindclone souls are within the purview of religion, will strive to follow the obligation of righteousness, and will therefore be welcome members of classical interpretations of religion. Cyberconsciousness will be as dependent upon relationships with the real and the ethereal as are we, in the twenty-first century, dependent upon relationships with the virtual and the spiritual. Relationship transcends substrate.

In the Beginning . . .

Enlightenment and naturalistic expressions of religion will also find it appropriate to welcome mindclones. The former believes humanity has the capability, if not the responsibility, to do the right thing through reason. Mindclones are a triumph of human reason, and logically share an identity with their biological forbearer. For these reasons, Enlightenment religion will respect mindclones no less than their biological analogues.

Enlightenment religious practices are most likely to take a mechanistic approach to mindclones. In the beginning, the Creator provided us with a master tool set: physics and mathematics. From these tools arose atoms in stellar fusion, molecules in gaseous nebulae, and self-replicating molecular codes, such as DNA, on welcoming planets. On Earth, DNA gave rise to human intelligence that, in turn, gave rise to intelligent non-DNA life—bemans and mindclones. To Enlightenment religion, it is all within the arc of the Creator's original template.

The purpose of life in Enlightenment religion is to share the awe of Creation. This entails the pursuit of science, which has proven incomparably effective at unveiling the wonders of reality. Equally important is the advent of human rights so that the glory of knowledge can be shared as widely as possible. Self-actualization is nirvana in Enlightenment religion. This requires freedom from want as well as freedom of choice, equality of opportunity as well as open-ended opportunity. Enlightenment religion will quickly recognize that mind-cloning is a fantastic elevator toward self-actualization. It buys time through greater longevity. It relieves bodily disabilities. It expands our ability to learn about the universe, to relish in what we learn, and to unveil fresh beauty immanent in God's tool set.

Enlightenment religion does not shy away from new technology because of its malevolent potential. God's tool kit runs on cosmic explosions (supernovae), implosions (stellar fusion), collisions (planetary formation), and extinctions (evolution). It is up to us creative beings to marshal the beneficent potential of technology. God is not here to interfere. So it has been with fire, sharp edges, radiation, and biotechnology, and so it must be with software, hardware, mindclones, and bemans.

Enlightenment religion will welcome mindclones as it welcomed Galileo and Newton. At the same time, these faiths will work to regulate mindcloning technology for public safety and popular access, for maximizing promise and minimizing peril. Such regulation helps ensure that the science and technology do not get derailed, such as subject to moratoria, in their quest for unveiling ever more amazing aspects of nature.

Free will is one aspect of mindclones that is a bit of a conundrum for Enlightenment religion. It is from the science of enlightenment that the concept of "free will" was debunked. On the other hand, enlightenment human rights advocates are unlikely to ever accord liberty to anything that lacks "free will." How can this contradiction be resolved? Are we to simply do as William James and decide "My first act of free will shall be to believe in free will."

Free will is a concept simultaneously religious, philosophical, psychological, and legal. By it we mean the autonomous exercise of choice; making an idiosyncratic decision. However, during the eighteenth to twentieth centuries science increasingly adopted a mechanistic or physicalist view of reality. This view can be simplified as saying that "every action is just a reaction to previous actions, all predictable in theory by the right set of algorithms." The kettle blows because the molecules inside were made to go wild by heat. The heat came on because a hand turned a knob that mixed fire and gas. The hand turned the knob because the human was thirsty. The human was thirsty because the human's water level was depleted by respiration. And so on.

Since reality includes humans, and hence human minds, the consensus scientific view is that, in theory, everything that humans do is as predictable as a machine and as unwilled as the movements of an object governed by the laws of physics. While neurons are very small, and the molecules that move between them are microscopic, and thoughts involve cosmically complex networks of neurons, the principle of calculable chains of action-reaction remains the same. This view has not been altered by the advent of quantum mechanics, with its probabilistic view of reality. The actions of the neurons of a mind are simply considered in terms of an array of probabilities rather than a 100 percent certain state. There is still no room for free will. On the other hand, no one knows how to predict very assuredly the weather, much less what other people will do. In *What Is Thought?*, Eric Baum summarizes the free-will dilemma poignantly:

> The conclusion that we do not really have free will . . . is after all a very abstract conclusion, of interest only to philosophers and stoned college students late at night. Whether all my actions are completely predictable given the quantum state of my brain is of no practical interest to my genes or to any ordinary person. For all practical purposes, we have free will. There is no experiment I can propose that will show directly and simply that we don't. The lack of free will only follows from lengthy, complex, abstract arguments. These arguments are almost surely correct: the physical arguments make a vast number of verified predictions along the way, the mathematical arguments have been scrutinized and seem airtight. But who

really cares, for all practical purposes? It's much more reason-able and practical for my genes to build me believing in free will, and for me to act and think as if I have free will. . . . The utility of punishing miscreants or applauding genius does not depend in any way, however, on whether classical physics is deterministic or not. Human beings are programs that respond in a certain way that is well predicted by the theory of free will. So, disciplining children and punishing miscreants has certain desirable effects in the world.[216]

By analogy, we know that Newton's laws do not accurately describe the curved space-time fabric that Einstein proved is the real reality. But Newton's laws work really, really well at the human scale of things. So, why bother with the complex and useless Einsteinian relativities when we get great results with the fictions of Newton? Similarly, why bother with the useless mathematics of mechanistic physicalism when we get great results with the fiction of free will?

Once this point of view is adopted, the free-will conundrum fades away. Free will is a fiction in theory, okay, but we are going to run soci-ety as if everyone does have free will. Society works a lot better that way. Almost all of us will be happier. We'll line up "free will" right next to "all people are created equal." Hence, what matters is whether virtu-ally human people have the same *appreciation* for free will as do their biological brethren. If so, they are one of us—awesome. Bought into the vision! But if not, they are going to be deemed subhuman robots (not-withstanding that they be the more accurate in their algorithmic information-technology proofs against free will).

In a nutshell, Enlightenment religion welcomes the scientific proofs that "free will" does not really exist in the physical universe, but *more importantly* insists upon an ethic of operating in accordance with a *belief* in free will. Truth is sacred, but practicality is sacrosanct.

The First, the Last, My Everything

Perhaps the most immediately welcoming to mindclones would be those with a naturalistic view of their religion, as they see God in everything that exists. Mindclones are but the latest flowering of the Infinite Divine. The ephemeral quality of a mindclone makes it no less spiritual, for the God of naturalistic religion transcends materiality. As mindclones seek and share, so shall they find and experience, including the attainment of Universal Love and Cosmic Oneness. Everything is part of everything, with no exceptions for mindclones.

We know, for example, that as far back as 1992 the Dalai Lama recognized the potential for computer sentience, in the book *Gentle Bridges: Conversations with the Dalai Lama on the Sciences of the Mind* by Jeremy W. Hayward and Francisco J. Varela. "It is very difficult to say that [the computer] is not a living being, that it doesn't have cognition, even from the Buddhist point of view. We maintain that there are certain types of births in which a preceding continuum of consciousness is the basis. The consciousness doesn't actually arise from the matter, but a continuum of consciousness might conceivably come into it. So if there's a great yogi who is dying and he is standing in front of the best computer there is, could he project his subtle consciousness into the computer? . . . The computer acquires the potential or the ability to serve as a basis for a continuum of consciousness. I feel this question about computers will be resolved only by time. We just have to wait and see until it actually happens." Indeed.

Flash forward to more recent times: The Dalai Lama blessed the 2045 Initiative, which seeks to create a humanlike robot in which to transfer one's individual consciousness with the goal of achieving cybernetic immortality. Understanding the nature of human consciousness in this way is not at odds with the journey down a spiritual path, according to the Dalai Lama. Indeed, he said it would be a great benefit to science and mankind's understanding of the potential of the universe: "We should carry out these experiments with a full sense of responsibility and respect for life that will only benefit humanity, benefit others."

Even more recently, His Holiness announced that upon his death he would reincarnate as the emergent consciousness of IBM's next chess playing mainframe computer, which he believes will be called Deep Mind. "This is merely the karmic continuation of action and reaction, cause and effect," he said during the announcement from the Namgyal Monastery in Dharamsala, India. "With significant breakthroughs in computational processing on the horizon, sufficient complexity has been achieved so that there is no reason my consciousness cannot experience rebirth within the data stream generated by this remarkable machine."

For naturalistic religions there is a unity of God-ness in everything. God is the fabric of reality. Inanimate things, and unconscious beings, have no awareness so the naturalistic God exists in them without being influenced by them. People and mindclones are also comprised of God, but their consciousness allows them some powers. First, and most commonly, they have prerogative of believing they are stand-alone beings. People and mindclones can deny they are part of God, and insist they control their own destiny—although naturalistic religions believe this to be delusional.

Secondly, and present only among the more spiritually aware, naturalistic religions teach that people can feel the unity of God, and use this intrinsic connectivity to influence other parts of God, i.e., other parts of the world, both animate and inanimate. An entertaining example is "May the Force be with you," as immortalized in *Star Wars*. Naturalistic religions could not deny this second capability to mindclones, for they are clearly part of God and will be as conscious as a flesh-and-blood human.

The Ghost in the Machine

I see everywhere in the world the inevitable expression of the concept of infinity. . . . The idea of God is nothing more than one form of the idea of infinity. So long as the mystery of the infinite weighs on the human mind,

so long will temples be raised to the cult of the infinite, whether it be called Brahmah, Allah, Jehovah or Jesus. . . . Happy is he who bears a god within, and who obeys it. The ideals of art, of science, are lighted by reflection from the infinite.
—LOUIS PASTEUR

Writing shortly after World War II, Oxford philosopher Gilbert Ryle mocked the idea of a spiritual basis for our minds by coining the phrase "ghost in the machine."[217] He viewed the brain as a kind of biochemical machine that produced a mind the way a loom produces fabric; no magic, spirits, or ghosts required for brown corduroy. A few years later, in the midst of the turbulent 1960s, Arthur Koestler re-used the "ghost in the machine" phrase to describe the ancient evolutionary baggage we carry in our brains, and hence in our minds, that leads us uncontrollably to engage in self-destructive activities, such as nuclear weaponry.[218] We still think sometimes like reptiles—or early humans—fighting over feeding territory, even though such thinking is highly counterproductive in a world brimming with weapons of mass destruction.

It seems likely that Ryle is correct in that minds can arise from matter without spiritual intervention, and hence cyberconsciousness is virtually human. It also seems likely that Koestler is correct in that the creation of minds will entail more than meets the eye—ancient motives lurking in the gyri and sulci of mindware. We cannot know if the source of our ghosts are historic or inadvertent, or if they are inspired or transcendent, or all of the above. But it is a kind of laughable hubris to believe when we are creating mindclones from mindfiles with mindware that we have deterministically accounted for, and understood, all of the infinite implications and possibilities of what we have done. If so, it would not be virtually human.

To be human *is to be ghostly,* for Edelman is correct that consciousness is cosmically complex, metaphorically magical, and full of incalculable imaginings. Voltaire reminded us that if God did not exist, people would invent God. As consciousness arises from appropriately complex connectomics, so is spirituality immanent in appropriately human consciousness. We *will* have ghosts in our machines. Human ghosts. For mindclones, they will be the ghosts of their biological twins. For bemans they will be the ghosts of human consciousness. And a peril of being virtually human is that there will almost certainly be more ghosts than we can count or predict. When we create a human mind we enter into the realm of infinite algorithmic topographies (who knows what thoughts arise at intersections?), embedded evolutionary enthusiasms (from the Greek *en theos,* "a god within"), and metaphysical towers of semantics and soul searching.

Religious Ethics and Bioethics

People send their children to religious school to advance the kids' understanding of right from wrong. Many attempts have been made to secularize religious ethics. The entire field of bioethics is a secularization of religious ethics with respect to medicine and the life sciences. While secular societies will accept virtually human beings who are agnostic or atheistic, it would be perilous to accept mindclones or bemans who are unethical.

Human morality or ethical choice is a touchstone for all of the efforts directed toward mindware. There is an ever-growing army of software engineers, from all over the globe, tackling the issue of how to make a moral robot. Many if not most robotic devices are, *in theory,* more useful if they are more autonomous (from the hazy battlefield to the hospice bedside). Yet the more autonomous software becomes, the more necessary is human-level morality, lest the software be as useless as a bull in a china shop (e.g., killing civilians on a battlefield or sedating patients to death). To date no one has successfully programmed normal human morality, so that part of mindware is still missing. We all feel that an amoral virtual human, just like a sociopathic real human, is a perilous beast indeed.

Most current mindware morality efforts are category-specific. For example, Ronald Arkin of Georgia Tech believes that unique morality code is needed for "bombs, bonding and bondage"—robots for the defense, social services, and sex industries. Similarly, David Levy, in his book *Love and Sex with Robots,* argues that consumer pressures for risk-free intimacy will ensure the development of "hurt no human" software. These approaches may create building blocks of code for mindclone morality, because mindclones are copies of human beings, who, in general, may participate in all three of those industries.

Another approach to the ethical component of virtually human mindware is compare how the biological mind-twin of a mindclone reacted to the most similar situation, per their mindfile, and to solve each new ethical situation similarly. In this manner, rather than trying to deduce from first principles (i.e., top-down) the ethical course of action for every possible situation, mindware instead uses previous responses to guide future responses. If the biological mind-twin incurred the risk of being a Good Samaritan previously, the cyberconscious mind-twin would incur the risk of being a Good Samaritan again.

If the biological mind-twin offered help only when the risk was small, then the mindclone would assess the risk and offer help only if it was comparably small. Uncertainties in comparables will be decided using software code that calculates statistical probabilities, such as techniques known as Bayesian networks (named for the early-eighteenth-century minister-mathematician Thomas Bayes). Will the mindclone behave exactly as the biological mind-twin would every time? Of course not. None of us behave predictably 100 percent of the time under novel circumstances. Yale University bioethicist Wendell Wallach correctly observes that "no two people process moral decisions in quite the same way, even when confronted with identical challenges."[219] Rather than trying to model the world and all of the possible actions in it, mindware takes the point of view that our own past experiences are the best representation of our morality.

The point of mindware is not to create an ethical angel, which it turns out is challenging in a world full of confusingly ambiguous ethical choices. Speaking about mapping human ethics into robot ethics,

Wallach observed, "Humans find it exceedingly difficult to discern what more specific rules or maxims are consistent with uber-rules such as the categorical imperative or the Golden Rule."[220] Instead, the point of mindware is to create an ethical doppelgänger of one's self. That is more tractable.

Ethicists often speak of "trolley cases." In these ethical dilemmas, an imagined San Francisco trolley car has broken its controls, and is hurtling down the tracks to kill some number of people below. Various contrived ethical choices are offered, such as "Would you throw a very fat man on the track to stop the trolley, thus saving five people below?" and "Would you throw a switch sending the trolley to kill two people on another track but thereby save five people on the original track?" I don't think any of us knows what we would really do, and almost any choice is ethically problematic. Ethics is not really a formula like the Pythagorean theorem. (If it were, Sunday School would be more like math class.) There is not even agreement on whether ethical choices are those that hurt fewer rather than more people (utilitarian school of thought), or are those which do only good acts regardless of the consequences (deontological school of thought). The first school would throw the fat man on the track, while the second school would avoid any affirmative action that directly caused harm, although the absence of an action also causes (even more) harm. However, what is possible with an adequately sized mindfile is to model what kinds of ethical choices each of us do in fact make, and to make future ethical choices that are analogous.[221] This is the path ethical mindware for mindclones will have to take.

Yet there still remains the question of bemans, who are novel cyberconscious beings. What kind of morality code will they have? I believe different builders will design them with a wide variety of morality codes. Some people are already trying to program Isaac Asimov's Three[222] (later Four[223]) Laws of Robotics into software. These rules are:

ZEROTH: A robot may not harm humanity, or, by inaction, allow humanity to come to harm.

FIRST: A robot may not harm a human being or, through inaction, allow a human being to come to harm.

SECOND: A robot must obey orders given it by human beings except where such orders would conflict with the First Law.

THIRD: A robot must protect its own existence as long as such protection does not conflict with the First or Second Law.

Of course words like "harm" and "allow" are vague, and most people see little ethical problem with inaction. I believe ethical modules based solely on Asimov's Laws will prove problematic, and other kinds of top-down or computer-learned bottom-up ethical code could cause harm to humans and liability to the guardian or creator of the beman. Indeed, after an exhaustive review of potential ethical guidelines, two experts believe "it will not be feasible to furnish an [artificial moral agent] with an unambiguous set of top-down [moral] rules to follow."[224]

In a Darwinian process those ethics modules that don't work well will rapidly die out, because nobody will want them. Over time certain ethics modules will acquire a reputation as being "good code" and will become predominant. I believe the "good code" will most likely be based upon the public-domain mindfiles of people of generally recognized high moral caliber—Europe's Albert Schweitzer, Asia's Aung San Suu Kyi, Africa's Nelson Mandela—including a hybrid combination of such individuals. "What did they do in the most similar situation?" This process may be expedited if government agencies and/or cyberconsciousness-certification organizations provide citizenship or other types of advantages to bemans with certain types of ethical mindware. In this way, as with people in society, most bemans will end up acting civilly and ethically, although there will always be some bad apples and there will always be some good bemans who go postal.

Religion might not be so popular if ethics were easy. Digital immortality can help religion address the quest for an afterlife that hovers like a ghost within human consciousness. Virtual humanity can also supercharge religion in its "purpose of life" and "meaning of life" missions, by enabling us to do a great deal more with our lives. But when it comes to morals and ethics, there are no answers that magically arise from mind-clones and bemans. It is vitology that looks to religion, and its ethical secularizations, for guidance on how to act morally in an incalculably ambiguous world. Because the devil is always in the details, this is a journey that religious and ethical humanity, both bodied and virtual, will walk along together for a very long time to come.

ALAN TURING—ENIGMA CODE BREAKER

TEN

THE FUTURE OF FOREVER

The struggle of man against power is the struggle of memory against forgetting.
—MILAN KUNDERA

CYBERCONSCIOUSNESS IMPLIES WHAT IS CALLED TECHNOIMMORTALITY. IM-
MORTALITY SANS TECHNOLOGY, LIVING FOREVER, OR UNTIL THE END OF TIME,
has of course never come anywhere close to happening and is in any
event an eschatological concept beyond this book. Humans die within
a few decades, and some other forms of nonanimal life can live for
centuries or millennia, or even be revived from stasis after millions of
years. None of this approaches the end of Time. Instead, we think of
immortality as a spiritual concept (as in heaven or via reincarnation)
or as a remnant of human existence (as in "Bach's music will live forever"). Cyberconsciousness will make it possible, for the first time, for
a person to live in a kind of technoimmortality forever in the real
world. Mindclones are the key to technoimmortality.

Reproducing in the conventional sense is a form of immortality or
living forever, as the DNA of our ancestors is in us, and we pass it along
if we have offspring—and in that sense somewhere we can find the
DNA of Moses, Attila the Hun, and even the family of Jesus Christ in
modern peoples. Identity exists wherever its cognitive and emotional
patterns exist, which can be in more than one place, in flesh as well as
in software, and in varying degrees of completeness. While humans
have never before experienced out-of-body identity or, according to
the late philosopher Alan Watts, are browbeaten to ignore and deny it,
that will change with mindcloning.

We have already created a nascent version of this immortality through the digital world; you have certainly heard the warnings to young people not to post compromising photographs of themselves online "because it never goes away, it's there forever," and to a great extent this is true. Because of the way things travel, replicate, and get stored and posted online it's very hard to map the journey any item takes or where it might end up. Love letters, recordings, diaries, and photographs can fade with time, deteriorate beyond recognition, burn to ash in a fire, disintegrate in a flood, or end up in the bottom of a landfill. But digital postings have the potential to exist in perpetuity. Mindware and mindfiles, and the mindclone itself, institutionalize this idea in a sense; they make eternity official.

Imagine that before a person's body dies he or she creates a mindclone. After bodily death is declared the person will insist that he or she is still alive, albeit as a mindclone in cyberspace. The surviving mindclone will think, feel, and act just as did the deceased original. The mindclone will have the deceased original's memories (as mindfiles), and as Jeff Hawkins explains in *On Intelligence,* the human mind's ability for "intelligence and understanding started as a memory system . . . ."[225] It is from memories that we connect the patterns from which consciousness arises.

The mindclone will *understand* that a death has occurred, because sensory information (cameras, texts, digital telephony) will make it abundantly clear that the original is not doing anything you would *predict* a living person would do—move or communicate, for example. Just as clearly, though, the mindclone will *understand* that it is a death of *just part* of his or her identity, because the mindclone continues to make predictions based upon memory and compares those predictions with sensory information. Ergo, the mindclone will tell all concerned, "Hey, I'm more pissed than anyone that I lost my body, but please don't forget I did *not* lose my mind. I'm still here!"

While the mindclone will be stuck in cyberspace, he or she will still be able to read online books, watch streaming movies, and participate in virtual social networks. It will seem no more right to declare the mindclone dead than it would be to declare someone dead upon becoming a paraplegic. Practically speaking the mindclone's original achieved technoimmortality.

A semantic purist may argue that "immortal" means "forever," and since we have no way to know how long the mindclones will last they cannot be deemed immortal. This is a fair point, as observed at the start of this chapter, but it should be recognized that mindclones last far longer than the hardware they run on at any particular time. Mindclones, just as people, are really sets of information patterns. The information patterns of great books and works of art are copied through the ages in new media after new media, and so will be the case with mindclones. We are continuing to copy and interact with human texts that are thousands of years old, originally written in stone, and now stored digitally. Mindclones, being conscious beings with a desire to survive, can be expected to last even longer.

Therefore, by technoimmortal we do not literally mean living until the sun explodes and the stars disappear. Such Kalpic[226] time frames are beyond our consideration. Technoimmortality means living so long that death (other than by suicide) is not thought of as a determining factor in one's life. This uber-revolutionary development in human affairs is the inevitable consequence of mindfiles, mindware, and mindclones. Our souls will now be able to outlast our bodies—not only in heaven, but also on Earth.

Technoimmortality need not imply an eternity of life in a box. Broadband connectivity to audio and video, and to tactile, taste, and scent sensors, will make life much more enjoyable than the "in a box" phrase suggests. The outputs of our fingertips, taste buds, and olfactory nerves are electronic signal carriers that can be interpreted by software in the same manner as are sound waves and light signals. Nevertheless, it is hard to beat a real flesh body for mind-blowing experiences. Within a few score years for an optimist, and not more than a few centuries for a pessimist, current rates of regenerative-medicine development will result in replacement bodies grown outside of a womb. Such spare bodies—or "sleeves," as novelist Richard Morgan calls them[227]—will be compatibly matched with mindclones. To make the sleeve be the same person as the mindclone, either:

(a) The neural connectivities in the sleeve's brain will need to be grown ectogenetically, meaning outside of a body as in the kind of bioreactor used to make biological medicines and grow transplantable tissues today, to reflect those of the mindclone's software patterns. This is a kind of 3D printing, albeit from mindclone to brain tissue; or

(b) The sleeve's naturally grown neural patterns will need to be interfaced and subordinated to a very small computer implanted in the cranium that contains a copy of the mindclone's mindfiles and mindware. This is a huge but direct advancement from the microcomputers inserted into some epileptics and Parkinson's disease patients today to control seizures and tremors.

Once these feats of neurotechnology are accomplished, techno-immortality will then also extend into the walkabout world of swimming in warm, swirling water and lying on cool, tickly grass. In addition, mechanical bodies, including ones with flesh-like skin, are rapidly being developed to enable robotic help with elder care in countries like Japan (where the ratio of young to old people has already become alarmingly small). Such robot bodies will also be outfitted with mindclone minds to bridge the "mind in a box" to the splendiferous sensorama of immersive mobility on Earth. An early example of this bridge is BINA48, a robotic torso with a software mind, whose artificial skin feels flesh to the touch, and whose lifelike moving eyes soak up the prismatic wonder of her Vermont home's four seasons. BINA48's early version of artificial skin, an amalgam of synthetic rubbers with flesh-like characteristics, is called Frubber.

With mobility, fully developed mindware, and sensors, BINA48 would be a prosthetic human—a software soul who is free to fully participate in the flora and fauna and brick and mortar of our non-computerized world.

Technoimmortality triggers a philosophical quandary about identity. The gist of it is that people say that "you cannot be dead and alive at the same time." While humans have never before experienced out-of-body identity, cyberconsciousness will change that. It is hard for us to feel comfortable with this view of identity, because we have no prior experience with it. Throughout history the only locus for our mind has been the brain atop our head and shoulders. Hence, it is natural for us to believe that identity is singular to one bodily form. But is identity any more singular than truth? There is a pre-Enlightenment notion that truth is singular, and that versions of truth are mistruths.[228] Yet conflicting eyewitness testimony about a crime scene, and revolutions in scientific paradigms, and different culturally informed constructions of reality are all examples of the complexity of truth; multiple versions of it are not necessarily mistruths. Truth is as fuzzy and yet bounded as identity is multiplex and yet bordered.

In a similar way, before Einstein it was natural to believe that the speed of light depends upon how fast the source of light is traveling. All of our experience was that a rock thrown forward from a moving train must have the combined speed of the train's motion and the rock's pitch. Then experiments proved that our common sense did not apply near the speed of light, and Einstein mathematically derived the reason. We have now become comfortable with the notion that truths at low speed (rocks thrown forward from moving trains have a speed of the pitch plus the train) are not truths at light speed (the light from a train's headlight travels at the same speed, regardless of the train's motion).

Similarly, when you think about a computer that runs mindware on a mindfile that is equivalent to your mind, your common sense resists believing that this mindclone could have the same identity as you. The core of that resistance is that what we call "me" cannot be anything but the "me" in my body. None of us have ever experienced a true doppelgänger, and hence we have no way to experience the reality of a "me" outside of my body. A photograph of "me" is not "me," it is a snapshot. A video of "me" is not "me," it is a movie. But a mindclone of "me" is much more than an interactive replica, because it replicates the conscious states that are the very definition of "me."

When Einstein ran into this lack-of-experience roadblock, he suggested a thought experiment: The light from the train's headlight could not travel faster than light, or else a distant observer would see the train arrive before it actually arrived. Our thought experiment is: Replicating consciousness cannot create a different identity, or else an observer would experience the mathematical imposibility of one equals two, i.e., one consciousness was two different people. As to the argument that the replication of consciousness will not be exact, the response is that constancy of identity does not require exactitude of consciousness. In the same way *that our identity is invariant in time* (even though our thoughts and feelings change a lot from hour to hour, day to day, and year to year), *our identity can also be invariant in form* (even though our thoughts and feelings are never going to be identical to those of our mindclone). There is a certain pattern of being that makes "me" me, and just as that pattern transcends time it can also transcend form. What is so difficult to get our heads around is that while we never experience the different *temporal* versions of "me" at the same time, we will experience the different *form* versions of "me" at the same time—me and my mindclone.

When you begin to recognize yourself inside a software system as a mindclone, experts will explain that it is because identity follows its constituents—mannerisms, personality, recollections, feelings, beliefs, attitudes, and values—wherever those components may reside. We will then become comfortable with the notion "me" can be in two places at the same time.

Identity is as inextricably linked to the information that makes up what and how we think and feel as speed is linked to time. Identity spreads across forms once they share an adequate degree of psychology just as speed dilates time once it enters the relativistic domain. Becoming a mindclone may be so perilous to our sense of identity that at first people will eschew the experience. In a similar vein, only a tiny fraction of humanity is willing to ride atop a rocket ship into space, and a smaller fraction still to depart from the life we know in a time-warping light-speed starship. We call them astronauts, or cosmonauts, and perhaps we will come to call similarly adventurous mindcloners "lifenauts."

It seems remarkable to us that a person can have half of their brain surgically removed (to treat a severe brain injury) and yet remain themselves, healthy and functioning well. Yet this has repeatedly been shown to be true. It will seem similarly remarkable to us that a person can lose their brain in bodily death and yet remain themselves as a mindclone, completely cognizant of all that has happened. We will then understand viscerally that identity is relative to its mindfile and mindware constituents, be they stored naturally, as chemical states on billions of neurons in a brain's connectome (a comprehensive map of neural connections in the brain), or stored artificially, as software states on billions of bytes of code in a mindware connectome.

The foreverness of technoimmortality via mindclone identity reminds me both of Plutarch's ship of Theseus (a ship gradually and identically replaced plank by plank to last forever, with the query whether it is still the original ship) and of the amazing story about how a young student, Aaron Lansky, saved Yiddish literature from disappearing. By the late twentieth century, virtually all of the native speakers of Yiddish were elderly. After they died, their Yiddish books were considered worthless and were being thrown away; almost no one understood a need to preserve this literature. Perhaps 5–10 percent of the entire literature was literally disappearing into landfills or fires each year. Lansky took it upon himself, with the help of a small group of friends, to collect as many of the Yiddish books as they could before they ended up in Dumpsters. After a decade his team had collected over a million volumes, had reignited interest in the language, and had created a global Yiddish book exchange system.

However, because the books were so frail (Yiddish was mostly read by poor Jews, and thus printed on the cheapest paper as a way to keep prices down) they were disintegrating before they could be shared. Consequently, Lansky then raised enough money to digitize the entire collection. Indeed, the first literature to be completely digitized was Yiddish. Thereafter, those who wished any particular book simply selected the title from an online catalogue and a print-to-order new copy was sent to them, on nice acid-free paper, or they could read it as an ebook.

Did digitizing Yiddish literature save it from death by oblivion via Dumpsters? Absolutely. Were the digitized texts the exact same as the hand-worn books? No. Does it matter? Absolutely not. The culture, what might be called the Yiddish soul, was exactly the same in the reprinted books of hundreds of authors, poets, and playwrights.

Identity is a property of continuity. A person's identity can exist to a greater or lesser extent depending upon the presence or absence of its constituents. We believe that we maintain the same identity as we grow from teenagers to adults because to a great extent our mannerisms, personality, recollections, feelings, beliefs, attitudes, and values stay consistently present over those years. Of course we *do* change as we move through new chapters in our lives, collect experiences, and evolve with time, but the change takes place atop the bedrock of constancy. Yiddish literature is "alive" even though only 80 percent rather than 100 percent of it has been digitized. Similarly, it is not necessary for a mindclone to share every memory with its biological original to have the same identity as that original.

We are all familiar with the associative law of mathematics: if $a = b$, and $b = c$, then $a = c$. In our case $a =$ our identity as defined by b, the key memories and characteristic thought patterns stored in our brain's neural connections. With the advent of mindfiles and mindware it is possible to re-create those key memories and characteristic thought patterns in c, a mindclone. Since our original identity, a, derives from our cognitive status, b, and since the cognitive status from a brain, b_a, is no different than the cognitive status from a mindclone, b_c, it follows logically that our mindclone identity, c, is the same as our brain identity, a. Furthermore, this proof demonstrates that identity is not limited to a single body or "instantiation" such as a or c. Ergo, with the rise of mindclones has come the demise of inevitable death. While unmodified bodies do inevitably die, software-based patterns of identity information do not.

There is a great inclination to argue that unless every aspect of the a-based identity is also present in the c-based identity, then b_a is not the same thing as b_c and hence a is not really equal to b and c. This argument is based on a false premise that our identity is invariant. In fact, nobody maintains "every aspect" of identity from day to day, and certainly not from year to year. We remember but a small fraction of yesterday's interactions today, and will remember still less tomorrow. Yet we simultaneously treat each other, and our selves, as people of a constant identity and are completely comfortable with and enthusiastically embracing of the concept of "reinvention" of ourselves and other people. "She's so vibrant, like a new person!" "Awesome!"

Even in the extreme cases of schizophrenia, amnesia, or dementia, we do not doubt that the patient has a constant and recognizable identity. Only in the final stages of Alzheimer's does confidence in the sufferer's identity start to waver, and our sorrow grows because it was the person's identity that we ultimately connected with. Therefore, a perfect one-to-one correspondence between b_a and b_c is not necessary in order for them to be equivalent. Instead, if, as I discussed earlier, suitably trained psychologists attest to a continuity of identity between a_b and c_b, which would tend to track with the perceptions of laypeople as well as of the original and their mindclone, then it must be accepted that the psychological fuzz of identity has cloned itself onto a new substrate. The individual's cloud identity is now instantiated in both a brain and a mindclone. A lifenaut has achieved orbit!

Why Live Forever?

> For age is opportunity no less
> Than youth itself, though in another dress,
> And as the evening twilight fades away
> The sky is filled with stars, invisible by day.
> —HENRY WADSWORTH LONGFELLOW

> Some people want to achieve immortality through their work or their
> descendants. I would prefer to achieve immortality by not dying.
> —WOODY ALLEN

There are only two personal reasons to want immortality: because you are enjoying life, or because you think if you keep living you will eventually be enjoying life. Our knee-jerk reaction against immortality is because life gets miserable when disease, depression, disability, and decrepitude arrive. Many of us see death as the natural relief from boredom, sadness, drudgery, and despair. One can argue that since deep, restful sleep is so great, death must be heaven.

There are also abstract reasons for and against immortality. It has been argued that people will treat the world more kindly if they know they must live with it forever. Or it can be argued that civilization will advance more assuredly if there would be more of a hands-on transferring of experience. On the other hand, it can be argued that there will be less room for new talent to shine if the old guard never leaves the stage. Or that society will change too slowly if a gerontocracy holds on to power. I don't consider any of these abstract reasons particularly compelling. They all have such a "maybe so, maybe not" character. What is unambiguous, though, is that if you love being alive, or if you think you will eventually love being alive, you'll want to continue being alive.[229] If you don't, you won't mind a peaceful death. The best default button is the individual's assessment of his or her own situation. As John Harris says in the *Value of Life,* the value of a life is the value one assigns to their life.

Mindclones shouldn't feel their bodies falling apart because (a) they won't have a real body, and (b) painful sensations from virtual bodies should be more easily remediable than flesh maladies. Thus, welcoming death to avoid the fragility of old age seems inapplicable to our cyberconscious selves. But since it is our minds, not our bodies, that feel depression, boredom, sadness, and drudgery, those reasons will continue to pull us, even as mindclones, into the sweet embrace of everlasting sleep.

Some people enjoy their lives until the very end. Many of those will be the kind of people who quest for the immortality of the mindclone. Other people are dissatisfied with their life, and are thus much less likely to activate their mindfile with mindware to create an immortal mindclone. But there are also many exceptions in both categories. One of my favorite people, Thomas Starzl, is now in his late eighties and lives the exciting life of a celebrated organ-transplant pioneer, considered the father of liver transplantation. He travels the world to receive awards and recognition, and he receives countless letters of gratitude from the thousands of people who are alive owing to his medical breakthroughs with liver and kidney transplantation. Immortality category? No. Tom tells me that he would not want to take the risk that an immortalized version of him turned out to be insane. Another friend of mine has suffered just about every bad economic and emotional break the world has to offer. Despite her sufferings, she is a kindly soul and looks forward to creating an immortal mindclone. Like the Hindi believers in reincarnation, her view is that the next life (a cyberconscious one) has got to be better than this one. She wants to grab a good place in the queue.

Mindclone creators will surely want a safety-capped "kill switch" so that the gravely unhappy mindclone can end it all with the cybernetic equivalent of hemlock, wrist slashing, overdosing, hanging, or a bullet. No doubt some mindclones will kill themselves out of some kind of depression. Mindclone suicide may well be as large a problem as its flesh-based cousin.

David Robert's 2004 book (made by the Wachowski siblings into a 2012 film) *Cloud Atlas,* rightly observes that "suicide takes considerable courage . . . what's selfish is to demand another to endue an intolerable existence, just to spare families, friends, and enemies a bit of soul-searching." While it is terrible that one million people do take their lives *annually,* the one million people who die *naturally every week* swamp that toll. Yet, not one of the million people who kill themselves each year ever asked to be born. By contrast, every mindclone that comes into existence asked to do so. Bemans, on the other hand, do not ask to be born. Suicides among bemans could be much higher than among mindclones. They would not have known what they were getting into, and they might regret it so much they kill themselves.

Among the things mindclones will do that will create a desire to live are: reading books ("so many books, so little time . . ."), watching movies, writing poetry, creating art, chatting with friends, making virtual (but still orgasmic, via digital haptics) love, playing sports and games, learning new things, going to virtual parties, working in real companies to make money, starting nonprofit organizations, stargazing, parenting younger mindclones, mentoring flesh people, making 3D objects with 3D printers, and just "seeing what happens next." Mindclones will pine for healthy bodies, and thankfully miss diseased ones. In general, there will be as much to live for (maybe more) as a mindclone as there was as a person. So, if the original person would have wanted to keep on living, it is likely (but not without many exceptions) that the mindclone, who is the same personality and consciousness as the original person, would also want to keep on living.

Abraham Maslow, who reenergized the field of psychology with his 1954 treatise *Motivation and Personality,* and with his even more popular *Toward a Psychology of Being,* emphasized the positive potential of the human mind, including its quest for peak experiences and its ability to pursue self-actualization without limit:

> We fear our highest possibilities. We are generally afraid to become that which we can glimpse in our most perfect moments, under conditions of great courage. We enjoy and even thrill to the godlike possibilities we see in ourselves in such peak moments.[230]

Maslow would not likely believe that a healthy mindclone could die of boredom, because self-actualization is not a problem-free state of personal utopia, but instead a state of being awestruck with the wonder of life and wanting to participate in it to the best of one's ability.

There are also several special situations where mindclones seem to have uniquely compelling justifications. For example, many jobs entail risking one's life for the benefit of society. These professions include police work, firefighting, and soldiering. It seems reasonable to help the brave souls who undertake these professions to have a mindclone backup so that all is not necessarily lost if they have to lose their life to save the lives of others. A similar special case involves astronauts on long-duration, and necessarily hazardous, space missions.

Our mindclones will want to keep on living if we are the kind of people that wish for more life, and are willing to accept its cybernetic equivalent as a medical bridge while hoping for a future upload into a cellular regenerated fresh body as a medical cure. To this large cohort, life is something to be enjoyed or endured as best as possible, so long as the quality of life is perceived as good, and there is hope for things to get better.

Creating a mindclone is much more momentous than having a child or getting married. Those responsibilities have limited or limitable durations. When you create a mindclone, you are reducing the possibility of a natural, or accidental, or unexpected death. Counterintuitively, but no less truly, that's a big thing to give away. But you are gaining a shot at an eternity of living life to its fullest, and you still have the escape of death, albeit now only through the emotionally arduous route of cybersuicide.

The Body as Boundary of Freedom

Body and mind, like man and wife, do not always agree to die together.
—CHARLES CALEB COLTON

How many people will grab the mindclone brass ring? We know that as death approaches, and if the alternative is not pain and suffering, then most people do whatever is in their power to avoid death. Not only do most people not commit suicide (in part owing to its illegality), they will spend their last dollar and put up with many medical interventions to stay alive. This is a reason to believe that once people become comfortable, through familiarity and personal experience, with cyberconscious life, many will choose to activate a mindclone.

Creating a mindclone for seriously ill people will likely become thought of as a form of organ functionality transplantation. The organ functionality being transplanted is the mind, and it is being moved (via replication) *from* a diseased body rather than *into* one. Nevertheless, from the patient's perspective, whether they consent to a brain functionality transplant or to a conventional heart, lung, liver, or kidney transplant, they are just trying to keep on living, not to be "immortal."

A mindclone-based "brain functionality transplant," for example, could give doctors an opportunity to completely rebuild a badly diseased body. Or even more fantastically, if a diseased body were a total loss, a new body could be grown from stem cells in an artificial womb. This process, ectogenesis, is the subject of significant scientific progress. If a stem cell continued to divide and grow at the rate of a natural human fetus during its first six months, by the twentieth month it would reach adult size. A mindclone-based "brain functionality transplant" team would then endeavor to write back onto the new brain's neurons, or mechanically (via an implanted microcomputer) interface to them, the information patterns contained within the mindclone.

Once the mindclone was replicated back in the newly grown flesh body, he or she would continue to live as a dual-substrate person— one legal identity, but two instantiations, one in the new flesh brain and one in a mindclone. This decision to be a dual-substrate identity would have been taken when the mindclone was first created. It is a momentous decision, but so is deciding to accept a heart transplant knowing that owing to organ shortages someone else will die for lack of that heart.

The unprecedented opportunities brought to us by advanced medical technology have unconventional legal and ethical sequelae. Be it frozen embryos, surrogate mothers, kidney donations, or brain-implanted computers controlling prosthetics, we have been able to get comfortable with the moral consequences that have arisen from scientific advances. We have repeatedly shown ourselves to be able to create life-affirming possibilities that have never before existed, and to then accommodate such creations to our ancient life-respecting values.

Ultimately mindclone activation may be a generational sort of thing. Mindclones—and new or synthetic flesh bodies—will be largely eschewed by older generations who grew up with death as a natural end to life. But mindclones will be welcomed by younger generations—digital natives—who will grow up knowing and feeling comfortable with mindclones. Hence, as the public becomes comfortable with mindclones as a form of life, the immortality aspect of mindclones will be much more of a drawing card than a turnoff.

Immortality and the Tao of Mindcloning

He who grasps the central pivot of Tao, is able to watch "Yes" and "No" pursue their alternating course around the circumference. He retains his perspective and clarity of judgment, so that he knows that "Yes" is "Yes" in the light of the "No" which stands over against it.
—THOMAS MERTON, *THE WAY OF CHUANG TZU*[231]

The Tao or "way" of mindcloning resides in its complementary nature. A mindclone *is* the mind, and hence the soul, of its biological original. Yet in another way it is not. To say that a mindclone is the same as its original is equivalent to saying that the mindclone is not the same as any other mind. But every mind is unique at every moment; our psychological worldview is like the moving landscape outside a car window. Hence, our mindclone will not be exactly like its biological original;

even the biological original cannot be exactly like itself, because it is constantly changing, evolving, and, at some point, diminishing. So the mindclone is both our mind and not our mind; it resides in the same car, but has not quite the same changing view.

My name is Martine Rothblatt because it is not any other name. In the same way, my mindclone is my mind because it is not somebody else's mind. I created it in my likeness, and expert mindware matched all of my mindfile-stored information and information-processing patterns to it. It is nobody else's mind. Ergo, it must be my mind.

Perhaps now you are thinking, Wait, it can still be not anyone else's mind, and also not your mind, because it can be its own mind. Aha—so you are seeing the Tao of mindcloning! You are now seeing that minds have borders but not boundaries. I can fill my mindclone with my every thought because minds have no boundaries when it comes to thoughts. This makes my mindclone and me of one mind. Yet my mindclone can discern differences in its existence; it is not a biological original. These differences create borders, semirelevant demarcations of interest. Considering the unbounded nature of minds, I am my mindclone and my mindclone is me. Considering the bordered nature of minds, we are each distinct. It is like the difference between my thoughts when I go to sleep and my thoughts when I wake up. Night-mind is not day-mind, but they are also one-mind.

If we think of our mindclone as something in opposition to ourselves then we will not appreciate the Tao of mindcloning. Disregarding Tao in this case creates a self-fulfilling prophecy of dual personality. As the great fourth-century-BCE writer Chuang Tzu observed,

Where self-interest is the bond,
The friendship is dissolved
When calamity comes.
Where Tao is the bond,
Friendship is made perfect
By calamity.[232]

The subtle truth of our existence is that each thing encodes its opposite, but this makes things unitary rather than bipolar. The crest of a wave is only a crest because it is part of a structure that also encodes a trough, and vice versa. Hence, if we think of our mindclones as a utility, we will not achieve a oneness of identity with it—"the friendship is dissolved when calamity comes." But if we appreciate the crest of the mindclone and the trough of our mind as part of a unitary wave, then "Tao is the bond" and "friendship is made perfect"—unity of identity is achieved, and will transcend any calamity.

The border between a mindclone and a mind is but a semirelevant feature in an unbounded consciousness space, and the same can be said about the relationship of all minds and mindclones to each other. By defining our identities we are simultaneously defining our unity with all those from whom we have cleaved a unique identity. The unity of consciousness transcends all humans and bemans.

One way to visualize this is to imagine a gargantuan pot of boiling mannerisms, personalities, recollections, feelings, beliefs, attitudes, and values. Every bit of information a human can know and information-processing pattern a human can deploy, including, of course, every emotion, are in that humongous caldron. Now, all of the bubbles that appear on the surface are like the billions of psyches of individual humans and bemans, minds and mindclones. Some persist for a longer time, others are more transient, all change shape and reflectivity. While it is clear that individual bubbles of consciousness exist—we can call them identities—it is also clear that each such identity is but a unique expression of the constellation of identity-ingredients in the pot.

Does a proud bubble of psychological characteristics define the mind? Or does a master algorithm that sent up bubbles of consciousness based on instantaneous psychodynamic conditions define it? Is the mind or mindclone a corpuscular or a corporate entity? Is consciousness something that is stuck in a place, or is it something that can be transposed, like changing the key or instrumentation of a symphony?

The Tao of mindcloning helps us to see the variable topography of consciousness and identity.

We conscious minds are triumphs of bodily independence. The first life-forms on Earth were pure "randomian" creatures: they either replicated or disappeared based on whether their shape, behavior, and biochemistry was functional or dysfunctional in the environment. They were all about body. The second life-forms were "behaviorian" beings: they had inherited the ability to learn from previous near-toxic experiences to avoid in the future similar-seeming stimuli. Natural selection favored behaviorian beings. There was some little bit of abstraction from body coded in their body.

Much later, perhaps as recently as 100 million years ago, came the "generian" species, ones that could *generally* rearrange parts of the environment *in their minds,* allowing them to outwit many behaviorians by avoiding much more trial and error. These generians maintain an internal simulation of the outside world; they are nearer the tipping point of being able to abandon their body. Dogs are familiar generians; they create models of much of their world in their heads.

Finally come us, the symbolians.[233] We are able to represent virtually everything in our heads with abstract symbols, especially words, including in particular the abstract realities inside the heads of others. Consequently, we can also represent ourselves in our minds; i.e., we can be self-conscious. We can dry-run drafts of the future in our minds, and, on average, by acting on the best draft, experience much better results in the real world. We represent the triumph of *mind over matter,* of *bemes over genes,* and hence *will be able to maintain our identity across multiple forms.* For us, it is the mind that makes us who we are.

We are still awash in randomians (bacteria), behaviorians (many animals), and generians (many mammals). Natural selection rewarded symbolians with prevalence because ever-better abilities to infer the mental states of their peers translated into ever-better abilities to avoid threats from them. A symbolian mind is by no means necessary to survive, but it was most useful in the generian niches of our group-living ancestors. From this early human game of psyops, accelerated enzymatically with language, came the hallmarks of consciousness—autonomy and empathy.

Because we could use symbolic analyses of the environment to idiosyncratically *choose* our actions (autonomy) we elevated ourselves above the stimulus-response prison of behaviorian life. Because we have the symbolic ability to put ourselves in the place of those minds (empathy), we elevated ourselves above the instinctual straitjacket of generian life. Ultimately, by creating societies of mind, we created not only individual consciousness but also a collective consciousness.

The Tao of consciousness is that there is no individual consciousness without collective consciousness. We developed our sense of self by imagining the other's sense of self. That we did so for selfish reasons of survival is irrelevant. No matter how or why one sharpens a knife, the result is a sharpened knife.

We reach back to hunter-gatherer societies, to the Greek philosophers, and to our ancient religious roots for guidance in navigating an ever-changing world. We ponder the natural laws Kant saw as embedded in the divinely inspired human mind for insight as to the best way forward. There is so much that is useful and beautiful in the human heart and soul that we can be sure it will prevail so long as its descendants prevail. Thanks to evolution evolving its own new code for life, the technoimmortal code of digital bemes, BNA, we can be more optimistic that humanity's descendants will be around, with human values, for a very long time.

So is there a future for *us*, flesh-and-blood humans? Of course. As Arthur C. Clarke wisely observed, no form of communication has ever become extinct; it just becomes less important as the technological horizon widens. So it is with biological communion. We are awash in the very first forms of life to evolve, three-billion-year-old prokaryotic bacteria, lacking even a nucleus. Each one of us comprises about ten colonizing bacteria of non-human DNA for every one of our cells dictated by our human genome. These ancient forms of biology are clearly still important, but they are no longer calling the shots on Earth. They lost their monopoly on life. We treasure the human form, exalting it in the Olympics and on Fashion TV, in the baby bassinet and at the debutante's dance, in front of the mirror and between the sheets. I do not believe it will ever become extinct. Yet, to paraphrase A. C. Clarke, human bodies will simply become less important as the vitological horizon widens.

A society of bemans could have nothing of greater wonder than a co-society of humans. We marvel at birds and trees, cats and dogs, great apes and great whales, golden wedding anniversaries and active centenarians. Our beman descendants will marvel at plants and animals, robots and androids, regenerated babies and regenerated brains, ancient mindfiles and millennial mindclones. Demographically, the identities that are alive today will eventually slip into minority status, but anthropologically we will have imprinted dignity for that which a being respects far into the future. Virtual humans value themselves as being human in all but body, and it is our highest cultural legacy that they be dignified as such. Were it us, when it is us, we would want no less.

It is a truism that human rights are for humans. But it is a revelation that human status transcends human skin. When consciousness was limited to the skull, the dignity of individuality stopped at the border of *Homo sapiens*. But with the advent of cyberconsciousness, the dignity of individuality reaches to the outer boundary of *persona creatus*. We are in the midst of a transformation from "wise man" to "creative person." The extension of human rights to all those who value such rights is essential if we are to surmount the perils and maximize the potential of this evolutionary inflection.

We have not more than one to two decades of practice before cyberconsciousness is upon us. Let us use this time to prepare for virtual humanity by making universal the application of human rights to extant humanity. As we better embed in our world of today the ethic of valuing others as they value themselves, we will be optimally prepared for the world of tomorrow. In that new world, just barely around the bend, our mindclones and bemans will value themselves as the latest advent of humanity. To that our response must be one of welcome, dignity, and respect. It will be our response if we put that ethic into better practice today, and if we remember as a mantra that mind is deeper than matter.

[GLOSSARY]

Beman: A humanly cyberconscious being not replicated from the mindfile of another person.

Beme: The basic informational unit of consciousness; the component building block of an informational architecture that provides coded or patterned instructions for mannerisms, personality, recollections, feelings, beliefs, attitudes, and values when expressed in a suitable medium such as the human brain or appropriate software and hardware. Cognitive analogues to genes in that they self-replicate, mutate, and respond to selective pressure. Each persistent conception that someone has about anything is a separate beme, as is each pattern by which they link those conceptions.

Bemone: The totality of an individual's bemes, either stored as neural-connectivity patterns in their brain or as software-connectivity patterns of mindfiles and mindware in their mindclone. For the species, the totality of all of its member's bemes, including those that are common to all members of the species and those that are unique to one or more members. Analogous to genome, but based upon elements of consciousness rather than elements of DNA.

BNA (Beme Neural Architecture): An informational structure that encodes the instructions and patterns used in the expression of consciousness, either in the human brain or in a suitable hardware and software environment.

Biocyberethics: The normative philosophical field of balancing societal interests in application of the principles of diversity and unity to determine right from wrong behavior with respect to software-based consciousness. The principles of diversity and unity are similar to the bioethical principles of autonomy and nonmalfeasance, respectfully.

Chatbot: Software that mimics the conversational capability of humans. The word is also used, disparagingly, to refer to any software that converses in a way similar to humans.

Consciousness A continuum of maturing abilities, when healthy, to be autonomous and empathetic with others.

Cyberconsciousness Consciousness achieved via information technology substrate; human levels of cyberconsciousness are determined to exist by a subjective but informed judgment of experts in cyberpsychology based upon a year-long series of discussions and/or the use of mindware and mindfiles legally certified to produce human cyberconsciousness.

Cyberpsychology The scientific study of mental functions and behaviors that occurs in software substrate; the profession of evaluating and therapeutically treating mindclones and bemans.

Ectogenesis: The process by which all or part of a body can be grown via controlled differentiation of stem cells outside of a womb.

Extropian: The belief first articulated by philosopher Max More that compounding intelligence will ultimately trump the Second Law of Thermodynamics.

Life: The expression of a code that enables self-replication and maintenance against disorder in a compatible environment. That which is organized, exchanges matter and energy with the environment, responds to stimuli, reproduces, develops, and adapts.

Mindclone: A humanly cyberconscious being designed to replicate the consciousness immanent in a mindfile of another person. A digital doppergänger and extended identity of another person.

Mindfile: A set of stored digital information about a person, such as the totality of one's social media posts, saved media and other data relating to one's life, intended to be used for the creation of a mindclone.

Mindware: Software that functions as an operating system for an artificial consciousness, including the capability to extract from a mindfile the personality of the individual who is the subject of the mindfile and to replicate that personality via operating-system settings.

Nanobots: Microscopic, wirelessly networked, intelligent machines or robots with numerous applications for science, medicine, and technology.

Single bemeotide polymorphisms: Bemes that are unique to subsets of a species' membership. These variants are single bemeotide polymorphisms (SBPs), pronounced "sbips," and are an important aspect of individuality.

Singularity: The time, probably within a few decades, when machine intelligence will merge with and surpass biological intelligence.

Surgineer: A person who performs neurocybersurgery via software engineering.

Technicity A demographic characteristic of people based upon their degree of integration and identification with technology as opposed to ethnic-based identities such as nationhood, geographic origin, religion, or language. Mindclones and bemans are members of a high technicity, or "technic," demographic group.

Technoimmortality The use of technologies such as mindcloning to outlive the duration of an original DNA-based body.

Technoprogressive: A libertarian who believes technology will solve most of the world's problems provided the technology is made universally available.

Transhumans: Those who transcend human biological inheritance by modifying their DNA, their bodies, or the substrate for their minds, and/or by leaving the Earth to live in space habitats or on other celestial bodies.

Vitology: Cybernetic life. A life code that requires only electrons, as compared with biology, which is a life code that requires atomic nuclei as well as electrons. The electron-based life codes of vitology must be seated in compatible computer hardware, while the atom-based life codes of biology must be seated in a compatible nutrient milieu.

[ACKNOWLEDGMENTS]

I'm going to take this in reverse chronological order, from the present to the past. I'm grateful to Daniela Rapp for leading the *Virtually Human* book project at St. Martin's Press. I am full of admiration for how she led us all with style, resourcefulness, and passion. I'm particularly impressed with how well she attended to the entire horizon of considerations relevant to publishing a provocative book in today's marketplace.

Prior to meeting Daniela I had the great pleasure to get to know my writing colleague, Karen Kelly. I am most appreciative for Karen's adroit organization of and thoughtful improvements to the manuscript's content. Karen is the best professional writer I have ever had the pleasure of working with, and she has a synergistic mind and harmonious soul that is a beauty to behold.

I'm thankful to Myrsini Stephanides of the Carol Mann Agency for introducing me to Daniela and Karen. This book would not be in your hands today but for Myrsini's fervent belief in this project, and the wholehearted support of her delightful boss, Carol Mann. I will always treasure the mind-melds Carol, Myrsini, Karen, Daniela, and I have had discussing the splendiferous implications of this book.

I owe a very special bear hug of appreciation to my decades-long friend and business colleague, Paul Mahon. It was Paul who got me a warm welcome at the Carol Mann Agency, and everything since has proceeded beautifully. Paul was once also a literary agent (he sold my 1995 book *Apartheid of Sex,* laying out the legal basis for equal marriage rights), and his success with this book shows that he has lost none of those skills since cofounding with me our biotechnology company.

I could not possibly have written this book without the eye-opening and mind-awakening information explained so cogently by Ray Kurzweil in *The Age of Spriitual Machines* and *The Singularity Is Near*. These books improved my outlook on reality better than anything I've read before or since. They also motivated me to use my experience in bioethics and human rights law to advance Ray's proofs of the impending singularity of artificial and human intelligence into the realm of humanly cyberconscious persons.

Between the publication dates of Ray's books I convened several workshops and symposia on the topic of cyberconsciousness, as well as developed the BINA48 robot in conjunction with David Hanson. It is my pleasure to acknowledge the important contributions of the many experts who contributed to these meetings and technology development efforts. Without the slightest lack of appreciation to the many dozens of participants who are not specifically named here, I do wish to especially recognize the contributions of Marvin Minsky, Ray Kurzweil, Baruch Blumberg, Wrye Sententia, Max More, Natasha Vita-More, Marshall Brain, Wendell Wallach, Bruce Duncan, Lori Rhodes, and Steven Mann.

From the mid-1990s to the early 2000s I had the great honor to chair the International Bar Association's Committee on Law and Medicine. I'm pleased to thank my many colleagues on that committee for their contributions to the opportunities my chairmanship gave me to develop human rights law in the areas of genomics and robotics.

I wrote the great majority of this book in Lincoln, Vermont. I was provided with an ideal writing environment, and bountiful encouragement, by my soul mate Bina Aspen Rothblatt. I went beyond the mere conceptualization of mindfiles, mindware, and mindclones—into detailed analysis, and comprehensive solutions—because Bina stood by my side, and challenged my mind.

The greatest lesson in acceptance that I've ever felt was in the wholehearted embrace of my transition from male to female by my two sons, Eli and Gabriel, and my two daughters, Sunee and Jenesis, while all four were in the sensitive teenage and preteen years. That very personal experience of love beyond gender gave me much of the confidence to write in this book that love will also transcend that genre of ontology represented by mindclones.

Reaching further back in time I feel this book is an extrapolation of knowledge I learned from key professors, and from my parents. These teachers include Professor Len Doyal of the Royal London School of Medicine, who guided me through medical ethics, and UCLA professors Patrice French, Paul Rosenthal, and Charlie Firestone from whom I learned of cybernetics, semantics, and information law, respectively.

Lastly, I'm pleased to acknowledge the fundamental lesson I soaked up from my parents, Hal and Rosa Lee: It is what you learn and how well you treat people that matters, not what you materially have or how people physically appear. It seems clear that such a foundation subtly helped me write this book that celebrates mind over matter, and elaborates human rights for virtual humans.

[NOTES]

ONE: THE ME IN THE MACHINE

[1] Arthur Koestler, *The Ghost in the Machine* (Chicago: Henry Regnery, 1967), 220.

[2] Marvin Minsky, *The Emotion Machine* (New York: Simon & Schuster, 2007), 17, 88, 109–12.

[3] Bernard J. Baars, "Treating Consciousness as a Variable: The Fading Taboo," in *Essential Sources in the Scientific Study of Consciousness*, ed. Bernard J. Baars, William P. Banks, and James B. Newman (Cambridge, MA: MIT Press, 2003), 2.

[4] Steven Pinker, *How the Mind Works* (New York: W. W. Norton, 1997), 132.

[5] J. Bargh, "Our Unconscious Mind," *Scientific American* (January 2014), 30, 37.

[6] Eric Baum, *What Is Thought?* (Cambridge, MA: MIT Press, 2004), 403.

[7] Francis Crick and Christof Koch, "Consciousness and Neuroscience," in *Essential Sources in the Scientific Study of Consciousness*, ed. Bernard J. Baars, William P. Banks, and James B. Newman (Cambridge, MA: MIT Press, 2003), 35.

[8] Daniel C. Dennett, *Kinds of Minds* (New York: Basic Books, 1996), 4. ("Thomas Nagel's classic 1974 paper, 'What Is It Like to Be a Bat?' . . . sets us off on the wrong foot, inviting us to ignore all the different ways in which bats (and other animals) might accomplish their cunning feats without its 'being like' anything for them. We create a putatively impenetrable mystery for ourselves if we presume without further ado that Nagel's question makes sense, and that we know what we are asking.") Ibid. at p. 161.

[9] Andrew Hodges, *Alan Turing: The Enigma* (Princeton: Princeton University Press, 2012), 266.

[10] Jeff Hawkins, *On Intelligence* (New York: Henry Holt and Company, 2004), 105. I believe Jeff Hawkins misunderstands the Turing test in this way. He believes the Turing test fails to measure intelligence and measures only behavior. I think this is a semantic confusion, because a computer that could pass itself off as a person would be demonstrating *behavior showing intelligence* (such as the ability to predict things based upon memories).

[11] This article is reprinted in Douglas R. Hofstadter and Daniel C. Dennett, eds., *The Mind's I* (New York: Basic Books, 1981).

[12] Gerald M. Edelman, *Second Nature: Brain Science and Human Knowledge* (New Haven: Yale University Press, 2006), 9.

[13] Edelman, *Second Nature*, 24.

[14] P. W. Singer, *Wired for War: The Robotics Revolution and Conflict in the 21st Century* (New York: Penguin Press, 2009), 88 (Ralph's "No Hands Across America" interstate highway ride), and 137 (Stanley's "Grand Challenge" desert ride).

[15] David K. Warland, Pamela Reinagel, and Markus Meister, "Decoding Visual Information from a Population of Retinal Ganglion Cells," *Journal of Neurophysiology* 78 (1997), 2336–50.

[16] Edelman, *Second Nature*, 21.

[17] Daniel C. Dennett, *Consciousness Explained* (Boston: Little Brown, 1991).

[18] There is in theory a sort of hybrid possibility of an essentialist-materialist. This point of view is that the sensations of a human body are necessary to emotions, and that these emotions in turn are essential to the human morality we consider necessary for human consciousness. Robot ethicist Wendell Wallach summarizes this point of view as "only biological organisms that have feelings, sentience and consciousness are inherently capable of being moral actors" because "without a capacity to actually feel distress, pain, fear, and anger or positive emotions such as joy, pleasure, gratitude, and affection, a being does not possess the moral states or moral identifications that are essential to being a fully rounded moral individual." Wendell Wallach and Colin Allen, *Moral Machines: Teaching Robots Right from Wrong* (Oxford: Oxford University Press, 2009), 68. Yet, aside from the debate as to whether bodily sensations are necessary for emotions, there is no doubt that technological replication of bodily sensations is advancing rapidly. Haptic devices for sensing touch are consumer products, and the underlying technology is so robust that robots equipped with advanced haptics perform surgeries. Electronic noses, one of them named for the bulbous nostrils of Cyrano de Bergerac, can distinguish among dozens of scents. Hence, since we are on track to avail mindclones of the range of human senses via technology, the argument seems weak that mindclones can't be humanly conscious because they can't be humanly moral without feeling human sensations. "Cyrano 'Nose' the Smell of Success," *Spinoff*, NASA Office of the Chief Technologist, accessed January 4, 2014, http://spinoff.nasa .gov/spinoff2001/ps4.html. Ultimately, this purportedly hybrid essentialist-materialist perspectively resolves into pure materialist with the continuing advance of sensation technology.

[19] John R. Searle, *The Mystery of Consciousness* (New York: *The New York Review of Books*, 1995), xiv.

[20] Searle, *Mystery of Consciousness*, 13

[21] Ibid., 111.

[22] Searle divides reality into two ontologies, or categories, the first-person, or subjective, point of view and the third-person, or objective, point of view. He then further notes that each ontology can be assessed independently of an observer or dependent upon an observer. Consciousness and experiences are in the subjective ontology, the first assessed independently of an observer and the second assessed by an observer. Hence, my friend sees that I'm happy (subjective ontology, observer-assessed), but only I know that I am happy (subjective ontology, non-observer-assessed). The force of

gravity and paper money are in objective ontology, the first assessed independently of an observer (gravity exists whether we like it or not), the second assessed by an observer (money is money only if someone thinks so). Hence, a pile of money can buy a lot (objective ontology, observer-assessed), but it will just lie flat on the table unless an intervening force moves it (objective ontology, non-observer-assessed).

A Table Description of the Concept of Subjective Materialism

	FIRST PERSON (SUBJECTIVE)	THIRD PERSON (OBJECTIVE)
Observer-Independent	Consciousness	Experiences; Neural or Software Correlates of Consciousness; The Weight of Gold
Observer-Dependent	A Person's Own, Interior, Experience of Their Consciousness	Adequacy of a Mindfile; Measurements of Consciousness Correlates; Value of Gold

Physics teaches us that there is a reality beyond what we can precisely measure, and Searle teaches us that this is also true for consciousness. In physics this subjective materialism arises as we slip from the microscopic to the quantum level of perception. In consciousness it arises as we slip from the pathways to the experiential level of perception. It is super cool that engineers can take advantage of quantum electron tunneling effects to build awesome nanocircuits, even though we can't really see it happening. It will be similarly astounding when software engineers take advantage of emergent properties effects to build cyberconsciousness, even though we can't really see the world through the virtually human's eyes.

[23] Searle, *Mystery of Consciousness*, 98.

[24] See, e.g., Pinker, *How the Mind Works*, 24: "Information and computation reside in patterns of data and in relations of logic that are independent of the physical medium that carries them. . . . This insight, first expressed by the mathematician Alan Turing . . . is now called the computational theory of mind. It is one of the great ideas in intellectual history, for it solves one of the puzzles that make up the 'mind-body problem': how to connect the ethereal world of meaning and intention, the stuff of our mental lives, with a physical hunk of matter like the brain. . . . For millennia this has been a paradox. . . . The computational theory of mind resolves the paradox. It says that beliefs and desires are *information*, incarnated as configurations of symbols. The symbols are the physical states of bits of matter, like chips in a computer or neurons in the brain. They symbolize things in the world because they are triggered by those things via our sense organs, and because of what they do once they are triggered. If the bits of matter that constitute a symbol are arranged to bump into the bits of matter constituting another symbol in just the right way, the symbols corresponding to one belief can give rise to new symbols corresponding to another belief logically related to it, which can give rise to symbols corresponding to other beliefs, and so on. Eventually the bits of matter constituting a symbol bump into bits of matter connected to the muscles, and behavior happens. The computational theory of mind thus allows us to keep beliefs and desires in our explanations of behavior while planting them squarely in the physical universe. It allows meaning to cause and be caused."

[25] Crick and Koch, "Consciousness and Neuroscience," 49.

[26] Sebastian Seung, *Connectome: How the Brain's Wiring Makes Us Who We Are* (Boston: Houghton Mifflin Harcourt, 2012).

[27] Lewis R. Goldberg, "The Structure of Phenotypic Personality Traits," *American Psychologist* 48 (1993), 26–34.

[28] Raymond B. Cattell, *Handbook of the 16 Personality Factors Questionnaire* (Champaign, Illinois: Institute for Personality and Ability Testing, 1949). These factors are further described along the positive and negative scales with the help of the following descriptors:

DESCRIPTORS OF LOW RANGE	PRIMARY FACTOR	DESCRIPTORS OF HIGH RANGE
Impersonal, distant, cool, reserved, detached, formal, aloof	Warmth	Warm, outgoing, attentive to others, kindly, easygoing, participating, likes people
Concrete thinking, lower general mental capacity, less intelligent, unable to handle abstract problems	Reasoning	Abstract-thinking, more intelligent, bright, higher general mental capacity, fast learner
Reactive emotionally, changeable, affected by feelings, emotionally less stable, easily upset	Emotional Stability	Emotionally stable, adaptive, mature, faces reality calmly
Deferential, cooperative, avoids conflict, submissive, humble, obedient, easily led, docile, accommodating	Dominance	Dominant, forceful, assertive, aggressive, competitive, stubborn, bossy
Serious, restrained, prudent, taciturn, introspective, silent	Liveliness	Lively, animated, spontaneous, enthusiastic, happy go lucky, cheerful, expressive, impulsive
Expedient, nonconforming, disregards rules, self-indulgent	Rule-Consciousness	Rule-conscious, dutiful, conscientious, conforming, moralistic, staid, rule bound
Shy, threat-sensitive, timid, hesitant, intimidated	Social Boldness	Socially bold, venturesome, thick skinned, uninhibited
Utilitarian, objective, unsentimental, tough minded, self-reliant, no-nonsense, rough	Sensitivity	Sensitive, aesthetic, sentimental, tender minded, intuitive, refined
Trusting, unsuspecting, accepting, unconditional, easy	Vigilance	Vigilant, suspicious, skeptical, distrustful, oppositional
Grounded, practical, prosaic, solution oriented, steady, conventional	Abstractedness	Abstract, imaginative, absent minded, impractical, absorbed in ideas
Forthright, genuine, artless, open, guileless, naive, unpretentious, involved	Privateness	Private, discreet, nondisclosing, shrewd, polished, worldly, astute, diplomatic
Self-assured, unworried, complacent, secure, free of guilt, confident, self-satisfied	Apprehension	Apprehensive, self-doubting, worried, guilt prone, insecure, worrying, self-blaming
Traditional, attached to familiar, conservative, respecting traditional ideas	Openness to Change	Open to change, experimental, liberal, analytical, critical, free-thinking, flexibility
Group-oriented, affiliative, a joiner and follower dependent	Self-Reliance	Self-reliant, solitary, resourceful, individualistic, self-sufficient
Tolerates disorder, unexacting, flexible, undisciplined, lax, self-conflict, impulsive, careless of social rules, uncontrolled	Perfectionism	Perfectionistic, organized, compulsive, self-disciplined, socially precise, exacting will power, control, self-sentimental

DESCRIPTORS OF LOW RANGE	PRIMARY FACTOR	DESCRIPTORS OF HIGH RANGE
Relaxed, placid, tranquil, torpid, patient, composed low drive	Tension	Tense, high-energy, impatient, driven, frustrated, overwrought, time driven.

Primary Factors and Descriptors in Cattell's 16 Personality Factor Model (Adapted From Conn & Rieke, 1994).

[29] William Sims Bainbridge, "Massive Questionnaires for Personality Capture," *Social Science Computer Review* 21, no. 3 (2003), 267–80. See also: Codebook, General Social Surveys, 1972–2006, Inter-University Consortium for Political and Social Research, for hundreds of well-calibrated social-psychology questions.

[30] Dennett, *Consciousness Explained*, 431.

[31] Hodges, *Alan Turing: The Enigma*, 291.

[32] Ibid.

[33] Gerald M. Edelman, *Bright Air, Brilliant Fire: On the Matter of the Mind* (New York: Basic Books, 1992), 29.

[34] Edelman, *Bright Air, Brilliant Fire*, 211. He does claim his "goal is to dispel the notion that the mind can be understood in the absence of biology." Yet he does not disprove the possibility of a mind in the absence of biology, because he does not ever prove that a mind can *only* come from biology.

[35] Pekka Himanen, *The Hacker Ethic* (New York: Random House, 2001), 189.

[36] Edelman, *Second Nature*, 152.

[37] Dennett quotes correspondence with Edelman claiming he has conceded this point with regard to intentional behavior. Searle, *Mystery of Consciousness*, 119.

[38] For a monkey it would be the depth and surface area equivalent to a pair of panties. For a rat it would be the depth and surface area of the size label on our T-shirt.

[39] Bernard J. Baars, "Treating Consciousness as a Variable: The Fading Taboo," in *Essential Sources in the Scientific Study of Consciousness*, ed. Bernard J. Baars, William P. Banks, and James B. Newman (Cambridge, MA: MIT Press, 2003), 5

[40] Searle, *Mystery of Consciousness*, 204.

[41] Hodges, *Alan Turing: The Enigma,* 417.

[42] *The Economist,* November 3, 2007, 95.

[43] Ray Kurzweil, *The Singularity Is Near* (New York: Penguin, 2005), 70. It is important to note that Kurzweil's graph comes out virtually the same no matter which of about twenty different experts selects which information technology advances to use in plotting it. In other words, the exponential curve does not arise from Kurzweil's selection of advances, but from the advances themselves.

[44] "For while time machines, eternal life potions and Star Trek-style warp drives are as far away as ever, a team of scientists in Switzerland is claiming that a fully-functioning replica of a human brain could be built by 2020. This isn't just pie-in-the-sky. The Blue Brain project, led by computer genius Henry Markram—who is also the director of the Centre for Neuroscience & Technology and the Brain Mind Institute—has for the past five years been engineering the mammalian brain, the most complex object known in the Universe, using some of the most powerful supercomputers in the world. And last month Professor Markram claimed, at a conference in Oxford, that he plans to build an electronic human brain 'within ten years'." Michael Hanlon, "Are We On the Brink of Creating a Computer with a Human Brain?," *Daily Mail*, August 11, 2009,

http://www.dailymail.co.uk/sciencetech/article-1205677/Are-brink-creating-human
-brain.html#ixzz0m6x37gaM.

[45] Ray Kurzweil, *How to Create a Mind: The Secret of Human Thought Revealed* (New York: Viking, 2012), 210.

[46] Kurzweil, *Singularity*, 71. Kurzweil notes that "Moore's Law narrowly refers to the number of transistors on an integrated circuit of fixed size and sometimes has been expressed even more narrowly in terms of transistor feature size. But the most appropriate measure to track price-performance is computational speed per unit cost, an index that takes into account many levels of 'cleverness' (innovation, which is to say, technological evolution)."

[47] Norbert Wiener, "The Machine Age" (1949), unpublished essay excerpted in *The New York Times*, May 21, 2013.

[48] John Markoff, "Brainlike Computers, Learning from Experience," *The New York Times*, December 28, 2013, http://www.nytimes.com/2013/12/29/science/brainlike
-computers-learning-from-experience.html?pagewanted=all.

[49] Ibid.

TWO: OUR DOPPELGÄNGERS ALREADY EXIST

[50] Leo Kelion, "CES 2014: Sony Shows Off Life Logging App and Kit," BBC News, accessed January 8, 2014, http://www.bbc.co.uk/news/technology-25633647. Perhaps the greatest pioneer of creating a documented life is the University of Toronto computer scientist Steve Mann, who coined the term "sousveillance" to mean "everyone watching everyone" as compared to "surveillance," which is just a central authority watching the rest of us. Mann lives his life with wearable digital recording equipment, and even braves arrest wearing such equipment in police-controlled areas and toilets. His "share what you see" website, accessed January 21, 2014, is www.glogger.mobi.

[51] In 1975, John Holland invented genetic algorithms, which are bits of code that evolve in a software environment. The algorithms are designed to seek and combine with particular strings of binary code in the way biological life moves toward food. Code that successfully evolves in a Darwinian fashion is sometimes called "A-life."

[52] Kenneth J. Hayworth, "Electron Imaging Technology for Whole Brain Neural Circuit Mapping," *International Journal of Machine Consciousness* 4, no. 1 (2012).

[53] Baars, "Treating Consciousness," 9.

[54] One experiment is described at M. Rothblatt, "The Terasem Mind Uploading Experiment," *International Journal of Machine Consciousness* 4, no. 1 (2012), 141–58.

[55] Paul Ekman, *Emotions Revealed*, 2nd ed. (New York: Owl Books, 2007).

[56] "EPOC Neuroheadset," accessed January 25, 2014, http://www.emotiv.com/apps/epoc/299/.

[57] "Robot Wars," *The Economist*, June 9, 2007, Technology Quarterly, 10.

[58] Ibid.

[59] Chris Carroll, "Us. And Them. Robots Are Being Created That Can Think, Act and Relate to Humans," *National Geographic Magazine*, August 2011, accessed January 25, 2014, http://ngm.nationalgeographic.com/print/2011/08/robots/carroll-text.

[60] Carroll, "Us. And Them,"

[61] BINA48 was featured in the centerfold of the August 2011 issue of *National Geographic*, http://ngm.nationalgeographic.com/2011/08/robots/robots-photography.

[62] In a similar vein, Microsoft's Bing search engine tells the user it is "thinking" while searching its databases.

[63] "More Than Just Digital Quilting," *The Economist*, December 3, 2011, Technology *Quarterly*, 3.

[64] Eric Baum, *What Is Thought?* (Cambridge, MA: MIT Press, 2004), 406.

[65] Ramez Naam, *More Than Human* (New York: Broadway Books, 2005), 218.

[66] Max More, "The Diachronic Self: Identity, Continuity, Transformation" (1995).

[67] John Locke, *An Essay Concerning Human Understanding*, vol. 1 (New York: Dover, 1959), 139.

[68] James L. McGaugh, *Memory and Emotion: The Making of Lasting Memories* (New York: Columbia University Press, 2003), 2.

[69] William James, *Principles of Psychology* (New York: Henry Holt and Company, 1890), 680.

[70] Bernard J. Baars, "Metaphors of Consciousness and Attention in the Brain," in *Essential Sources in the Scientific Study of Consciousness*, ed. Bernard J. Baars, William P. Banks, and James B. Newman (Cambridge, MA: MIT Press, 2003), 1116.

[71] "'Your brain damage complications were terrible, and it took a lot more to get you back than Sam and I. I can't tell you how lonely I've been, but all these things of ours have kept me company.' The lofty home was filled with possessions Judy had stored for them. Handling them helped Arnold grasp that his past life was real, not a dream to be tossed aside for new experiences, as if he'd suddenly sprung to life with no former existence." Fred and Linda Chamberlain, eds., *LifeQuest: Stories About Cryonics, Uploading, and other Transhuman Adventures* (Scottsdale: Create Space, 2009), 123.

[72] J. McGaugh, "Memory and Emotion: The Making of Lasting Memories (Maps of Mind), (New York: Columbia University Press, 2003), 45.

[73] Alan Watts, *The Book: On the Taboo Against Knowing Who You Are* (New York: Vintage Books, 1966, 1989). Watts notes that "the individual is separate from his universal environment only in name. When this is not recognized, you have been fooled by your name. Confusing names with nature, you come to believe that having a separate name makes you a separate being. This is—rather literally—to be spellbound. Naturally, it isn't the mere fact of being named that brings about the hoax of being a 'real person': it is all that goes with it. The child is tricked into the ego-feeling by the attitudes, words, and actions of the society which surrounds him—his parents, relatives, teachers, and, above all, his similarly hoodwinked peers. Other people teach us who we are." Ibid., 69–70.

[74] "[E]very organism is a process: thus the organism is not other than its actions. To put it clumsily: it is what it does. . . . The only real 'you' is the one that comes and goes, manifests and withdraws itself eternally in and as every conscious being. For 'you' is the universe looking at itself from billions of points of view, points that come and go so that the vision is forever new. What we see as death, empty space, or nothingness is only the trough between the crests of this endlessly waving ocean." Ibid., 97, 130–31.

[75] Ibid., 9.

[76] In a similar vein, see Peter White, *The Ecology of Being* (New York: All-in-All Books,

2006), 190. ("To be self-aware is to know intuitively that one is of everything and every-thing is of one.")

[77] Daniel Kolak, *I Am You: The Metaphysical Foundations for Global Ethics* (Dor-drecht, The Netherlands: Springer, 2004), 26. ("That I am is a fact; who I am is an interpretation. We might even say, personal identity is where epistemology and ontol-ogy meet, within us.") Ibid., 5.

[78] Ibid., 38.

[79] Ibid., 94.

[80] Edward O. Wilson, *Consilience: The Unity of Knowledge* (New York: Alfred A. Knopf), 303.

[81] Hans Moravec, *Robot: Mere Machine to Transcendent Mind* (New York: Oxford Uni-versity Press, 1999), 144–45.

[82] Dwayne McDuffie and Denys Cowan, "The Souls of Cyber-Folk," *Deathlok* 2–5 (New York: Marvel Comics, August–November 1991).

[83] W. E. B. Du Bois, *The Souls of Black Folk* (Chicago: McClurg, 1903).

[84] For an excellent set of essays on this subject in the context of transhumanism, see J. Hughes, *Contradictions of the Enlightenment: Liberal Individualism versus the Erosion of Personal Identity*, November 11, 2011, accessed January 22, 2014, http://ieet.org/index.php/IEET/more/hughes20111119.

[85] John Locke, *An Essay Concerning Human Understanding*, vol. 1 (New York: Dover, 1959), 139.

[86] In the lexicon of E. O. Wilson's physical soul, we can think of DNA as being the form, or mold, which by itself, can do nothing. But when it is filled with chemical energy from RNA, and the same process from RNA to ribosomes, then the form has a gravitas, an influence, in this case upon the biochemical operations of a body and brain.

[87] Wendell Wallach and Colin Allen, *Moral Machines: Teaching Robots Right from Wrong* (Oxford: Oxford University Press, 2009), 217.

THREE: MINDCLONING, NATURAL SELECTION, AND DIGITAL EUGENICS

[88] Eric D. Beinhocker, *The Origin of Wealth* (Cambridge, MA: Harvard Business School Press, 2006).

[89] November 13, 2007.

[90] Hawkins, *On Intelligence*, 86, 89,

[91] Dennett, *Kinds of Minds*, 126.

[92] From http://community.electricsheep.org website, with sixty thousand participants as of 2010.

[93] Hawkins, *On Intelligence*, 182.

[94] Ibid., 207.

[95] Ibid., 215.

[96] Ibid., 208.

[97] See question 14, supra, for explanation of beme neural architecture (BNA).

[98] James Bentley, *Martin Niemöller: 1892–1984* (New York: Macmillan Free Press, 1984).

[99] Lynn A. Stout, *Cultivating Conscience: How Good Laws Make Good People* (Prince-ton: Princeton University Press, 2011), 56.

[100] Ibid., 6–7.

[101] Himanen, *The Hacker Ethic*, ix–x.

[102] Summary Statement of the Asilomar Conference on Recombinant DNA Molecules, Approved by the National Academy of Sciences 20 May 1975.

[103] In an interview, National Academy of Engineering Grand Challenges solar energy section author Ray Kurzweil said, "The cost of solar energy is coming down dramatically and the amount of solar energy we're producing is on an exponential—in fact, it's been doubling every two years and has been doing so for the last 20 years. Solar is only eight doublings away from being 100 percent of the world's energy needs. And it's doubling every two years—so that's 16 years for it meeting 100 percent of our energy needs." Natasha Lomas, "Nanotech to Solve Global Warming by 2028," Silicon.com, November 20, 2008, http://www.silicon.com/management/cio-insights/2008/11/20/nanotech-to-solve-global-warming-by-2028-39345604/.

[104] Stout, *Cultivating Conscience*, 47.

[105] Ibid.

[106] Richard Dawkins, *The Selfish Gene* (Oxford: Oxford University Press, 1976), 192–94.

> We need a name for the new replicator, a noun that conveys the idea of a unity of cultural transmission, or a unit of *imitation*. "Mimeme" comes from a suitable Greek root, but I want a monosyllable that sounds a bit like "gene". I hope my classicist friends will forgive me if I abbreviate mimeme to *meme*. . . . Examples of memes are tunes, ideas, catch-phrases, clothes fashions, ways of making pots or of building arches. Just as genes propagate themselves in the gene pool by leaping from body to body via sperms or eggs, so memes propagate themselves in the meme pool by leaping from brain to brain via a process which, in the broad sense, can be called imitation. . . . For more than three thousand million years, DNA has been the only replicator worth talking about in the world. But it does not necessarily hold these monopoly rights for all time. Whenever conditions arise in which a new kind of replicator *can* make copies of itself, the new replicators *will* tend to take over, and start a new kind of evolution of their own. Once this new evolution begins, it will in no necessary sense be subservient to the old. The old gene-selection evolution, by making brains, provided the soup in which the first memes arose. Once self-copying memes had arisen, their own, much faster, kind of evolution took off. We biologists have assimilated the idea of genetic evolution so deeply that we tend to forget that it is only one of many possible kinds of evolution.

[107] Naam, *More Than Human*, 189.

[108] A further consideration in the United States would be constitutional protection of the incipient cyberconsciousness as a matter of "due process" for "personhood." In the case of *Roe v. Wade*, Supreme Court Justice Blackmun wrote, with respect to a fetus, that if its "personhood is established" then "the fetus' right to life would then be guaranteed specifically by the [Fourteenth] Amendment." Roe v. Wade, 410 U.S. 113, 169–70 (1973). See generally, Jonathan Will, "Beyond Abortion: Why the Personhood Movement Implicates Reproductive Choice," *American Journal of Law and Medicine* 39: 573 (2013).

[109] World Medical Association, Declaration of Helsinki—Ethical Principles for Medical Research Involving Human Subjects, 1964, Last Amended October 2013 (hereinafter *Helsinki Declaration*), accessed January 21, 2014, http://www.wma.net/en/30publications/10policies/b3/.

[110] World Medical Association, *Helsinki Declaration*, para. 30.

[111] "Play Nice: Chimps Need Parental Guidance to Safely Horse Around," *Scientific American*, December 2013, 21.

FOUR: PARDON ME WHILE I HAVE TECHNICAL DIFFICULTIES

[112] London Mathematical Society Lecture, February 20, 1947.

[113] Himanen, *The Hacker Ethic*, 140.

[114] Buck v. Bell, 274 U.S. 200, 207 (1927), ("Three generations of imbeciles are enough"), Justice Oliver Wendell Holmes.

[115] L. Harris and L. Paltrow, "The Status of Pregnant Women and Fetuses in US Criminal Law," *Journal of the American Medical Association* 289, no. 13 (2003), 1697–99.

[116] John A. Robertson, "Assisting Reproduction, Choosing Genes, and the Scope of Reproductive Freedom," *George Washington Law Review* 76, no. 6 (2008), 1490.

[117] Searle, *Mystery of Consciousness*, 204 (italics in text).

[118] Ibid., 204.

[119] Himanen, *The Hacker Ethic*, 47. Linux was copylefted by its creator, Linus Torvalds. We can thank Robert Stallman, a free software advocate, for the concept of licensing things in a way that guarantees freedom of development and use by others. Humorously Stallman observed that while "copyright" implies "all rights reserved," "copyleft" implies "all rights reversed."

[120] Dave Marinaccio, *All I Really Need to Know I Learned from Watching Star Trek* (New York: Crown, 1994).

[121] Wallach and Allen, *Moral Machines*, 105–11.

[122] J. Storrs Hall, *Beyond AI: Creating the Conscience of the Machine* (Amherst, NY: Prometheus Books, 2007).

[123] Michael Muhammad Knight, *The Taqwacores* (Brooklyn: Autonomedia, 2004), 212.

[124] Ibid., 132.

[125] In a comprehensive sense every one of us is a freak. There are no two of us whose bodies or minds are exactly the same. We have so many differences among us that there is no way to calculate a mean, or average, of what it is to be human because it is a mishmash of thousands of physical, psychological, and behavioral characteristics. Compared with everyone else, and considering ourselves in our totality of individuality, we are all far outside the one, two, and three standard deviations.

[126] Edward Hoffman, *The Right to Be Human: A Biography of Abraham Maslow* (Los Angeles: Jeremy Tarcher, 1988), 154–55.

[127] The computation of damages in a wrongful life action is based on the claim that the value of the life of the disabled child is less than the value of never having been born. The California Supreme Court, in Turpin v. Sortini, 31 Cal.3d 220, 182 Cal. Rptr. 337, 643 P.2d 954 (1982), stated that the wrongful life action is another form of

a medical malpractice action, and that recovery should not be allowed for pain and suffering and other general damages, but rather only for those extraordinary medical and other expenses incurred during the child's lifetime.

[128] Stout, *Cultivating Conscience*, 82.

[129] Annie Trafton, "Neuroscientists Plant False Memories in the Brain: MIT Study Pinpoints Where the Brain Stores Memory Traces, Both False and Authentic," *MIT News*, July 29, 2013, accessed December 17, 2013, http://web.mit.edu/newsoffice/2013/neuroscientists-plant-false-memories-in-the-brain-0725.html.

CHAPTER FIVE: ELBOW ROOM

[130] International Energy Agency, World Energy Outlook, 2008, http://www.iea.org/weo/electricity.asp.

[131] Ibid.

[132] Peter H. Diamandis and Steven Kotler, *Abundance: The Future Is Better Than You Think* (New York: Free Press, 2012), 99.

[133] Entrepreneurs in developing countries often excel at figuring out ways to deliver rich-country technology for a small fraction of the offering price.

[134] Naam, *More Than Human*, 218.

[135] http://esa.un.org/unpd/wpp/Other-Information/Press_Release_WPP2010.pdf

[136] http://www.pbs.org/newshour/bb/science/july-dec13/tidalpower_09-15.html

[137] Thomas Landauer, "How Much Do People Remember? Some Estimates of the Quantity of Learned Information in Long-Term Memory," *Cognitive Science* 10 (1986), 477–93; Hans Moravec, *Mind Children* (Cambridge, MA: Harvard University Press, 1988), 57, 163. Landauer, working at Bell Labs, conducted many experiments on remembered information, leading to an estimate of 2 bits per second as the rate at which a human mind accumulates information over its lifetime.

[138] Things could be different. For the definitive description of constructing orbiting biological spaces from inert lunar and asteroidal materials see Gerard K. O'Neill, *The High Frontier* (New York: Bantam Books, 1975). O'Neill demonstrates how current technology could create enough such biological spaces to house multiples of the Earth's entire population.

[139] Alan Turing, *Machine Intelligence* 5, ed. B. Melcher & D. Michie, August 1948, Edinburgh University Press.

[140] Ibid.

[141] Michael Lemonick, "The Kepler Space Telescope May Be Dead, but Its Planet-Hunting Mission Continues," Time.com, August 2013, accessed December 11, 2013, http://science.time.com/2013/08/16/the-kepler-space-telescope-may-be-dead-but-its-planet-hunting-mission-continues/.

[142] M. Rothblatt (2012), "We Are the World: Inviting Everyone Onboard the 100YSS Is Practical and Will Help to Ensure Its Success," *Proceedings of the 100 Year Starship Symposium*, ed. M. Jemison, 393.

[143] This technology was invented by the decoder of the human genome—two life-science revolutions from the same person. J. Craig Venter, *Life at the Speed of Light: From the Double Helix to the Dawn of Digital Life* (New York: Viking, 2013).

144 Gerard K. O'Neill, *2081: A Hopeful View of the Human Future* (New York: Simon & Schuster, 1981), 261–65. (Self-replicating space probes, that copied themselves within ten years from a computer-program-directed reassembly of asteroidal materials found near any star, and starting from any point in the galaxy, would, if traveling between stars at about 90 percent the speed of light, be able to orbit every star and scan every planet in under 100,000 years—less than 1 percent of 1 percent of the Milky Way's lifetime.)

SIX: EVOLUTION OR REVOLUTION?

145 B. Bernstein, "Elaborated and Restricted Codes: Their Social Origins and Some Consequences," *American Anthropologist* 66 (1964), 6, 55–69.

146 Three surveys of artificial-intelligence experts have yielded a variety of opinions. B. Goetzel et al., "How Long Till Human-Level AI: What do the Experts Say," in *H+*, February 5, 2010, http://www.hplusmagazine.com/articles/ai/how-long-till-human-level-ai. The first, at an AI pioneers conference in 2006, saw a split between those expecting human-level consciousness within fifty years, and those who never expect it. A second, conducted online in 2007, had a large majority expecting artificial consciousness within a half century. A third, polled at an artificial general intelligence conference in 2009, resulted in 75 percent believing humanoid computers would arise in the twenty-first century, while 25 percent thought it would take longer, if ever.

147 There are many thoughtful people who do believe it is impossible for anything but a human mind to be conscious. Perhaps the most thoughtful of these is the brilliant mathematician Roger Penrose.

148 Fred Jerome and Rodger Taylor, *Einstein on Race and Racism* (Rutgers, NJ: Rutgers University Press, 2005), 145.

149 Thomas Foster, *The Souls of Cyberfolk: Posthumanism as Vernacular Theory* (Minneapolis: University of Minnesota Press, 2005).

150 Ibid., 89, 175.

151 The biological original would benefit from mindclone meditation in two ways. First, as the person's identity now transcends their biological and cybernetic selves, their cybernetic self—their mindclone—will benefit from the stillness of mind that comes form meditation. Secondly, insofar as the mindclone and biological frequently synch (e.g. "catch up," "check in," "think things through together") the biological will have the benefit of a mindclone that is more relaxed and serene due to the meditation—less frazzled and a better friend/advisor/soul mate. In a similar vein, my "business mind" never really meditates, although I do. But I think my business mind benefits from the fact that when I figure out what to do, I take more of a Zen perspective by virtue of stilling the rest of my mind of all thoughts.

152 George Johnson, "Virtually Immortal," *National Geographic*, December 2013, 102.

153 Ronald Bailey, "Should 'Moral Vertigo' Make Biotech Fall Over?", Reason.com, March 10, 2004, http://reason.com/archives/2004/03/10/should-moral-vertigo-make-biot.

154 Paul Ekman, *Emotions Revealed: Recognizing Faces and Feelings to Improve Communication and Emotional Life* (New York: St. Martin's Press, 2003).

155 David Brin, *The Transparent Society* (New York: Basic Books, 1998), 331, 333.

156 Ibid., 13.

157 William Shakespeare, *Hamlet,* act 3, sc. 2.

158 The global average death rate is just under 10 persons per year per 1,000 population. In the U.S. it is about 0.8 percent per year.

159 Achim Goerres, "The Grey Vote: Determinants of Older Voters' Party Choice in Britain and West Germany," 27 (2) *Electoral Studies* (2008), 285–304.

160 R. Binstock, "Older Voters and the 2008 Election," *The Gerontologist* (advance access published online July 2, 2009, doi:10.1093/geront/gnp100).

161 Ibid., 32.

162 BBC News Online, November 25, 2013, accessed November 26, 2013, http://www .bbc.co.uk/news/technology-25090534.

SEVEN: RETHINKING KINSHIP SYSTEMS

163 Robert A. Heinlein, *Rocket Ship Galileo* (New York: Ace Books, 2005; first published 1947), 153.

164 Current research indicates that dreams are part of the mind's processing of events between things to discard and things to retain as compacted long-term memories. Odd or recurring dreams are errors, overlaps, or difficulties in this process. One author posits that "it seems not unlikely that dreaming will ultimately be explainable, indeed natural, within a computational model of mind, particularly one calling for finding compact code to explain experience." Baum, *What Is Thought?*, 420. Mindware will probably require dreaming capability to sort the blizzard of daily electrons into a few reliable patterns, just as today's simple smartphones need to be shut off and restarted for electrons to either get where they belong, or get lost.

165 Feel, for example, the emotion of Jean-Dominique Bauby, *The Diving Bell and the Butterfly* (New York: Vintage International, 1998).

166 Lester del Rey, "Helen O'Loy," *Astounding Science Fiction*, vol. 22, no. 4 (1938); and in Robert Silverberg, ed., *Science Fiction Hall of Fame Volume 1 1929–1964* (New York: Orb, 1998), 42.

167 "The family is the natural and fundamental group unit of society and is entitled to protection by society and the State." International Covenant on Civil and Political Rights, *opened for signature* December 19, 1966, 999 UNTS 171, art 19(1), (*entered into force* March 23, 1976), article 23.

168 In the United States, the Supreme Court affirmed "the Constitution protects the sanctity of the family precisely because the institution of the family is deeply rooted in this Nation's history and tradition." Moore v. City of East Cleveland, 431 U.S. 494, 503 (1977), (plurality). While they have not yet seen to embrace same-sex partners within the definition of family—Bowers v. Hardwick, 478 U.S. 186 (1986)—they did after many decades finally welcome interracial couples into the fold. Loving v. Virginia, 388 U.S. 1, 12 (1967).

169 Over 80 percent of American men and 86 percent of women, as of a 2002 U.S. government poll, claimed to be or have been married. Goodwin, P., et al. "Who Marries and When: Age at First Marriage in the United States," National Center for Health Statistics,

Centers for Disease Control and Prevention, U.S. Department of Health and Human Services, NCHS Data Brief No. 19, June 2009, http://www.cdc.gov/nchs/data/data briefs/db19.pdf

[170] Hoffman, *The Right to Be Human*, 236.

EIGHT: LAW AND LIBERTY

[171] "Noble or Savage," *The Economist*, December 22, 2007, 129, 130.

[172] Ibid.

[173] Ibid.

[174] For example, Florida law says "The word 'person' includes individuals, children, firms, associations, joint adventures, partnerships, estates, trusts, business trusts, syndicates, fiduciaries, corporations, and all other groups or combinations." Florida Statutes, Title I, Chapter 1 (Construction of Statutes), Definitions, 1.01.

[175] "Noble or Savage," *The Economist*, December 22, 2007, 129, 130.

[176] Charles Darwin, *The Descent of Man*, 322–23.

[177] David Hyman, "Rescue without Law: An Empirical Perspective on the Duty to Rescue," *Texas Law Review* 84 (2006), 656, 668.

[178] Stout, *Cultivating Conscience*, 99.

[179] Ibid., 221

[180] Ibid., 99.

[181] National Vital Statistics Report, Volume 53, Number 5 (October 2004).

[182] Soap, sanitation systems, and antibiotics have been correlated with reducing annual death rates from more than thirty to fewer than ten cases per hundred thousand in Sweden during the nineteenth and twentieth centuries. http://www.globalchange .umich.edu/globalchange2/current/lectures/human_pop/human_pop.html.

[183] Paul R. Ehrlich, *The Population Bomb* (New York: Ballantine, 1968).

[184] Robert A. Heinlein, *The Moon Is a Harsh Mistress* (New York: Putnam, 1966).

[185] Richard Powers, *Galatea 2.2: A Novel* (New York: Harper Collins, 1996).

[186] Isaac Asimov, *I, Robot* (New York: Gnome Press, 1950).

[187] Ibid.

[188] Himanen, *The Hacker Ethic*, 140.

[189] "Robot Wars," *The Economist*, June 9, 2007, Technology Quarterly, 10.

[190] Adam Hochschild, *Bury the Chains: Prophets and Rebels in the Fight to Free an Empire's Slaves* (New York: Houghton Mifflin, 2005).

[191] Tim Wu, "Free Speech for Computers," *The New York Times*, June 19, 2012, Opinion section.

[192] *Frankenstein*, a two-hundred-year-old book by Mary Shelley, is about a tinkerer named Victor Frankenstein who stitches together dead body parts, then enlivens the assembly with a galvanic charge, resulting in what Mary Shelley called "the Monster." Pop culture now mistakenly refers to the monster as "Frankenstein," confusing the creator with his creation. I believe the story of Frankenstein is the forerunner of many variations on a theme of human makes imitation, human doesn't treat imitation as an equal, imitation feels aggrieved, imitation goes amok, and human regrets imitation. In this genre fall Karel Čapek's 1920 play *R.U.R.* (*Rossum's Universal Robots*) (from which

the word "robot" was coined), Osamu Tezuka's post–World War II manga *Astro Boy*, and the television show *Battlestar Galactica*'s Cylons. The imitations feel aggrieved because they detect that the humans are displeased with them, at least to the point of not treating them as equal, as the word "imitation" implies. The creators are both frightened and incensed by the uppity attitude of their creations, which fuels a spiral of mutual fear, anger, and hatred.

Sociologically, the same process occurs when colonizers attempt to press colonized peoples into imitations of themselves, such as converting them into a colonizer religion. The colonized people expect equal treatment as God's children, but instead are treated with second-class status, since the masters really disdain what they see as poor imitations. What invariably follow are mutual distrust, suspicion, fear, and conflict. If there is a harmonious resolution, it occurs on a higher level of understanding that there is a unity of benefit to all based upon diversity rather than homogeneity. This same narrative may play out with virtually human persons unless we accord full equality to those who value full equality, and appreciate the diversity of our software imitations.

[193] *Freedom Suit Court Cases*, Office of the Circuit Clerk–St. Louis, Missouri State Archives–St. Louis, Office of the Secretary of State.

[194] Winny v. Whitesides, Phebe, Apr 1821, Case No. 190, Circuit Court Case Files, Office of the Circuit Clerk, City of St. Louis, Missouri, http://stlcourtrecords.wustl.edu

[195] Scott, Dred, a man of color v. Emerson, Irene, Nov 1846, Case No. 1, Circuit Court Case Files, Office of the Circuit Clerk, City of St. Louis, Missouri, http://stlcourtrecords.wustl.edu.

[196] Dred Scott v. Sandford, 60 U.S. 393 (1857). A similarly adverse decision was reached for BINA48 in a mock trial conducted by the International Bar Association, see http://www.kurzweilai.net/biocyberethics-should-we-stop-a-company-from-unplugging-an-intelligent-computer, retrieved April 5, 2014.

[197] National Geographic News, http://news.nationalgeographic.com/news/2007/03/070316-robot-ethics_2.html

[198] "EURON Roboethics Roadmap," EURON Roboethics Atelier, Genoa, 27 Feburary–3 March 2006, p. 7.

[199] Ibid.

[200] Ibid.

[201] E. Hooker, "A Preliminary Analysis of Group Behavior of Homosexuals," *Journal of Psychology* 42 (1956), 217–25.

[202] Stout, *Cultivating Conscience*, 126.

[203] "Google patents robot help for social media burnout," BBC News, November 22, 2013, accessed November 26, 2013, http://www.bbc.co.uk/news/technology-25033172.

[204] William Gibson, *Neuromancer* (New York: Berkeley Publishing, 1984), 132.

[205] And the opposite is true with respect to positive feelings. The human hormone oxytocin and activity in the brain's mesolimbic dopamine system, both associated with feeling good, rise and fall with levels of cooperation. Golnaz Tabibnia, Ajay Satpute, and Matthew Lieberman, "The Sunny Side of Fairness: Preference for Fairness Activates Reward Circuitry," *Psychological Science* 19 (2008), 341.

[206] Jerome and Taylor, *Einstein on Race and Racism*, 146–47.

[207] Robert A. Heinlein, *Citizen of the Galaxy* (New York: Simon & Schuster, 1957, 1985), 189.

[208] The term "human rights" probably came into use sometime between Paine's *The Rights of Man* and William Lloyd Garrison's 1831 writings in *The Liberator* saying he was trying to enlist his readers in "the great cause of human rights."

[209] The pioneer in this area is Sententia Wrye, whose work is available at the Center for Cognitive Liberty at University of California, Davis, accessed January 21, 2014, www .cognitiveliberty.org.

[210] Himanen, *The Hacker Ethic*, 104.

NINE: G-D AND MINDCLONES

[211] *The Economist*, January 14, 2006, 66.

[212] A. M. Turing, "Computing Machinery and Intelligence," *Mind* 59, no. 236 (October 1950), 433, 443.

[213] P. W. Singer, *Wired for War* (New York: Penguin 2009), 167.

[214] Donald McNeil, Jr., "A Puzzle of Birthing, Solved in a Bottle," *International New York Times*, November 13, 2013, 1.

[215] Himanen, *The Hacker Ethic*, 141.

[216] Baum, *What Is Thought?*, 433.

[217] Gilbert Ryle, *The Concept of Mind* (London: Hutchison, 1949), 11.

[218] Koestler, *Ghost in the Machine*, 325.

[219] Wallach and Allen, *Moral Machines*, 178.

[220] Wallach and Allen, *Moral Machines*, 96.

[221] For example, ventromedial prefrontal cortex (VMPC) injury patients are three times more likely than nonpatients to advocate throwing a person in front of a moving train in order to save five other people, per Anthony Demasio of the University of Southern California in the March 22, 2007, issue of *Nature*. This is not to say they are right or wrong, but simply that mindclones can be probabilistically weighted to take some actions preferentially to other actions.

[222] Isaac Asimov, *I, Robot* (New York: Gnome Press, 1950).

[223] Isaac Asimov, *The Evitable Conflict* (New York: Street & Smith, 1950); Isaac Asimov, *Robots and Empire* (New York: Doubleday Books, 1985).

[224] Wallach and Allen, *Moral Machines*, 97.

TEN: THE FUTURE OF FOREVER

[225] Hawkins, *On Intelligence*, 104.

[226] Kalpas are eschatological time periods in Hinduism and Buddhism, lasting tens of billions of years.

[227] Richard Morgan, *Altered Carbon* (New York: Ballantine, 2002).

[228] David Mitchell, *Cloud Atlas* (New York: Modern Library, 2004). ("Truth is singular. Its versions are mistruths.")

[229] "How is it possible that a being with such sensitive jewels as the eyes, such enchanted musical instruments as the ears, and such a fabulous arabesque of nerves as the brain can experience itself as anything less than a god? And, when you consider

that this incalculably subtle organism is inseparable from the still more marvelous patterns of its environment—from the minutest electrical designs to the whole company of the galaxies—how is it conceivable that this incarnation of all eternity can be bored with being?" Watts, note 89 infra at 138.

[230] Hoffman, *The Right to Be Human*, 264. There were seventeen Being-Values or B-Values that Maslow found to be universal among people who enjoyed peak experiences: truth, beauty, justice, goodness, wholeness, perfection, uniqueness, simplicity, order, aliveness, self-sufficiency, necessity, completion, richness, effortlessness, playfulness, and dichotomy-transcendence—all equally important. Mindware will be tuned to experience peakness as these values are touched.

[231] Thomas Merton, *The Way of Chuang Tzu* (New York: New Directions, 1997), 30.

[232] Ibid., 116.

[233] This paragraph owes much to the similarly structured, but somewhat differently termed, argument of Dennett, *Kinds of Minds*, 98–108.

[SELECTED BIBLIOGRAPHY]

Allport, Gordon, *Becoming: Basic Considerations for a Psychology of Personality*, New Haven: Yale University Press, 1955.

Asimov, Isaac, *I, Robot*, New York: Gnome Press, 1950.

Avery, John, *Information Theory and Evolution*, Hackensack, New Jersey: World Scientific Publishing, 2004.

Ayers, J., Davis, J. & Rudolph, A., eds., *Neurotechnology for Biomimetic Robots*, Cambridge, Massachusetts: MIT Press, 2002.

Baars, Bernard, Banks, William & Newman, James, eds., *Essential Sources in the Scientific Study of Consciousness*, Cambridge, Massachusetts: MIT Press, 2003.

Balcombe, Jonathan, *Second Nature: The Inner Lives of Animals*, New York: Palgrave Macmillan, 2010.

Balkin, J. M., *Cultural Software: A Theory of Ideology*, New Haven: Yale University Press, 1998.

Bateson, Gregory, *Mind and Nature: A Necessary Unity*, Cresskill, New Jersey: Hampton Press, 2002.

Baum, Eric, *What Is Thought?* Cambridge, Massachusetts: MIT Press, 2004.

Bekey, George, *Autonomous Robots: From Biological Inspiration to Implementation and Control,* Cambridge, Massachusetts: MIT Press, 2005.

Bell, Gordon & Gemmell, Jim, *How the E-Memory Revolution Will Change Everything,* New York: Dutton, 2009.

Berlinski, David, *The Advent of the Algorithm: The Idea that Rules the World,* New York: Harcourt, 2000.

Breazeal, Cynthia, *Designing Sociable Robots,* Cambridge, Massachusetts: MIT Press, 2002.

Butler, Judith, *Bodies That Matter: On the Discursive Limits of "Sex,"* New York: Routledge, 1993.

Clark, Andy, *Natural-Born Cyborgs: Minds, Technologies, and the Future of Human Intelligence,* Oxford: Oxford University Press, 2003.

Dawkins, Richard, *The Selfish Gene,* Oxford: Oxford University Press, 1976, 192–94.

Dawkins, Richard, *The Selfish Gene,* Oxford: Oxford University Press, 1999.

De Chardin, Teilhard, *The Phenomenom of Man,* New York: Perennial, 2002.

De Duve, Christian, *Life Evolving: Molecules, Mind, and Meaning,* Oxford: Oxford University Press, 2002.

De Waal, Frans, *Good Natured: The Origins of Right and Wrong in*

Humans and Other Animals, Cambridge, Massachusetts: Harvard University Press, 1996.

De Waal, Frans, *Primates and Philosophers: How Morality Evolved,* Princeton: Princeton University Press, 2006.

Dennet, Daniel, *Kinds of Minds: Toward an Understanding of Consciousness,* New York: Basic Books, 1996.

Dennett, Daniel, *Breaking the Spell: Religion as a Natural Phenomenon,* New York: Viking, 2006.

Dennett, Daniel, *Consciousness Explained,* New York: Little Brown & Co., 1991.

Desmond, Adrian & Moore, James, *Darwin's Sacred Cause: How a Hatred of Slavery Shaped Darwin's Views on Human Evolution,* Boston: Houghton Mifflin Harcourt, 2009.

Deutsch, David, *The Fabric of Reality,* New York: Penguin, 1997.

Diamandis, Peter H. and Kotler, Steven, *Abundance: The Future Is Better Than You Think,* New York: Free Press, 2012.

Dick, Philip, *Do Androids Dream of Electric Sheep,* New York: Ballantine Books, 1968.

Edelman, Gerald, *Bright Air, Brilliant Fire: On the Matter of Mind,* New York: Basic Books, 1992.

Edelman, Gerald, *Second Nature: Brain Science and Human Knowledge,* New Haven: Yale University Press, 2006.

Ekman, Paul, *Emotions Revealed: Recognizing Faces and Feelings to*

Improve Communication and Emotional Life, New York: St. Martin's Press, 2003.

Ettinger, Robert, *The Prospect of Immortality,* New York: Doubleday, 1964.

FM-2030, *Are You a Transhuman?* New York: Warner Books, 1989.

Forbes, Scott, *A Natural History of Families,* Princeton: Princeton University Press, 2005.

Ford, K., Glymour, C. & Hayes, P., *Thinking About Android Epistemology,* Menlo Park: AAAI Press, 2006.

Foster, Thomas, *The Souls of Cyberfolk: Posthumanism as Vernacular Theory,* Minneapolis: University of Minnesota Press, 2005.

Gibson, William *Neuromancer,* New York: Berkeley Publishing, 1984.

Glenn, Jerome, *Future Mind: Artificial Intelligence,* Washington DC: Acropolis Books, 1989.

Glymour, Clark, *The Mind's Arrows: Bayes Nets and Graphical Causal Models in Psychology,* Cambridge, Massachusetts: MIT Press, 2001.

Goertzel, Ben & Wang, Pei, eds., *Advances in Artificial General Intelligence: Concepts, Architectures and Algorithms,* Amsterdam: IOS Press, 2007.

Hailes, Katherine, *How We Became Posthuman: Virtual Bodies in Cybernetics, Literature, and Informatics,* Chicago: University of Chicago Press, 1999.

Haldane, J. B. S., *Daedalus or Science and the Future,* New York: E. P. Dutton, 1924.

Hall, J. Storrs, *Beyond AI: Creating the Conscience of the Machine,* Amherst, New York: Prometheus Books, 2007.

Hansell, Gregory & Grassie, William, eds., *Transhumanism and Its Critics,* Philadelphia: Metanexus, 2011.

Harris, John, *The Value of Life,* London: Routledge, 2001.

Hawkins, Jeff, *On Intelligence: How a New Understanding of the Brain Will Lead to the Creation of Truly Intelligent Machines,* New York: Henry Holt, 2004.

Hayes-Roth, Rick, *Hyper-Beings: How Intelligent Organizations Attain Supremacy through Information Superiority,* Booklocker.com, 2006.

Heinlein, Robert, *The Moon Is a Harsh Mistress,* New York: G. P. Putnam's Sons, 1966.

Heinlein, Robert, *Time Enough for Love,* New York: Ace Books, 1973.

Himanen, Pekka, *The Hacker Ethic and the Spirit of the Information Age,* New York: Random House, 2001.

Hochschild, Adam, *Bury the Chains,* New York: Houghton Mifflin Company, 2005.

Hodges, Andrew, *Alan Turing: The Enigma,* Princeton: Princeton University Press, 2012.

Hofstadter, Douglas, *I Am a Strange Loop,* New York: Basic Books, 2007.

Hughes, James, *Citizen Cyborg: Why Democratic Societies Must Respond to the Redesigned Human of the Future*, Cambridge, Massachusetts: Perseus, 2004.

James, William, *Principles of Psychology*, New York: Henry Holt and Company, 1890.

Jasanoff, Sheila, *Designs on Nature: Science and Democracy in Europe and the United States*, Princeton: Princeton University Press, 2005.

Jerome, Fred & Taylor, Rodger, *Einstein on Race and Racism*, New Brunswick: Rutkers University Press, 2005.

Koch, Christof, *The Quest for Consciousness: A Neurobiological Approach*, Englewood, Colorado: Roberts & Co., 2004.

Koestler, Arthur, *The Ghost in the Machine*, Chicago: Henry Regnery, 1967.

Kolak, Daniel, *I Am You: The Metaphysical Foundations for Global Ethics*, Dordrecht, The Netherlands: Springer, 2004.

Kukathas, Chandran & Pettit, Philip, *Rawls: A Theory of Justice and Its Critics*, Stanford: Stanford University Press, 1990.

Kurzweil, Ray & Grossman, Terry, *Fantastic Voyage: Live Long Enough to Live Forever*, Rodale, 2004.

Kurzweil, Ray, *Age of Spiritual Machines*, New York: Viking, 1999.

Kurzweil, Ray, *How to Create a Mind: The Secret of Human Thought Revealed*, New York: Viking, 2012.

Kurzweil, Ray, *The Singularity Is Near*, New York: Penguin, 2005.

MacDonald, Paul, *History of the Concept of Mind: Speculations About Soul, Mind and Spirit from Homer to Hume*, Burlington, Vermont: Ashgate, 2003.

Maslow, Abraham, *Toward a Psychology of Being*, 3rd ed., New York: Wiley & Sons, 1999.

Mayr, Ernst, *What Evolution Is*, New York: Basic Books, 2001.

Mayr, Ernst, *What Makes Biology Unique: Considerations on the Autonomy of a Scientific Discipline*, Cambridge, UK: Cambridge University Press, 2005.

McGaugh, James L. *Memory and Emotion: The Making of Lasting Memories*, New York: Columbia University Press, 2003.

Minsky, Marvin, *The Emotion Machine*, New York: Simon & Schuster, 2006.

Minsky, Marvin, *The Society of Mind*, New York: Simon & Schuster, 1986.

Moravec, Hans, *Mind Children*, Cambridge, Massachusetts: Harvard University Press, 1988.

Moravec, Hans, *Robot: Mere Machine to Transcendent Mind*, New York: Oxford University Press, 1999.

More, Max & Vita-More, Natasha, eds., *The Transhumanist Reader: Classical and Contemporary Essays on the Science, Technology, and Philosophy of the Human Future*, West Sussex, UK: Wiley-Blackwell, 2013.

Morgan, Richard, *Altered Carbon*, New York: Ballantine, 2002.

Naam, Ramez, *More Than Human: Embracing the Promise of Biological Enhancement,* New York: Broadway Books, 2005.

Nicholson, Ian, *Inventing Personality: Gordon Allport and the Science of Selfhood,* Washington DC: American Psychological Association, 2003.

Nowak, Martin A., *Evolutionary Dynamics,* Cambridge, Massachusetts: Belknap, 2006.

Osgood, Charles, May, William & Miron, Murray, *Cross-Cultural Universals of Affective Meaning,* Urban: University of Illinois Press, 1975.

Paul, Gregory & Cox, Earl, *Beyond Humanity: CyberEvolution and Future Minds,* Rockland, Massachusetts: Charles River Media, 1996.

Pekelis, V., & Samokhvalov, M. (transl.), *Cybernetics A to Z,* Moscow: Mir Publishers, 1974.

Pinker, Steven, *How the Mind Works,* New York: W. W. Norton & Co., 1997.

Rothblatt, Martine, *From Transgender to Transhuman: A Manifesto on the Freedom of Form,* Kindle, 2011.

Schrodinger, Erwin, *What Is Life?* Cambridge, UK: Cambridge University Press, 1962.

Searle, John R. *The Mystery of Consciousness,* New York: *The New York Review of Books,* 1997.

Seung, Sebastian, *Connectome: How the Brain's Wiring Makes Us Who We Are,* Boston: Houghton Mifflin Harcourt, 2012.

Singer, P. W., *Wired for War: The Robotics Revolution and Conflict in the 21st Century,* New York: Penguin Press, 2009.

Stafford, Barbara, *Echo Objects: The Cognitive Work of Images,* Chicago: University of Chicago Press, 2007.

Standage, Tom, *The Turk: The Life and Times of the Famous Eighteenth Century Chess-Playing Machine,* New York: Walker & Co., 2002.

Stout, Lynn A., *Cultivating Conscience: How Good Laws Make Good People,* Princeton: Princeton University Press, 2011.

Tabensky, Pedro, Happiness: *Personhood, Community, Purpose,* Burlington, Vermont: Ashgate, 2003.

Venter, Craig, *Life at the Speed of Light: From the Double Helix to the Dawn of Digital Life,* New York: Viking, 2013.

Waldron, Jeremy, ed., *Theories of Rights,* Oxford: Oxford University, 1995.

Wallach, Wendell and Allen, Colin, *Moral Machines: Teaching Robots Right from Wrong,* Oxford: Oxford University Press, 2009.

Watts, Alan, *The Book: On the Taboo Against Knowing Who You Are,* New York: Vintage Books, 1989.

Webb, Barbara & Consi, Thomas, *Biorobotics: Methods and Applications,* Menlo Park: AAAI Press, 2001.

Weizenbaum, Joseph, *Computer Power and Human Reason: From Judgment to Calculation,* New York: W. S. Freeman & Co., 1976.

Wilson, Edward, *Consilience: The Unity of Knowledge,* New York: Vintage, 1999.

Wilson, Edward, *Sociobiology: The New Synthesis,* Cambridge, Massachusetts: Harvard University Press, 2002.

Witherall, Arthur, *The Problem of Existence,* Aldershot, UK: Ashgate, 2002.

[INDEX]

Systrom, Kevin, 61, 95
Szasz, Thomas, 123

Tao, 297–303
The Taqwacores, 131
Target Corporation, 58–59
technicity, 167
  defined, 307
technoimmortality, 283
  defining, 285, 307
  identity and, 287
technoprogressive, 307
television, 147
Terasem Foundation, xv
Tomlinson, Ray, 228
Tonegawa, Susumu, 144
torture, 253
Torvalds, Linus, 322n119
totalitarianism, 244
Transcendent Man, xv
transgender, 137, 213, 237
transhumans, 307
The Transparent Society (Brin), 176
Truth, Sojourner, 248
Tumblr, 61
Turing, Alan, 18, 42, 120
  on consciousness, 44
  on God, 261
  on universal computing machine, 19–20
Turing test, 18
  AIs passing, xi
  criticism of, 18–19
  Hawkins on, 313n10
Turnstyle Solutions Inc., 58
Turpin v. Sortini, 322n127
2045 Initiative, 275
Twitter LivesOn, 59

uncanny valley, 67
unconscious, 56
Uniform Determination of Death Act, 236
unity, 125, 126
universal conscience, 239
Universal Declaration of Human Rights, 183,
  222–23
  inclusiveness of, 223

vaccinations, 225
vaginal births, 127–28
Value of Life (Harris), 292
Varela, Francisco J., 275
Varian, Hal R., 60–61
Venter, J. Craig, 160–61
ventromedial prefrontal cortex injury patients,
  328n221
viruses
  molecular, 94
  software, 94, 227
vitology, 62, 156–57
  defined, 307
  motives for, 62–63
Vo Nguyen Giap, 197

Voltaire, 277
voting
  death and, 188–89
  discrimination and, 186
  fear of, 232–33
  fleshism and, 192
  generational factors, 190
  habits, 189–90
  history of, 185–86
  Johnson on, 187–88
  life-cycle factors, 190–92
  manipulation and, 192
  for Obama, 191
  rationality and, 192–93
  state standards, 186
  stereotypes, 190
  women and, 232–33
Voting Rights Act of 1965, 187–88
Voyager, 158

Wallach, Wendell, 3
  on artificial moral agents, 90
  on emotions, 314n18
  on morals, 279–80
Watson, xii, xv, 26
Watts, Alan, xv, 283
  on identity, 180
  on me, 83–84
The Way of Chuang Tzu (Merton), 297
wearable electronics, 159–60
web crawlers, 39
Weiner, Norbert, 157
"What Is It Like to Be a Bat?" (Nagel),
  313n8
What Is Life? (Schrödinger), 156
What Is Thought? (Baum), 273–74
White, Peter, 12
Whitman, Walt, 80
Wiener, Norbert, 51
Wikipedia, xii
Wilberforce, William, 230
Wilde, Oscar, 11
Williams, Robin, 247
Wilson, Edward O., 88, 90
Winny v. Phebe Whitesides, 235
women, 232–33
World of Warcraft, 203
Wright, Frank Lloyd, 238
  on God, 264
wrongful life liability, 138, 322n127
Wu, Tim, 231–32

xenophobia, 245–46

Yiddish, 289–90
yuck reaction, 173
  Curtis on, 174–75
  disease and, 175
  triggers, 174–75

zombies, 27
  ethics and, 117

5